Dear David and
Thank you for you
in the past ye

Writing on the Wall

Scenario development in times of discontinuity

Writing on the Wall

Scenario development in times of discontinuity

Philip van Notten

DISSERTATION.COM

Boca Raton / Florida / USA

ISBN: 1-58112-265-9

published by Dissertation.com, Boca Raton, Florida, USA
printed by Thela Thesis, Amsterdam, The Netherlands

© Philip van Notten 2005. All rights reserved. No part of the material protected by this copyright notice may be reproduced or utilised in any form or by any means, electronic or mechanical, including photocopying, recording or by any information storage and retrieval system, without written permission from the copyright owner.

cover, graphic design and editing by ZWAAR WATER, Amsterdam, The Netherlands

For my wonderful son, Damiaan

CONTENTS

	Acknowledgements	page	XIII

CHAPTER 1 — INTRODUCTION — page 1
1. Times of discontinuity — page 3
2. Foresight and Integrated Assessment — page 4
3. Focus of the research — page 7
4. Framework of the research — page 8
5. Audience and structure — page 11

CHAPTER 2 — SCENARIO DEVELOPMENT TODAY — page 15
1. Introduction — page 17
2. Definition — page 18
3. Study of contemporary scenario practice — page 20
   - 3.1 Scenario diversity — page 20
   - 3.2 A comparative review and a typology for scenarios — page 22
4. Macro characteristics — page 24
   - 4.1 Goal — page 24
   - 4.2 Process design — page 25
   - 4.3 Scenario content — page 29
5. Micro characteristics — page 30
   - 5.1 Project-goal characteristics — page 30
   - 5.2 Process design characteristics — page 33
   - 5.3 Scenario content characteristics — page 35
6. Towards an overview of contemporary scenario practice — page 37
7. Concluding remarks — page 40

CHAPTER 3 — DISCONTINUITY — page 41
1. Introduction — page 43
2. Research approach — page 44
3. Literature review — page 44
   - 3.1 Surprise — page 47
   - 3.2 Wild card — page 49
4. Reflection on the literature — page 50
   - 4.1 Beyond events — page 51
   - 4.2 Interactions — page 53
   - 4.3 Immaterial influences — page 54
   - 4.4 Steady or instantaneous change? — page 54

5	A concept of discontinuity for foresight		page	55
	5.1 Abrupt discontinuity		page	55
	5.2 Gradual discontinuity		page	56
6	Illustrating the concept		page	57
	6.1 '9/11'		page	58
	6.2 The emergence of the environment as a societal concern		page	63
7	Concluding remarks		page	66

CHAPTER 4 **DISCONTINUITY AND SCENARIO PRACTICE** page 69

1 Introduction		page	71
2 Concepts for exploring discontinuity in scenario development: are there any?		page	71
3 Methods for exploring discontinuity in scenario development: are there any?		page	74
4 Discontinuity in contemporary scenario practice		page	77
4.1 Studies that omit discontinuity		page	77
4.2 Analysis of studies that omit discontinuity		page	81
4.3 Discontinuity in exploratory studies		page	83
4.4 Discontinuity in pre-policy research studies		page	88
4.5 Analysis of studies that included discontinuity		page	91
5 Reflection		page	93
6 Concluding remarks		page	96

CHAPTER 5 **DISCONTINUITY IN SCENARIO PRACTICE** page 99
A RECONSTRUCTION OF THE VISIONS SCENARIO STUDY

1 Introduction		page	101
2 Research approach		page	102
3 An introduction to visions		page	103
4 VISIONS and discontinuity		page	104
5 Chronology		page	106
5.1 Storylines		page	106
5.2 From storylines to scenarios		page	108
5.3 Bifurcations		page	110
5.4 From scenarios to visons		page	112
6 VISIONS in hindsight		page	113
6.1 People: partners, participants, and team members		page	115
6.2 Methods, and concepts		page	117
6.3 Procedural issues		page	120

7	Reflections	page	122
	7.1 Inspiring factors	page	122
	7.2 Impairing factors	page	123
	7.3 Double-edged factors	page	124
8	Concluding remarks	page	125

CHAPTER 6 EXPLORING DISCONTINUITY: AN EXPERIMENT — page 127

1	Introduction	page	129
2	Salmon aquaculture	page	129
	2.1 Driving forces behind European salmon aquaculture	page	130
	2.2 Ecological impacts	page	131
	2.3 Economic impacts	page	133
	2.4 Socio-cultural impacts	page	133
	2.5 Possible solutions?	page	134
3	Organisation of the experiment	page	135
4	Discontinuity-oriented process design	page	136
	4.1 Basic framework	page	136
	4.2 Discontinuity-oriented design: mobilising inspiring factors	page	137
	4.2.1 Group composition	page	138
	4.2.2 Discontinuity guardianship	page	140
	4.2.3 Open structure	page	141
	4.2.4 Underdeveloped methods: A general observation	page	142
	4.3 DISCO 1.0: prototype for discontinuity-oriented scenario development	page	149
5	Output of the DISCO 1.0 experiment	page	149
	5.1 Staggered brainwriting	page	149
	5.2 Analogies	page	151
	5.3 Perspective-based imaging	page	152
6	Analysis of the DISCO 1.0 experiment	page	153
	6.1 Methods: Staggered brainwriting	page	153
	6.2 Methods: Analogies	page	154
	6.3 Methods: Perspective-based imaging	page	155
	6.4 Open structure	page	155
	6.5 Group variety	page	156
	6.6 Discontinuity guardianship	page	157
7	Concluding remarks	page	158

CHAPTER 7 **TOWARDS DISCONTINUITY-ORIENTED SCENARIO DEVELOPMENT** — page 159
    1 Summary of findings — page 161
    2 Hurdles for discontinuity-oriented scenario development — page 165
    3 Rising to the challenge: fostering cultures of curiosity — page 167
    4 Issues for further interdisciplinary research — page 170
    5 Towards deciphering the writing on the wall — page 172

REFERENCES References for chapter 1 — page 173
    References for chapter 2 — page 176
    References for chapter 3 — page 181
    References for chapter 4 — page 185
    References for chapter 5 — page 189
    References for chapter 6 — page 191
    References for chapter 7 — page 193

APPENDIX 1 Sources of consulted scenario studies — page 195
APPENDIX 2 Interview format for VISIONS process reconstruction — page 205
    Curriculum vitae — page 207
    Index — page 209

ACKNOWLEDGEMENTS

The past four years have involved working with an inspiring group of people. I am grateful to my colleagues at Maastricht University's International Centre for Integrative Studies (ICIS) for making life as a researcher both enjoyable and stimulating. In particular, I would like to thank my supervisor, Jan Rotmans. His inspirational ideas regularly helped overcome bottlenecks, oversights and my often mistaken belief that the research for this thesis was complete.

My research was funded by the Innovational Research Incentive Scheme on foresight methodology, which was awarded to my co-supervisor Marjolein van Asselt by the Netherlands Organisation for Scientific Research in 2001. The research described in this thesis is a contribution to the scheme together with Marjolein's own work on uncertainty and Susan van 't Klooster's on plurality. I am indebted to Marjolein for her dedication to her task as co-supervisor. Thanks also to Am Sleegers whose Master´s research contributed to this thesis's Chapter 4!

The research for Chapter 6 was funded by KLICT (Netchains, Logistics, and Information and Communication Technology), to whom I express my gratitude. The research was conducted in partnership with Wageningen University's Agro-technology and Food Innovations (A&F). My thanks go to A&F's Sietze Vellema, Conny van der Heijden and Daniella Stijnen as well as my ICIS colleagues Jan Stel and Derk Loorbach.

The close cooperation with others is a reason for the use of the first person plural 'we' as opposed to the first person singular 'I', despite of the fact that this thesis carries only my name. The second reason is that the first person plural is the preferred style at ICIS.

Besides formal partnerships, I have benefited from regular, informal exchanges with professionals involved in foresight and integrative assessment (IA). These include members of the ICIS network, especially Chris Anastasi, Jerry Ravetz, Frank Ruff, Bernd Kasemir, and the late Poul Harremoës. The COST European Network for Foresight Methodology, funded by the European Commission and hosted by the European Science Foundation, has also been a source of inspiration. My thanks go to the network's management committee especially Dale Rothman, Ted Fuller, Jennifer Cassingena-Harper, and Ruud van der Helm. The Dutch foresight network (NTV) was a watering hole for ideas as well. I enjoyed discussions with Paul Rademaker, Ig Snellen, Thomas Corver, and Bart van Steenbergen, among others. I have also enjoyed the contacts with a group of professionals connected through Shell International's and Global Business Network's scenario work, in particular Joop de Vries, Kees van der Heijden, Robert Bood, Paul de Ruijter, Jaap Leemhuis, and Napier Collyns.

Towards the later stages of my research, I worked with the Organisation for Economic Cooperation and Development (OECD) and the United Nations Environment Programme (UNEP). My thanks in particular go to Riel Miller, Edna Yahil, and Marion Cheatle for the enjoyable experience.

I would like to thank those that were involved in the editing, graphic design and printing of my thesis: Susan van 't Klooster, Brian Waniewski, Esther Mosselman, René Janssen, Marin de Swart, Shereen Siddiqui and Auke van den Berg.

Besides professional acknowledgements I would also like to express my gratitude to friends and family. First and foremost among those is my son, Damiaan. Watching my cheerful little boy develop in his first two years has been a wonderful experience. It is to Damiaan that I dedicate this thesis.

I also thank Elisabeth Dobbinga, Damiaan's mother, for her professional and personal support during my research years. I am confident that raising Damiaan together will be an enriching experience for both of us.

I am grateful for the support of my cousins Ariane and Harald, Isabelle and David, Henriette and Reindert, and Aunt Tina. My thanks also goes to Aunts Henriette and Mia for helping with the publication of my thesis. Many thanks also to my ever-supportive sister, Florentine, and to her partner, Marnix, and his family. I would also like to thank my parents, Eleonore and Ferdinand, for their enduring love.

There are a host of friends that I would like to thank. They include those from my years at Leiden University, particularly Rutger Kalsbeek, Ward Schalekamp, Henrik Postma, Remco Aalbers, Michiel den Hertog, Patrick Rutgers and their partners. My thanks also to Jurriaan Lempers and Karen Rethmeier, Juriaan Lahr and Francine Stigter! Friends beyond the university context that I would like to thank are Mats Holmberg, Jacco van Uden, Mechteld Bentinck, Ariel and Karin Sobelman, and Simon and Gemma Bird. I would also like to thank the company of friends at the Plankstraat in Maastricht, especially Thijs Peters, Bas Bakermans and Ed Spanjaard. A special thank you to Eduard Kimman for his extraordinary generosity over the years!

In 2001, I had the privilege of being a visiting scientist to the European Environment Agency (EEA) in Copenhagen. My friends in Denmark have been very supportive in often difficult times. I would like to thank my former EEA colleagues, notably Teresa Ribeiro, David Stanners, Charlotte Islev, Eva Carlson, Sofia Guedes Vaz, Ann Dom, Jan Erik Petersen, Peter Gabrielsen, Tony Carritt, Aphrodite Mourelatou, Gorm and Mette Dige, and Peter Bosch and Janet Rodenburg. Special thanks go to David Gee and Vivienne-Taylor Gee who have gone to great lengths to help me and make me feel at home. Thanks also to other, 'non-EEA' friends in Denmark: Cynthia and Mikkel Selin, the Bothmanns – Gyrithe, Kirstin and Hans Christian –, Hanne Shapiro, Kristian Borch and Christina Dall! I am especially grateful to the Moltkes, my family away from home. Lastly, I want to commemorate Michele Fontana, with whom I shared an office at the EEA, whose untimely death on October 8th, 2001 was a great shock. I wish his partner, Chiara, and their sons Leonardo and Martino, strength in the future.

The Hague, November 2004

1
introduction

I INTRODUCTION

1 Times of discontinuity

"Night fell on a different world"[1] on September 11th, 2001, so argued President George W. Bush in an address to Congress shortly after the attacks in New York, Washington, and Pennsylvania. The September 11th attacks were daring, spectacular, and effective. In the US, the immediate direct effects of '9/11' included stock market depreciations, declines in New York property prices, cancellations of Hollywood productions, and soaring political fortunes of the president. Indirect effects worldwide included the upsurge in the value of the Pakistani rupee, the bankruptcy of two European airlines, revival of the Northern Ireland peace talks, and the fall of the Taliban regime in Afghanistan.

Many of the attacks' immediate effects were temporary, but some of them were more enduring. Schwartz[2] argued that the attacks changed history irrevocably, singling out the damage that they have done to the American and global economy, claiming that the West will be paying a "bin Laden surtax" for years to come. Two years after the attacks, George Soros[3] argued that '9/11' changed the course of history because it "introduced a discontinuity into American foreign policy", which involved the president using 9/11 as an excuse for implementing a radical foreign policy agenda. The assumptions on which the discontinuity was based predated the tragedy, according to Soros. The origins of these assumptions can be traced back to such myths of American culture as the 'White Man's Burden', 'Destiny', and 'Providence'[4], which have often influenced past US foreign policy. On a structural level, then, the September 11th attacks are arguably symptomatic of the 'clash of civilizations'[5] and such forces as globalism and tribalism[6] manifested in tensions between US' and other cultures' and interests. It remains to be seen what the meaning of '9/11' is on a broader historical level.

Although the significance of '9/11' is subject to debate, it is symbolic of a general sentiment of discontinuity whereby we feel vulnerable to undefined and highly disruptive events. Recent catalysts of this sentiment are eye-catching developments such as the SARS (Severe Acute Respiratory Syndrome) and bird flu outbreaks, the Enron and Parmalat scandals, political assassinations in Sweden and the Netherlands, regime changes in Iraq and Afghanistan, and terrorist attacks in Bali, Istanbul, Madrid, and various parts of the Middle East. Nowotny et al.[7] argue that:

> Gone [...] is the belief in simple cause-effect relationships often embodying implicit assumptions about [...] linearity; in their place is an acknowledgement that many - perhaps most - relationships are non-linear and subject to ever changing patterns of unpredictability.

However, recent discontinuities should not be seen as evidence that discontinuities occur more frequently now than they did before. Looking back in history we see that disruptive processes are common. For example, 25 years ago few Europeans would have predicted the upcoming upheavals on their own continent: the collapse of communism, Berlin as the capital of a reunited Germany, the wars in the former Yugoslavia, the single European currency, and the near doubling of the number of European Union member states. Changes elsewhere have been no less discontinuous and unforeseen: the fall of the Asian tigers, the emergence of the Internet and mobile telecommunication, and the presidency of Nelson Mandela.

Discontinuity is a notion that features in a variety of contexts and disciplines ranging from law to geology to mathematics. What we call societal discontinuity involves the interaction of events and processes such as those described above that involve or produce some form of structural change in society. Globalisation, technological innovation, increased knowledge about our world, and temporal acceleration[8] make for an increasingly complex or interconnected world. Greater interconnection means that events and developments can have a further reach, as the occurrence of the West Nile virus in the New York area illustrates. The virus was never seen in the US before 1999 and it was most likely carried to New York from Africa through an infected person or an imported bird. The warm summer of 1999 provided the conditions for the spread of the virus, leading to 62 severe reported cases of disease, resulting in six deaths. In 2002, nearly 2000 cases were reported, of which 94 were deaths. The broad reach and rapid spread of computer viruses is another example of interconnectedness. Increased interconnection means that small changes can have discontinuous effects.

Past cases of discontinuities invite the question whether discontinuity and its complex societal manifestations can be understood and perhaps anticipated. Such publications as *The Age of Discontinuity*[9], *The Fourth Discontinuity*[10], *The Great Disruption*[11], and *Inevitable Surprises*[2] have sought to do just that. Although several of these analyses have been influential in stimulating debate, dealing with the possibility of discontinuous, contingent, and unexpected developments in policy-development is a relatively new area of interest[12;13]. The September 11th attacks and subsequent events have further stimulated the interest in discontinuities.

2 Foresight and Integrated Assessment

Society has contemplated its future for centuries as illustrated by classic novels such as Thomas More's *Utopia* (1516), Edward Bellamy's *Looking Backward: 2000 – 1887* (1887), H.G. Well's *The Time Machine* (1895), Aldous Huxley's *Brave New World* (1932), and George Orwell's *Nineteen Eighty-Four* (1949), as well as the science fiction work of Jules Verne and Isaac Asimov. More recently a genre involving the popular scientific, often utopic predictions of technology-driven, future prosperity has emerged[14]. Examples of these publications are McLuhan's *Understanding Media* (1964) and Toffler's *Future Shock*[15]. However, according to De Wilde, this type of future exploration is problematic because of its neo-liberal finalism and its simplistic view of societal progress. The literary and popular scientific interest in contemplating the future has been joined by the study of the future and the complex interaction of processes that shape it. Early signs of an academic interest in the future can be traced back to H.G. Wells' article in Nature[16]. Herman Kahn's work at RAND and the Hudson Institute[17;18;19;20;21] arguably laid an important foundation for modern day study of futures-oriented issues.

Such terms as foresight, futurology, futures research, prospective analysis, and future studies refer to the research of futures-oriented issues. The distinctions between the terms are often ambiguous. One definition of foresight is the skill of making meaning of looking ahead[22]. Another is:

The process of developing a range of views of possible ways in which the future could develop, and understanding these sufficiently well to be able to decide what decisions can be taken today to create the best possible tomorrow[23].

In comparison, future studies aims to "discover or invent, examine and evaluate, and propose possible, probable and preferable futures"[24]. We do not express a preference for one term over another, in part because we have no interest in joining the semantic debate. For the purposes of consistency in our research, we use the term foresight to refer to the study of the future.

Cross-disciplinary by nature, foresight addresses relationships among complex societal problems from as wide as possible a point of view. It draws on such disciplines as psychology, history, policy science, economics, environmental science, and business administration. Whether foresight is a field or discipline in its own right is subject to debate. Marien[25] argues that if ever foresight was, its diversity ensures that it is certainly not a discipline now. Others disagree[26;27], with some arguing that although foresight as a scientific discipline has not yet reached maturity, it is no longer in its adolescence[28].

Foresight emerged in decision-making contexts following the Second World War, in US military strategic planning at the RAND Corporation, and in French spatial planning at DATAR. In the 1960s, General Electric and Royal Dutch/Shell introduced foresight techniques to their corporate planning procedures. In the 1970s, foresight was applied in speculating about socio-economic and environmental futures. The 1972 Club of Rome report *The Limits to Growth*[29] is perhaps the most renowned and controversial example of a foresight study in the public domain. Today, foresight initiatives are undertaken in a range of contexts[30], from small and middle enterprises (SMEs), to regional and national foresight studies such as the UK foresight programme[31;32;33], from environmental assessments for public policy such as the United Nations Environmental Programme's Global Environmental Outlook[34] to the outlooks of the RIVM Netherlands Institute of Public Health and the Environment[35].

I INTRODUCTION

Foresight aims to make complex societal problems understandable in order to speculate about their possible development. Persistent[36], messy[37] and 'wicked'[35;38;39;40;41], complex societal problems are characterised by their unstructured, unsolvable nature. They can merely be contained or managed. They are the subject of conflict due to divergent interests and perspectives of those people they involve, but also to the urgency of the problem, which prevents their comprehensive analysis. Complex problems are also described as composed of a tangled web of interconnected problems: multi-disciplinary, cutting across various disciplines and socio- cultural, economic, technological, environmental, and institutional, which separate in various spatial or geographical scales. Complex problems are relevant for our research because the interaction of events and processes in society might lead to discontinuity.

The study of complex problems is also the focus of a school of thought called Integrated Assessment (IA)[35;42;43;44]. IA is a structured process of dealing with complex issues that uses knowledge from various scientific disciplines and/or stakeholders to offer integrated insights to decision-makers[1]. IA attempts to shed light on complex issues by illuminating a wide analysis of causal relationships and strategic options. In doing so, IA analyses the evolution of problems in their past, present, and future contexts. Holism rather than reductionism is the philosophy underlying IA.

IA originated in the USA and in Europe in the seventies[8]. In Europe, it stemmed from demographic and environmental research; in the USA, from economic cost-benefit analyses of environmental problems. The approach is connected to such fields as technology assessment[45], risk analysis[46], and policy studies[47]. However, IA distinguishes itself from these disciplines by using the idea of integration as its point of departure[8]. One can distinguish between two categories of IA methods[35;42;43]. First, there are analytical techniques such as models and risk assessments involving a rigorous research method. Second, there are participatory techniques such as policy exercises and focus groups. Judging from experimentation with IA methods, the engagement of stakeholders in participatory processes helps to improve the quality of IA by drawing on non-scientific knowledge, values, and preferences[48] but many of its methods are still under development.

Where foresight is more future-oriented, IA focuses on making complexity manageable for policy making. The IA community has a more natural scientific orientation than the various foresight schools, which are dominated by social scientists, but the two communities overlap with regard to methods that they use. Both use

---

[1] References to Integrated Assessment literature proposed by Van Asselt, Rotmans, & Rothman (2004) include: Dowlatabadi and Morgan (1993), Parson (1996), Bailey et al. (1996), Morgan and Dowlatabadi (1996), Robinson (1996), Rotmans and van Asselt (1996), Weyant et al (1996), Schneider (1997), Rotmans (1998), Jäger (1998), Tol and Vellinga (1998), Toth and Hizsnyik (1998), Rotmans and Dowlatabadi (1998), Kasemir et al. (1999), van Asselt (2000), Rotmans and van Asselt (2002) and Kasemir et al (2003).

mathematical projections and scenario development, and they share the opinion that methods are best used in combination with one another[49].

Societal discontinuity is a relatively new area of concern in IA[50;51;52] and foresight. Since the 1970s the consideration of change and discontinuity has gained some ground over predictive forecasting[53], which tended to reason from continuous developments and linear processes. It is argued that although studies of the future traditionally reasoned from the idea of continuous developments and linear processes. A departure from this historical or evolutionary determinism seems to have occured[54] as well as interest created to reflect systematically on discontinuity.

3 Focus of the research

The research described in our thesis focuses on the idea of discontinuity in the context of IA and foresight methodology. It is argued that foresight methodology has hardly been reflected on[12;55;56]. Reflection on IA methodology is considered similarly appropriate[35;43;57] especially in view of the interest in societal discontinuity in contemporary public debate. We chose to focus on methodological aspects of IA and foresight in order to gain insight into current practice. In the context of IA and foresight, methodology addresses the means whereby a study is conducted. This includes not only method, but also issues of context, timing, objective, facilitation, logistics, participants and expertise, and scientific philosophy. Subsequently, we did not focus exclusively on methods or techniques in our research. Rather, we were interested in the full range of factors that influence the process of exploring discontinuity with a view to contributing to the methodological improvement of IA and foresight[2].

We chose as the centrepiece of our research the investigation of the ways in which discontinuity is addressed in scenario development. We did so for two reasons. First, scenario development is arguably the most common approach in foresight[58] and it is also regularly applied in IA. Therefore, short of a comprehensive and undoable analysis of IA and foresight in the current thesis, an analysis of contemporary scenario development was appropriate. Second, according to the literature, scenario development is an approach that is well suited to exploring the idea of discontinuity[32;59] and therefore an analysis of contemporary scenario practice and its treatment of discontinuity also seemed fitting.

Scenarios are coherent descriptions of alternative hypothetical futures that reflect different perspectives on past, present, and future developments, which can serve as a basis for action[60]. Scenario development aims to combine analytical knowledge with creative thinking in an effort to capture a wide range of possible future developments in a limited number of outlooks. Scenario development assumes that the future is

---

2   Other methodological issues such as uncertainty and plurality are addressed in the Netherlands Organisation for Scientific Research's (NWO) Foresight Methodology programme, led by Dr. Marjolein van Asselt, of which this research is a part. See also Van Asselt et al (2003).

uncertain and the directions in which current developments might range from the conventional to the revolutionary[3]. Scenario development can be interpreted as a strictly defined method or as a more general philosophy, applicable in a variety of manners. We maintained the latter interpretation in the research described in this thesis.

The RAND Corporation was the first to use scenarios for decision-making purposes in post-Second World War military strategic planning[54;61;62]. Since then scenario uses, users, methods, and audiences have greatly diversified. The use of scenarios is referred to by various names each stressing numerous applications and contexts: scenario planning, scenario analysis, scenario thinking, and scenario learning. Because the focus of our research is on methodological aspects of scenarios, we prefer to use the term scenario development.

The thesis' title *Writing on the Wall* is a reference to the warning of impending discontinuity in the biblical tale of Belshazzar, King of Babylon, described in the book of Daniel. Belshazzar hosted a lavish feast for more than a thousand dignitaries for which he had used gold and silver goblets taken from the temple in Jerusalem years before by the Babylonians. The goblets were sacred but the king and his guests drank from them anyway. During the feast a hand appeared and wrote an inscription on a wall, "Mene mene tekel u-pharsin". The terrified king called on his magicians to explain what the writing on the wall meant. Only Daniel, the head of the king's magicians, could decipher it: "You have been weighed in the scales of God's judgement and have been found too light." Daniel explained that the writing was a warning to Belshazzar that his days as king were numbered because of his arrogance towards God, and that his kingdom would be split in two. This dramatic turn of events was not long in coming. Babylon was overrun that same night, the king was killed, and his kingdom was divided between the Medes and the Persians. Sudden, structural change such as the end of Belshazzar's kingdom is a feature of discontinuity. The challenge is to decipher the writing on the wall.

The title *Writing on the Wall* also refers to the popular method of group brainstorming, used in scenario development. In scenario workshops, brainstorming is used to produce ideas about possible future events and developments. These ideas are put in writing on paper or post-its, which are then posted on a wall for all involved to see and consider.

4 Framework of the research
Research objective
The research described in the current thesis seeks to establish an understanding of the meaning of discontinuity in the context of IA and foresight in general and in particular

---

[3] For research of uncertainty in IA see Van Asselt (2000), Van der Sluijs (1997), and Walker et al (2003).

the manner in which it is addressed in scenario development. By doing so, we aim to contribute to the improvement of discontinuity-oriented methodology. To do so we addressed such research questions as:

- What types of scenarios are there? What are their functions? How are they developed?
- How is discontinuity interpreted in the context of IA and foresight in general, and in scenario practice in particular?
- To what extent can contemporary scenarios be considered discontinuity-rich? How are such scenarios developed?
- What factors should be taken into account in discontinuity-oriented scenario development?

We did not set ourselves the task of assessing the overall value of scenario development. Because it is already commonly used we considered methodological questions to be more useful and interesting than existential questions. Only where discontinuity is concerned did we address existential issues to a limited degree. Furthermore, we did not aim to judge the output and use of individual scenario studies. Instead, our focus was on whether and how discontinuity is or can be addressed in scenario development. Lastly, our aim was not to invent the ultimate scenario method for identifying future discontinuity. Instead, we used a broad methodological scope to investigate how the idea of discontinuity is addressed in scenario development and what factors might inspire or impair discontinuity-oriented scenario development, as a basis for a methodological proposal.

Research methodology

To our knowledge no scientific investigation of scenario development has addressed the issue of discontinuity. Accordingly, we argue that a theoretical basis for scenario development in relation to discontinuity is necessary before hypotheses could be formulated with a view to falsification[63]. Although we suspect that the idea of discontinuity is not as embedded in scenario practice as sources in scenario literature[32;64;65;66;67] suggest, our research aimed to generate hypotheses without a particular premise as a leading principle.

Consequently, the first steps in the research have an exploratory or 'self-conceptualising' character, aiming to develop a conceptual framework rather than to test one[4]. The exploratory process led to a conceptualisation of the idea of discontinuity

---

[4] A distinction was made between self-conceptualising and pre-conceptualised research by Kees van der Heijden in a peer review workshop for the Futures Methodology programme (September, 2003, Maastricht). He explained that self-conceptualising research was open and exploratory in nature and free of a predetermined frame of reference or set of assumptions regarding the subject of study. In contrast, pre-conceptualised research does reason from a common theory or framework.

for scenario development. The concept allowed us to investigate the degree to which contemporary scenarios are discontinuity-rich. It also provided the basis for evaluation. The evaluative part of the research involved an empirical investigation of factors that inspire and impair discontinuity-oriented scenario development. Establishing a body of knowledge informed by both theoretical and empirical insights allowed for the formulation and testing of a hypothesis in an experiment. The hypothesis derived from our research was framed as:

> *Discontinuity-oriented scenario development involves fostering the interplay of influential factors whereby inspiring ones are mobilised and impairing ones are quashed.*

Factors that inspire are those that stimulate the exploration of discontinuity. In contrast, impairing factors hinder discontinuity-thinking. Influential factors might also have a 'double-edged' effect with both inspirational and impairing aspects, depending on the influence of other factors. The hypothesis implies that one can create conditions for the exploration of discontinuity. We aimed to do that in a systematic manner in order to make a discontinuity-oriented scenario process reproducible.

Research Methods

Reviews of foresight and scenario literature underlay our research and the empirical findings are based on interviews and an experiment.

A review of IA and foresight literature was necessary in the first, exploratory stages of the research in order to develop a conceptual framework. This literature helped to establish the history and basic principles of scenario development and various interpretations of the idea of discontinuity. In the latter case, we extended our scope of investigation to include such fields as history, policy studies, and the natural sciences in order to develop our conceptual basis.

We reasoned that general statements about scenario development could not be made without first establishing an overview of contemporary scenario practice. The rare examples of structured overviews of scenario processes[68;69;70;71;72;73] generally focus on particular aspects of scenario development. Therefore, we carried out a rudimentary overview of 100 scenario studies conducted in the past 20 years along with an in-depth analysis of 30, by analysing such documentation as project reports and publications. In some cases interviews were conducted in order to support the details of the documentation. This research led to a development of a typology for scenarios with which scenario studies might be compared. The typology was used to investigate how contemporary scenario studies address discontinuity.

A combination of interviews, archive research, and unsystematic participant observation was used in the reconstruction of one discontinuity-rich scenario study entitled 'VISIONS for a sustainable Europe'. VISIONS was the study of choice because we judged the scenarios it produced to be relatively discontinuity-rich and because the study was extensively documented. Much use was made of such primary sources as papers, progress reports, workshop proceedings, and correspondence. We chose to conduct interviews with members of the VISIONS scenario team in the expectation that they would provide 'behind the scenes'-commentary and reflections on the process to complement the information in the archive material. Unsystematic participant observation involved the participation of the author in a number of VISIONS meetings.

In the VISIONS reconstruction, the various methods were used in combination with one another in accordance with the research strategy of triangulation[74]. The strategy involves the use of different methods and sources of information so that the validity of the observations from one source can be checked and complemented by observations from another. In the classical use of the term triangulation a distinction is made between the principal source of study and the supporting source. However, in the VISIONS reconstruction we did not distinguish between principle and supporting sources. Instead, we used the idea of triangulation in a manner which allowed us to switch between different types of sources and methods[75]. In doing so, differences between the output of the various sources were used as leads for further investigation.

The comparative review and the reconstruction provided the basis for the formulation of the above-mentioned hypothesis about discontinuity-oriented scenario development, which we tested in an experiment. We chose an experimental approach because it provided the opportunity for real-time observation. The experiment involved the preparation, conduct, and analysis of two workshops with a diverse group of participants in order to simulate a natural scenario exercise as best as possible. The design was developed on the basis of general characteristics of the discontinuity-oriented scenario studies that we identified in developing our typology of scenarios, and on insights regarding the inspiring and impairing factors that we derived from the VISIONS reconstruction. Four observers, an audio recorder and a video camera recorded the experiment. The subject of study was the future of the controversial European salmon aquaculture industry where the potential for discontinuity is considered great.

The steps taken in our research and the output that it delivered are described in Figure 1.

5 Audience and structure

Scenario development and its various applications are discussed in Chapter 2. We first address the basic principles of scenario development. In large part, the chapter relates to the common features and differences between the various types of contemporary scenarios. These are organised in a typology for scenarios, presented in the form of a 'scenario cartwheel'. Chapter 3 discusses various interpretations of the idea of discontinuity in scenario development, and in related sources. The chapter closes with a conceptualisation of discontinuity in the context of IA and foresight that acts as a guiding principle for the empirical research, described in the following chapters. The comparative review of scenario studies and the manner in which they address discontinuity is presented in Chapter 4. The VISIONS study is reconstructed

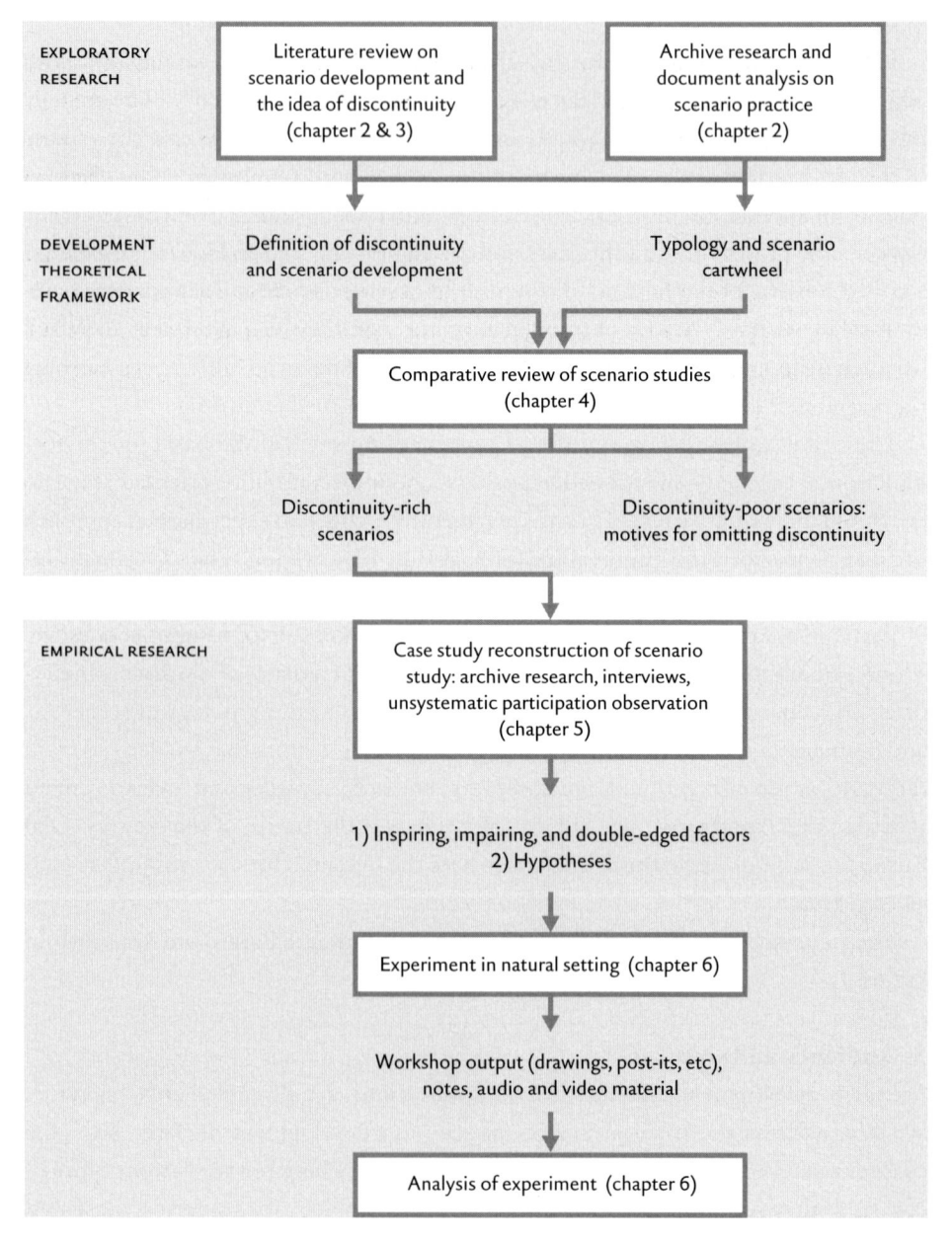

```
EXPLORATORY      Literature review on              Archive research and
RESEARCH         scenario development and          document analysis on
                 the idea of discontinuity         scenario practice
                 (chapter 2 & 3)                   (chapter 2)
                          ↓                                 ↓
DEVELOPMENT      Definition of discontinuity       Typology and scenario
THEORETICAL      and scenario development          cartwheel
FRAMEWORK
                          ↓         ↓
                 Comparative review of scenario studies
                                (chapter 4)
                          ↓                      ↓
                 Discontinuity-rich          Discontinuity-poor scenarios:
                 scenarios                   motives for omitting discontinuity
                          ↓
EMPIRICAL RESEARCH   Case study reconstruction of scenario
                     study: archive research, interviews,
                     unsystematic participation observation
                                (chapter 5)
                                   ↓
                 1) Inspiring, impairing, and double-edged factors
                 2) Hypotheses
                                   ↓
                 Experiment in natural setting (chapter 6)
                                   ↓
                 Workshop output (drawings, post-its, etc),
                 notes, audio and video material
                                   ↓
                 Analysis of experiment (chapter 6)
```

Figure 1 *The steps of the research. The type of research that was conducted is presented in boxes. The output of each step is denoted in the captions between the boxes.*

and the factors that inspired and those that impaired the exploration of discontinuity are described in detail in Chapter 5. The conclusions from Chapters 4 and 5 form the basis for the experiment in discontinuity-oriented research described in Chapter 6, which was intended to test the hypothesis mentioned above. In Chapter 7, we conclude by summarising and reflecting on our research as well as offering issues for further research.

The research is intended for several audiences. First, given its scientific context, the thesis is aimed at fellow academics, in particular those involved in IA, foresight, risk analysis, policy analysis, and strategic management. We argue that it is also relevant to historians interested in considering possible future implications of historic events and processes. A second audience is the group of scenario practitioners who develop scenarios on a regular basis. Lastly, the research is aimed at decision-makers and their advisers in public, private, and non-governmental organisations who develop and use scenarios. We contend that a better understanding of the idea of discontinuity and of scenario practice might help them in using scenarios in their decision-making.

2
scenario development today

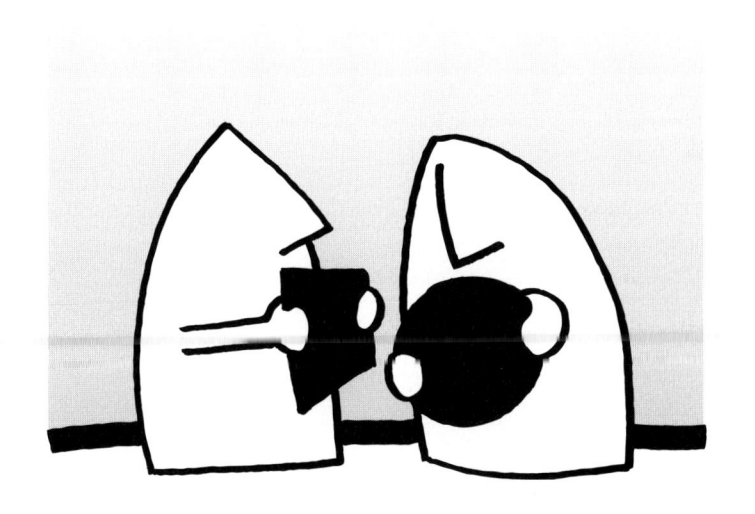

2 SCENARIO DEVELOPMENT TODAY

1 Introduction

Throughout its 50-year history scenario development has been applied in an increasing number of sectors and disciplines[1;2;3]. Scenario development originated within the field of military strategic planning[4] with Herman Kahn's technique of 'future-now thinking' at the RAND Corporation[2][1]. The technique combined detailed analysis with the use of the imagination to produce a report such as people living in the future might have written. Kahn reasoned that imagination had always been integral to the contemplation of the future, and that scenarios were a way of stimulating and disciplining imaginative thinking[5]. Inspired by Kahn, Royal Dutch/Shell established its Group Planning unit in 1964. The identification of the possibility of a sharp rise in oil prices on the eve of the 1973 Oil Crisis distinguished Shell's work with scenarios[6;7]. On the basis of his experiences of the oil crisis, Pierre Wack, Shell's scenario director, broadened the decision-oriented approach to scenarios to include the idea of learning. Since the seventies the educational function of scenarios has gained in importance[8].

Today, a diverse group of people develop and use scenarios in a variety of ways[1;9]. Numerous communities of scenario practitioners have developed over the years, each focusing on different types of scenario approaches[10]. Scenario development techniques have evolved and their popularity has waxed and waned[8]. Although we did not investigate the causes of these waves of popularity, the evolving nature of scenario practice made it desirable to establish an overview of the current state of the art in order to develop a basis for the rest of our research. Another motivation is Masini's and Vasquez's[11] observation that scenario development has become "a Swiss pocket knife of multiple uses, or a magic wand" that is often waved by inexperienced and unskilled consultants and professionals. They argue that this treatment of scenario approaches is damaging to the scenario community. The research described in the current chapter is intended establish an overview of contemporary scenario practice as a first step in our investigation of scenario methodology.

The chapter first examines the numerous definitions of scenarios with the aim of developing a working definition. Second, the chapter describes how we investigated the current state of scenario practice. The research was conducted through a comparative review of scenario studies of the past fifteen years, which led to the development of a typology for scenarios. The typology was then used as a heuristic for the evaluation of scenario practice.

---

[1] RAND is an acronym for Research And Development. RAND is a US-based policy advisory organisation.

2 Definition

The word scenario is derived from the Latin 'scaena', meaning scene[1;2]. The term scenario was originally used in the context of such performing arts as theatre and film. Kahn adopted the term because of its emphasis on storytelling. Since then the use of the term has changed somewhat. Sparrow[12] notes four contemporary uses of the word. One is synonymous with sensitivity analysis, whether in cash flow management, broader risk assessment, or project management. The second, used in the context of military strategic planning, is synonymous with the idea of a contingency plan that defines who is to do what during a particular crisis. This interpretation of the term scenario can also be found in the context of planning for civil emergency situations. In a third meaning, derived from military planning and used in the context of decision-making in public policy or commercial strategy, the scenario is also synonymous with a contingency plan. Sparrow argues that those who advise decision-makers hold a fourth interpretation, which regards scenarios in a more exploratory light. By planners' definition, a scenario is less a strategy than a coherently structured speculation. However, the distinction is not always recognised[13;14]. The fourth meaning nevertheless forms the focus of our research.

In the following paragraphs we examine scenario development as an exploratory approach by analysing approximately twenty definitions found in the scenario literature. Eleven representative definitions are cited here to describe the main characteristics of a scenario. For clarity's sake, we highlited the central characteristics in the definitions.

There are numerous views on how to define scenarios among those involved in scenario development, but on one point there is a consensus: they are not predictions[4;8]. They are instead descriptions of hypothetical situations that can be used to consider possible future actions[3]. In De Geus'[3] words:

The only relevant questions about the future are those where we succeed in shifting the question from whether something will happen to what we would do if it did happen.

According to Jungermann[15;16], scenarios communicate what might be expected to happen. He elaborates as follows:

Scenarios are descriptions of alternative HYPOTHETICAL *futures. They do not describe what the future will look like but rather what possible futures we might expect, depending on our actions (or inactions) in the present*[17].

Some definitions consider a scenario to be a description of an end state whereas others concentrate on the path to the end state. In addressing this issue Jungermann[17] distinguishes between snapshot scenarios and chain scenarios.

Snapshot scenario: *An outline of one conceivable* STATE OF AFFAIRS, *given certain assumptions about the present and the course of events in the intervening period.*

Chain scenario: *Hypothetical* SEQUENCES OF EVENTS *constructed for the purpose of focussing attention on* CAUSAL PROCESSES *and* DECISION POINTS [18].

Kahn and Wiener[18] do not consider snapshot scenarios to be scenarios at all, preferring to call them alternative futures. Kahn and Wiener's reference to causal processes is also found in Schoemaker's[19a] definition among others:

> *[Scenarios are] concrete, CAUSALLY COHERENT narratives woven around strands of evidence (a causal tapestry)*

A causal interpretation is also provided by Utrecht University's Department of Planning and Policy[19b]:

> *A scenario describes the present situation in (segments of) society together with the likely and desirable future states of this society and series of EVENTS (OR TRANSITION PATHS), WHICH MAY CONNECT THE PRESENT SITUATION AND THE FUTURE states of society*

Like Kahn and Wiener, Godet and Roubelat[20] refer to the idea that scenarios enable their users to take decisions and shape their futures:

> *A scenario is the set formed by the description of a future situation and the course of events that enables one to PROGRESS from the original situation to the future situation.*

Having established the causal and decision making aspects of several scenario definitions, we return to Schoemaker's definition to point out another feature of scenarios. Schoemaker refers to scenarios as narratives, an idea that is also supported by Van der Heijden's definition among others:

> *Scenarios [...] are STORIES describing the current and future states of the business environment*[21].

Postma[22] presents the notion of the internal consistency of scenarios, which is arguably connected to the idea of causal coherence that Schoemaker describes:

> *[Scenarios] are descriptions of internally CONSISTENT pictures of future events and/ or situations.*

Fahey and Randall[23] address the notion that scenarios should be plausible:

> *Scenarios are descriptive narratives of PLAUSIBLE alternative projections of a specific part of the future.*

Some definitions introduce the idea that a scenario is an interpretation of the future by the people who develop it:

> *Scenarios are tools for reordering ones PERCEPTIONS about alternative future environments in which today's decisions might be played out*[24].

Rotmans[25] and Van Asselt elaborate by introducing the idea of perspectives. Furthermore, whereas many definitions highlight a scenario's connection of the present with the future, Rotmans and Van Asselt introduce the idea that the past is relevant as well:

> *Scenarios are archetypal descriptions of alternative images of the future, created from mental maps or models that reflect DIFFERENT PERSPECTIVES on PAST, present and future developments.*

We do not subscribe to any one of these definitions in view of the diversity that we observe above. Nonetheless, in order to be explicit about our point of departure for

our research we propose a general, inclusive working definition of scenarios, based on the various characteristics of scenarios described above. The scenario's main characteristics are their:
- Hypothetical nature;
- Description of alternative futures;
- Description of a future end-state or a path to an end-state;
- Causal coherence and Internal consistency
- Possible use as a basis for action;
- Descriptive nature;
- Plausibility;
- Interpretative nature;
- Connection between past, present and future.

We contend that plausibility is not a manageable characteristic for our definition due to its normative nature. If the aim of scenarios is not to ask what will happen in the future, as De Geus[3] indicates, then plausibility is a problematic criterion because it requires a premature judgement on the probability of future developments.

We have attempted to draw on all the other listed characteristics in composing the following definition:

Scenarios are coherent descriptions of alternative hypothetical futures that reflect different perspectives on past, present, and future developments, which can serve as a basis for action.

3 Study of contemporary scenario practice

Having established a definitional point of departure, we turn to the investigation of contemporary scenario practice. Like in the examination of definitions of scenarios, we also observed a diversity of the contexts in which scenarios are used. The observed diversity is a point of departure for our research, as we will explain below.

3.1 Scenario diversity

An indication of the variety of contemporary scenario practice is its wide application: multinationals[26], local governments[27] and such temporary bodies as national foresight programmes[28]. A limited number of private organisations such as Shell[29] and DaimlerChrysler[30] have institutionalised the use of scenarios. However, they are developed and applied on an ad-hoc basis by many organisations including those in short-term oriented markets, such as the telecom companies KPN, Ericsson, and Vodafone. Scenario development is not common with SMEs[31], although two documented examples are the mail-order company Smith & Hawken[32] and Flight Directors, a broker between airlines and holiday companies[31]. Another form of scenario work developed in the last 15 years through inter-company co-operation, facilitated by organisations such as Global Business Network (GBN) and the World Business Council for Sustainable Development (WBCSD).

The public sector also contains a large variety of users. Scenario studies are conducted by global organisations such as the World Bank[33] and the United Nations Environmental Programme[34]. Activities on a continental level include the European Commission's Institute for Prospective Technological Studies and such European Union programmes as EForsee and the COST European Network for Foresight Methodology. Numerous ad-hoc intergovernmental platforms have been set up to conduct multi-stakeholder foresight programmes not only on the regional and national levels, such as in Finland[35] but also popular on the local level such those studies conducted in the Dutch cities Den Bosch[36] and Rotterdam[27].

The participation of civil society in exploratory scenario studies is a development of the last fifteen years. So-called civic scenario studies have been conducted in South Africa[37;38], Colombia[39], and Kenya[40] among others. They involved a wide range of participants including guerrillas, religious organisations, political parties, businessmen, and trade union members.

The academic community is also increasingly active in scenario research. The work of the Global Scenario Group[41] and that of the Intergovernmental Panel on Climate Change (IPCC)[42] are examples of on-going scenario work in a largely academic context.

Given the diversity of current scenario practice, there needs to be a regular exchange of ideas and a development of a shared understanding between the various communities of scenario practitioners if fragmentation is to be avoided. The issue of fragmentation in foresight was explored in issues of Futures[10;43;44;45] in which Marien[10] argued that the foresight 'field' is a misnomer. He warned that foresight practice is vulnerable to fragmentation because its shared theoretical basis is limited. He argues that fragmentation might lead to the reinvention of wheels.

There are a limited number of publications that present a collection of case studies such as Ringland[1;26;27] and Fahey and Randall[46], but these tend not to compare scenario studies. The only comparative studies that we are aware of are Cloudy Crystal Balls: An assessment of recent European and global scenario studies and models[9], Political Experiments of the 1990s: The Use of Scenarios in the Public Domain[47;48], the Dutch Terugblik op toekomstverkenningen (A retrospective look at future studies)[49] and a discussion in a Futures special issue[50]. However, these comparative studies generally focus on particular aspects of scenario development and do not capture the widely differing understandings of contemporary practice. Due to the general lack of an overview of approaches, scenario communities might unknowingly be engaged in similar work and, as Marien argues, they risk reinventing the wheel.

3.2 A comparative review and a typology for scenarios

Critical reflection on current practice is useful given the diversity of examples it provides and the opportunities it offers. We expected that in conducting a comparative review of scenario studies we might establish a basis for our methodological research. The review was conducted in combination with the development of a typology, which we then used as a heuristic for the evaluation of scenario practice. A common framework was necessary in order to evaluate the similarities and differences in contemporary scenario practices in a consistent manner. In order to do justice to the variety of approaches and contexts it was necessary to investigate a relatively large number of studies.

We aimed to establish an overview of scenario practice through a comparative review of approximately 100 studies carried out since 1985 and listed in Appendix 1. Not all the studies we consulted were used in equal measure for the development of the typology due to the variation in their documentation. Accordingly a selection of 30 scenario studies was made from the initial set of 100 studies based on the adequacy of the documentation for our purposes. Information about the studies was drawn from primary and secondary sources, ranging from reviews of recent scenario processes to interviews with people involved in those studies. A research constraint was the shortage of available sources for decision-oriented scenarios developed for commercial organisations. An explanation for the shortage might be that commercial organisations are reluctant to share information in case they reveal sensitive strategic material.

The studies were conducted in a variety of organisational contexts, including businesses such as the British Airways and KPMG; 'inter-company' co-operative efforts such as the Dutch Management Association (NIVE) and the World Business Council for Sustainable Development (WBCSD); governmental organisations such as the Rotterdam port authority; broad based participatory efforts such as those in South Africa and Colombia; and academic settings such as the Intergovernmental Panel on Climate Change (IPCC) and the research institutes of the VISIONS project. The studies covered a variety of topics, including sectoral studies for transport, telecom, and nutrition; country studies and a regional study; and issue-based studies that address gender equality, the labour market, climate change, and leadership. Given the variety of the selected studies, we argue that they are representative enough to act as an empirical basis for our assessment of current scenario practice.

The diversity of contemporary scenario practice made it necessary to develop a heuristic broad and comprehensive enough to highlight the variety of scenario approaches in use today. A number of earlier typologies were consulted, such as those proposed by Ducot and Lubben[51], Duncan and Wack[52], Godet and Roubelat[13], Postma et al.[22], and Heugens and Van Oosterhout[53]. Each of these put forward fundamental distinctions between scenario types, but because typologies reflect a field's state of play at a fixed point in time, they become outdated as the field they address evolves. This is why we chose not to adopt Ducot and Lubben's detailed typology of 1980. Another problem is that most typologies do not capture sufficiently the diversity and flexibility in contemporary scenario development. Heugens' and Van Oosterhout's typology, although more recent than Ducot and Lubben's, is less detailed. Another drawback is the limited scope of some typologies. For example, business-oriented classifications such as Duncan's and Wack's do not acknowledge differences between macro-economic and environmental scenarios. We concluded that the existing classifications are a source of inspiration but not detailed enough for an in-depth analysis, nor broad enough to do justice to the variety of today's scenario development approaches. Consequently, it was decided to develop a new typology on the basis of earlier typologies and insights from the comparative review.

The comparative review and the typology development were conducted simultaneously in an iterative process. The selected studies were used to form the basis of the typology. Many other studies were used to illustrate parts of the typology, as the rest of the chapter will show. The comparative review and typology development resulted in what we call a 'scenario cartwheel', a graphic representation of the analysed studies on the basis of their similarities and differences. The cartwheel is presented in Figure 3, later in this chapter.

The establishment of the boundaries of the typology was a challenge. In determining the boundaries of a scenario process, we decided not to include dissemination as a characteristic in the typology because, although important in the communication of scenarios, it was not an integral part of the scenario development process itself. Similarly, we decided to exclude from the typology a scenario project's resources such as funding and the institutional conditions within which a scenario process takes place[21;49;54;55]. These aspects of scenario development are crucial to the success of scenario development but rather than investigating the nature of the choices behind these aspects, we chose to focus on methodology and the implications of methodological choices[2]. In addition, it was sometimes difficult to find terminology precise and clear enough to communicate distinctions between the typology's elements. Although we feel we have clarified in the large array of scenario terminology, some terms in the typology remain illusive when viewed out of the context of the others. Another challenge was to strike a balance between detail and

---

[2] An investigation of how and why decisions are made would require a more ethnographic type of research as Dobbinga (2001) demonstrates in her study of the Questa scenario process at the Dutch Ministry of Transport. A similar approach is also being taken in an investigation of scenario processes at the Dutch Spatial Planning Bureau and the Netherlands Energy Centre as part of the Innovational Research Incentive Scheme on foresight methodology.

generalisation. It is for this reason that we chose to develop a two-tiered typology. One level describes three general distinctions or 'macro characteristics' among scenarios and a second describes nine distinguishing characteristics or 'micro characteristics'. The scenario cartwheel only features the macro-characteristics since the use of micro-characteristics in order to capture nuances might diminish the graphic's communicative power.

The typology is explained in detail in the following two sections. It is illustrated using studies from the comparative review. Dimensions indicating the poles of the macro and micro characteristics provide further detail. The poles represent the possible extremes in scenario types. In practice, however, hybrid forms are common, as examples will show.

4 Macro characteristics

The typology proceeds from three macro characteristics comprising central aspects of scenario development. The macro characteristics apply both to sets of scenarios and to individual scenarios. We identified the macro characteristics in terms of the "why?" the "how?" and the "what?"; in other words, the project goal, the process design, and the scenario content. The project goal influences the process design, which, in turn, influences the scenario content.

4.1 Goal

The first macro characteristic addresses the scenario study's goal. Since the seventies, the educational function of scenarios has gained importance in relation to its function as a planning tool of earlier years[1;2;3]. Scenarios started to be used more for exploratory than predicative ends as illustrated by Royal Dutch/Shells' 1972 scenarios, which aimed to draw managers' attention to the possibility of a transformation in the supply chain for oil production. With the founding of Global Business Network (GBN) in 1987 some scenario practitioners abandoned the planning aspect of scenario development altogether choosing instead to use scenarios primarily for purposes of the learning and communication[24].

Policy planning is still a feature in some scenario contexts such as the French 'la prospective'; which aims to combine the exploratory with the decision-oriented[20]. Nevertheless, the decision-orientation of scenarios has broadened and tends to resemble pre-policy research rather than classical planning. Duncan and Wack[52] describe this evolution as follows:

> Over the years scenario planners have learned not to start with such a narrow focus [as with decision-oriented scenarios] since doing so increases the chances of missing key determinants of future conditions or events. You must first use a wide-angled lens to look at the big picture – afterward you can zoom in on the details.

Through the historical overview and the comparative review we observe that there are two poles of the spectrum of goals of a scenario study: exploration and pre-policy research. **Exploration** includes ends such as learning, awareness raising, the stimulation of creative thinking, and investigating the interaction of societal processes[1;9;21;32;56;57]. In an exploratory scenario exercise, the process is often as important as the product. The study 'Which World?: Scenarios for the 21st century'[58] is one of many examples of an exploratory exercise with its investigation of possible paths to alternative futures.

At the opposite end of the spectrum is the project goal of **pre-policy research**. Here scenarios are used to examine paths to futures that vary according to their desirability. Decision-support scenarios contain value-laden combinations of scenarios described as desirable, optimistic, high-road, or utopic; conventional or middle-of-the-road; and undesirable, pessimistic, low-road, dystopic, or doom scenarios. High- and low-road scenarios were developed in the Scenarios for Scotland study[59;60;61], and they are implied in the Mont Fleur[37;38] and the Destino Colombia scenarios[39]. Contemporary pre-policy research scenarios can propose concrete strategic options for decision-making purposes. Examples are the scenarios developed by AMD[62] and a nutrition company in 2000[63;64]3. More common today in pre-policy research scenarios is to provide implicit policy recommendations. For example, the most desirable Mont Fleur scenario, the Flight of the Flamingos, describes a South Africa successfully negotiating the post-apartheid transition period, but does so only in general policy terms[1;37;38].

In practice, many studies are hybrids that straddle the two poles of exploration and pre-policy research[13;21]. In a first phase, scenarios are developed in an exploration of certain topics. The resulting scenarios are often too general to function as a basis for decision-making. Therefore new scenarios developed using the broad exploratory basis of the first phase to zoom in on aspects relevant to strategy development. For example, at Royal Dutch/Shell, global scenarios are developed on a corporate level[21]. These scenarios are then used as input for the development of a second set of scenarios that focus on the strategic issues most relevant to individual Shell operating companies.

4.2 Process design

The second macro characteristic is a scenario exercise's process design, which addresses the methodological aspects of scenario development. Numerous scenario communities have developed over the years, and each focuses on different types of scenario approaches[10]. For example, the European environmental scenario

---

3   We withhold the name of the company in accordance with agreements about confidentiality.

community, which include such organisations as the Stockholm Environment Institute (SEI), the Austrian-based International Institute for Applied Systems Analysis (IIASA), and the Dutch National Institute of Public Health and the Environment (RIVM), often use computer simulations[65]. Meanwhile, the security and defence sector draws on the RAND Corporation's scenario work among others. The business community strongly relates to the Anglo-American approaches developed by Royal Dutch/Shell and GBN, although the French approach of 'la prospective' leans more strongly on computer software than its Anglo-American counterpart. German scenario work is known for its analytical rigour, as demonstrated by the work of DaimlerChrysler's Society and Technology Research Group[66] and Scenario Management International (ScMI)[67;68].

On the one end of the process design spectrum we find the **intuitive** approach. The intuitive scenario process strongly depends on qualitative knowledge and insights from which scenarios are developed. Such creative techniques as the development of stories or storylines in workshops are typical approaches to intuitive scenario development[21;32;69]. The intuitive approach suggests that scenario development is an art form; a viewpoint corroborated by such publication titles as The Art of the Long View[32] and The Art of Strategic Conversation[21;32]. There are a number of basic steps in an intuitive scenario process, according to Bood and Postma[70]:

- Identification of subject or problem area
- Description of relevant factors
- Prioritisation and selection of relevant factors
- Creation of scenarios

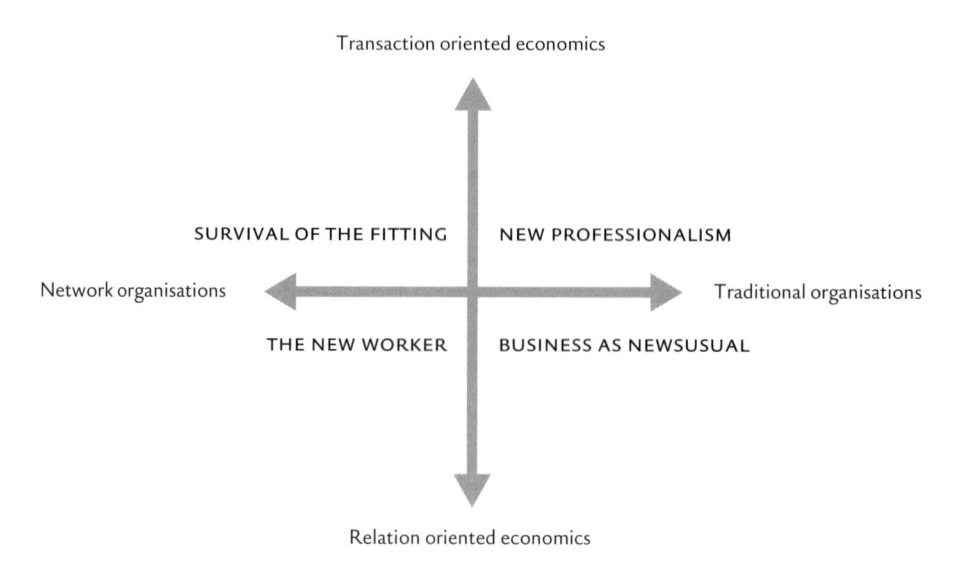

Figure 1 *The KPMG Ebbinge scenarios*

2020 PATENTS ON
'CANCER BUSTERS' EXPIRE

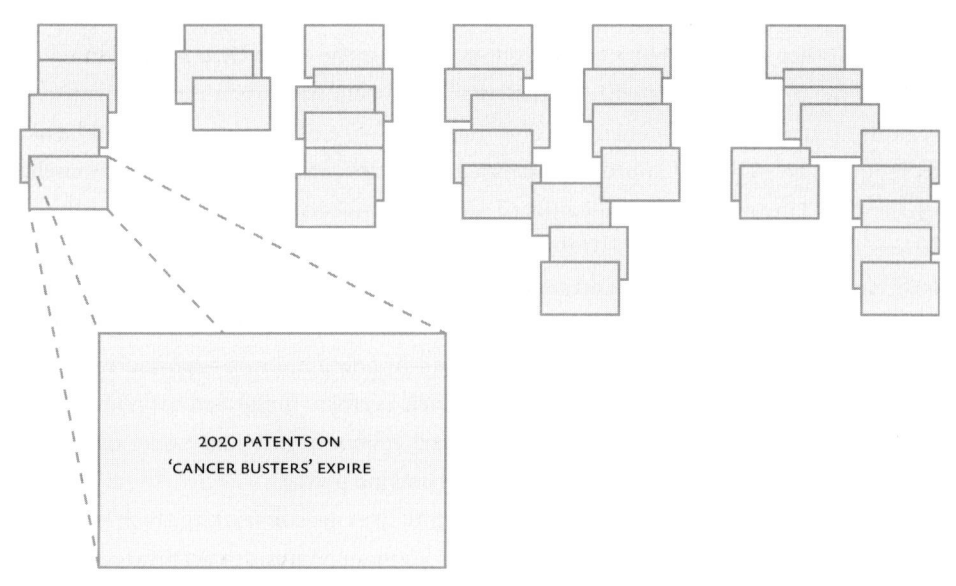

Figure 2 *Sequences of post-its form storylines*

A subsequent step might be the evaluation of the scenarios with a view to pre-policy research[70]. The above steps are usually performed in one of two manners: deductively or inductively[21]. The deductive manner aims to create a framework early on in the process with which to structure the rest of the scenario exercise. A two dimensional matrix is a common method used in the deductive approach. Such a framework is created by identifying the two most influential factors for the future of concern. Other relevant factors are then arranged around the framework. The scenarios on the future of the Dutch job market developed by KPMG Ebbinge[71;72] were developed with the help of such a matrix, as illustrated in Figure 1[4]. The dominant factors considered here are economic relationships and organisation types. The two future possibilities of each factor are represented by transaction- and relation-oriented economic relationships, as well as by network and traditional organisations. These form the basis for the development of four scenarios.

An inductive approach, on the other hand, does not use such a framework to impose a structure on the scenario process. Instead, scenarios are created in a freer process, whereby coherent stories are developed from associations, inferred causal patterns and other ideas. When inductive approaches are used in workshops the ideas are often represented in a series of post-it notes arranged sequentially to form storylines, as illustrated in Figure 2[5]. The VISIONS[56;73] scenarios were developed in such a manner, although some use was made of a so-called 'factor, actor, sector'-framework, which provided an additional structure for thinking about the future.

4   KPMG Ebbinge is now called Ebbinge & Company.
5   The squares in the figure represent possible future developments.

At the other end of the process design spectrum is the **analytical** approach. Contrary to the intuitive approach, the analytical approach, such as 'la prospective'[13;74], regards scenario development as an analytical and systematic exercise. Model-based techniques are analytical approaches derived from the earliest scenario development methods and involving a quantification of prominent uncertainties[6]. Computer simulations are more rigorous and less flexible than intuitive approaches[11]. For instance, it is difficult and costly to repeat certain steps taken in 'la prospective's' approach[11], and often relevant causal relationships cannot be addressed in model-based approaches. Examples of computer simulation models used in contemporary scenario work include TARGETS[75;76] and Threshold 21[9], which perform integrated assessments of sustainability; and WORLDSCAN[9;77], an macro-economic oriented model applied to economic, energy, transport, trade, and environmental policy[6].

Another type of analytical scenario development is desk research, which involves the development of scenarios on the basis of document analysis or archival research. This process is less formalised and systematic than model-based approaches, but is often just as rigorous. Examples of scenario studies based on desk research include Bobbitt's[78], The Shield of Achilles, Schwartz et al.'s[130] The Long Boom, and McRae's[79] global scenario described in The World in 2020.

It is possible to combine intuitive and analytical approaches. To illustrate, desk research often forms a part of extensive intuitive scenario exercises. These exercises use scenario workshops to generate creative ideas, and a core scenario team conducts desk research to elaborate and process the workshop ideas. Examples of studies that used intuitive processes in combination with desk research include the VISIONS process[56;73], during which much time was spent elaborating material from workshops. There are also examples of scenario studies that attempted to combine intuitive process designs with model-based approaches. For example, in the development of the IPCC emissions scenarios, intuitive techniques supported a predominantly analytical approach insofar as drafting narratives formed the first step in the development of quantified, model-based scenarios, followed by a consultation process with experts worldwide[42]. Equally, the analytical might support the intuitive, as demonstrated by the GEO – 3 scenarios[34][7]. The IPCC and UNEP have conducted several model-based environmental scenarios since the early nineties. Each successive scenario study that these organisations conduct involves increasingly intuitive techniques in combination with models. Nevertheless, the combining of intuitive approaches with model-based techniques is relatively new and subject to experimentation.

Intuitive designs are commonly used for exploratory purposes while analytical designs are more often used in pre-policy research exercises. The NIVE study[80]

---

[6] TARGETS and WORLDSCAN are acronyms for Tool to Assess Regional and Global Environmental and Health Targets for Sustainability and WORLD model for SCenario ANalysis respectively.

on the future of leadership is an example of an exploratory exercise conducted in an intuitive manner. Similarly, examples of analytical techniques used in pre-policy research exercises are the Battelle Institute's BASICS and 'la prospective's' MICMAC approach[1;74;81][8]. Both probabilistic computer-based approaches are used to identify cross-impacts between variables.

4.3 Scenario content
The third and final macro characteristic involves the content or composition of the developed scenarios. We distinguish between **complex** and **simple** scenarios. Applied to the context of scenario development, a complex scenario is composed of an intricate web of causally related, interwoven events and processes; while a simple scenario is more limited. The subject of simple scenarios might be a particular niche, such as chipmaker AMD's scenarios to anticipate the possible reactions of its competitor Intel to the introduction of a computer chip[62]. Alternatively, simple scenarios may limit themselves to the extrapolation of a limited set of isolated trends, such

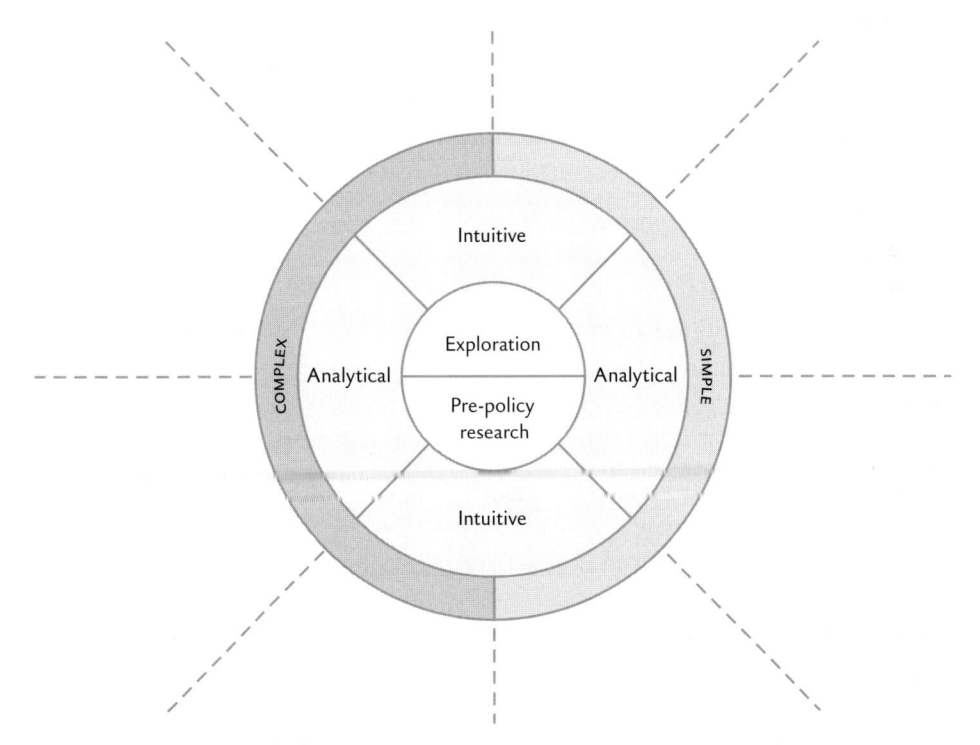

Figure 3 *The scenario cartwheel*

[7] GEO is an acronym for Global Environmental Outlook. GEO-3 is the third in the GEO series of UNEP-outlooks.
[8] BASICS and MICMAC are acronyms for Battelle Scenario Inputs to Corporate Strategy and Matrice d'Impacts Croisés Multiplication Appliquée à un Classement respectively. In English: Cross-Impact Matrix Multiplication Applied to Classification.

as the European Environment Agency's baseline scenario on the future of Europe's environment[82]. The term 'simple' in the context of scenario development does not indicate poor quality. Indeed, scenarios are sometimes criticised for being overly complicated and incomprehensible 'black boxes'. A simple scenario can be more effective and less demanding in terms of resources than its complex counterpart[83].

The macro characteristics are presented in figure 3 which we refer to as the scenario cartwheel, which can be used as a heuristic to distinguish between different types of scenario studies.

5 Micro characteristics

A rudimentary comparison of scenario analyses might confine itself to the use of the macro characteristics. A more in-depth comparison demands a greater appreciation of detail, which can be gained with the help of nine micro characteristics, described in the following paragraphs, and arranged according to the macro characteristic with which they are closest associated. The micro characteristics are denoted in bold; the range of possibilities within the context of each characteristic is denoted in italics.

5.1 Project-goal characteristics

A first characteristic addresses the **function** of the scenario exercise. Functions can be either related to the scenario development *process* or to the *product* of its output. Process-oriented scenario development has the following functions:
- Learning;
- Communication; and,
- Improving observational skills.

The educational function of a scenario process involves informing people[4;84] by deciphering the often confusing information of the present[52] and arranging possible future events and developments in consistent pictures of the future[85]. Making sense of the future in this manner involves challenging mental models[6] and prevailing mindsets[86], learning from the past[70], and investigating fundamental uncertainties[19] about the future. The educational aspect of scenario development arguably helps improve peoples' intellectual and creative skills[8;19;21;70]. Ultimately, scenarios might serve as a vehicle to create an awareness of the future in society[8].

In addition to an educational function, scenarios might also have a communicative function[4;11]. The process of scenario development provides a common reference point for discussion[21;87] across disciplinary boundaries. In organisations it can provide a basis for 'strategic conversations'[21;32] through which to address threats and opportunities, and to develop strategy on the basis of a shared mental model. Learning through social interaction in a scenario process arguably helps an organisation improve its perceptive ability and thereby anticipate difficult times and cash in on opportunities[32]. In doing so an organisation might act or react more vigilantly to unexpected events[88] and thus avoid being caught off guard in the future[87].

Product-oriented scenario studies are more concerned with the nature and quality of the output than with the manner in which the output arose. Functions of product-oriented scenarios are:
- Identification of driving forces and signs of emerging trends;
- Development of policy; and
- Testing of policy.

Scenarios can be used to identify and evaluate the potential dangers and opportunities behind prominent events and processes, as well as emerging ones[11;70;85]. This function is related to the aforementioned perceptive skills. The signs of emerging developments are also referred to as weak signals[30;89], early warnings[90;91], seeds[90] or traces[92]. The evaluation of events and processes can be an aid in policy development[4;21;46;93]. Furthermore, scenarios might also be a tool for evaluating decisions and testing policy options[21;53;70;85;87;93]. Using scenarios to do 'practice runs' of possible future situations, might indicate possible effects of present-day decisions.

A second micro characteristic focuses on the degree a scenario is **normative**. The issue of norms and values is contentious, since all scenarios are arguably normative, insofar as they consist of the interpretations, values, and interests of those involved in the scenario exercise. We distinguish between *descriptive* scenarios, which explore possible futures, and *normative* scenarios, which are explicitly normative because of their description of probable or preferable futures. Types of descriptive scenarios in the literature on the subject include baseline, reference, or non-intervention scenarios. Interpretations of these terms vary[13;22;51;94;95] as do the terms that refer to normative scenarios: prospective, strategy, policy or intervention scenarios. Most current scenario studies are descriptive[9]. For example, Royal Dutch/Shell's 2001 global scenarios entitled Business Class and Prism are descriptive in their outline of two possible futures free from indications of desirability[96]. In contrast, the 'Balanced Growth' scenario in The Netherlands in Triplicate study[97] is normative because it aims to show that, given certain conditions, economic growth need not exclude environmental protection.

Whether a scenario looks forwards from a particular present situation or backwards from a particular point in the future might have an influence on whether it is considered normative. For instance, the backward-looking 'backcasting'[9;13;51;56;85;94;95;98;99;100] scenario is explicitly normative in its analysis of policy measures and other developments needed to reach a particular desirable future. An example of a backcasting study is the POSSUM project[9;101] in which sustainable transport targets for the year 2020 were formulated. However, not all backward-looking scenarios are explicitly normative as the descriptions in the literature on anticipatory[16;51;94] scenarios demonstrate.

Scenarios also differ according to the **subject** or problem area addressed by a scenario study. The subject provides focus to a scenario study, narrowed down by the time scale in question[9;56]. The perception of time is context-dependent. Ten years is considered long-term in the fashion industry whereas it is relatively short-term for many environmental issues. As a general rule, a long-term scale for a scenario is 25 years or more, as used by the World Business Council for Sustainable Development's (WBCSD) global scenarios to the year 2050[102;103]. A short-term scale is 3 – 10 years, as used in the year 2000 scenario study of the food and beverage market for 2005 by a Dutch nutrition company[63;64]. Due to its context-dependency, we do not use time as a micro characteristic in its own right. However, time scale is relevant for establishing focus with regards to the *issue*, the geographical *area* and/or the *institution* addressed by the scenarios.

Issue-based scenarios take societal questions as the subject of study. Examples of issue-based scenario analyses are those on the future of television[104], of crime[105], and of women[106].

Area-based scenarios explore a particular geographical region, such as a country, a sub-national region, or a city. Examples of scenarios that address the global scale are the OECD scenarios The World in 2020[9] and the IPCC scenarios[42;75;94]. There are also a large number of scenario studies that address the national level, such as the Japan[107;108] and Destino Colombia[39] scenarios; and The Netherlands in 2030, a study that developed scenarios of possible spatial planning futures[39;49;109]. An example of regional scenarios is the Dutch study Scenarios for Agriculture and Land-Use in Noord Brabant[49]9.

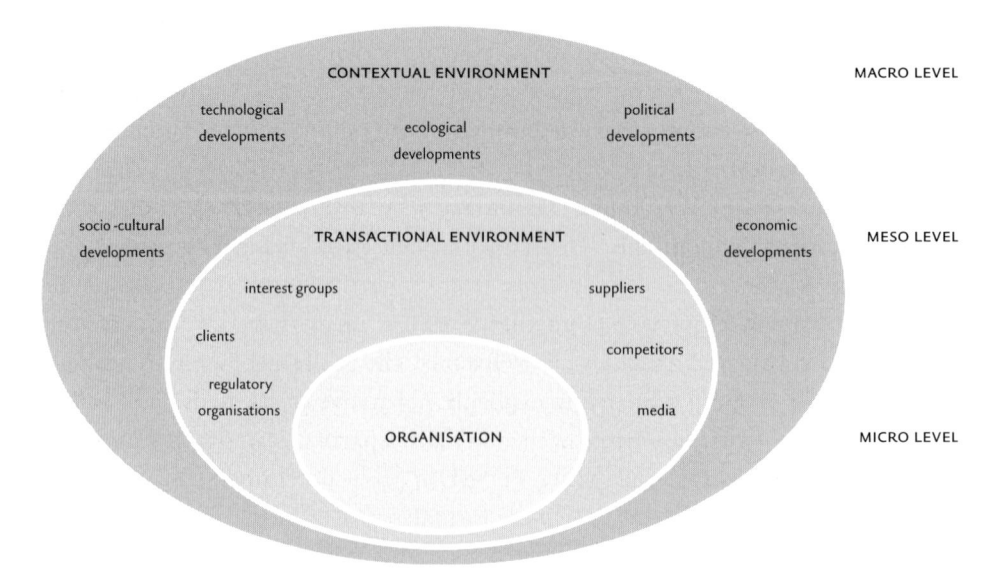

Figure 4 *Breakdown of institution-based spheres*

Institution-based scenarios address the spheres of interest of an organisation, group of organisations, or sector. This type of scenario can be broadly sub-divided into so-called macro or contextual scenarios on the one hand, and focused or transactional scenarios on the other[21;22;52;94;110][10]. The contextual scenario describes the institution's macro-environment: the issues that are not directly influenced by the institution that conducts the scenario development. Contextual analyses might be used to explore unfamiliar or expansive terrain, such as Shell's global scenarios[21]. A transactional scenario describes the institution's meso-environment[13;21]. This type of scenario focuses on the interactions between variables and dynamics within a particular field. Whether an issue addresses the contextual or transactional environment is determined by whether the institution can directly influence the issue under study. The institution-based spheres are illustrated in Figure 4. However, the distinction between the contextual and transactional environments is sometimes vague[53].

A study can consist of combinations of issue-based, area-based, and institution-based scenarios. For example, the VISIONS scenarios[56] are both area-based and issue-based in their exploration of such issues as equity, employment, and consumption in a European context; and the drinks company United Distillers' scenarios of India and South Africa are both institution-based and area-based[1].

5.2 Process design characteristics

Different types of scenario development can also be distinguished on the basis of the type of **input** used. We distinguish between *qualitative* or *quantitative*[9;56;94] input. Qualitative input is appropriate in the analysis of uncertain and complex situations and when relevant information cannot be entirely quantified. Relevant qualitative information might include opinions about human values and behaviour invariably used in such intuitive processes as the NIVE[80], Beyond Hunger[111], and Surprising Futures studies[112]. Quantitative input is used in computer models[113;114], developed to explore the fields of energy, technology, macro-economy, and the environment[9;82;115;116]. Examples of the studies based on quantitative input include the scenarios developed by the Netherlands Bureau for Economic Policy Analysis (CPB)[77] and by the IPCC[42].

Combining qualitative and quantitative input can make a scenario more consistent and robust[9;54;56;71]. A quantitative scenario might be enriched with the use of qualitative information. Likewise, a qualitative scenario might be tested for plausibility through the quantification of information, if possible. However, the fusion of quantitative and qualitative data in scenarios remains a methodological challenge.

---

[9] Noord Brabant is one of the Netherlands' 13 provinces.
[10] Terms related to macro scenarios are 'global', 'archetypal', 'framework' and 'external'. Terms related to meso scenarios are 'decision' and 'internal' scenarios.

A promising technique in this regard is agent-based modelling, which aims to incorporate such qualitative elements as actors' behavioural patterns in the otherwise quantitative realm of computer simulation[117;118;119].

The **methods** describe the approaches used in the scenario process. The poles in scenario development methods are the *participatory* approach on the one hand and *model-based* approach on the other. In the participatory approach, ideas for scenarios are collected in a participatory process[120;121;122]. A participatory approach might draw on a broad range of experts such as with the development of the KPMG Ebbinge scenarios on the future of the Dutch job market[71]; or only on stakeholders, as in the case of the workshop with local inhabitants for the VISIONS Green Heart scenario study[123;124;125]. Today, a common approach to participatory scenario development is a workshop involving stakeholders. Sometimes outsiders such as artists, writers, journalists, and specialists from other fields are involved to help improve the quality of the discussion. Workshop activities are easily adaptable to the needs that emerge from earlier steps in the scenario development process[21;22]. Other participatory techniques[121] include focus groups, citizens' juries[126] and envisioning workshops[127]. Participatory approaches are suitable for the generation of ideas. However, those ideas often need processing in order to become coherent.

The analytical approach often uses conceptual or computational models to examine possible future interactions between a select set of variables. The computational modelling approach works mainly from quantified data. Model-based process designs usually involve a set of well-defined and predetermined steps. Thus the process is rigid and intolerant towards those iterations that are common in intuitive processes. Conceptual modelling involves such structured intellectual procedures as the cross-impact and morphological analyses involved in the French 'la prospective'[13;74], the causal diagrams developed by Vennix[128] at Nijmegen University, as well as the techniques applied in Germany by DaimlerChrysler[66] and ScMI[67;68]. However, the structured approach is an especially strong feature of such computational models as TARGETS[75], Threshold 21[9;129], and WORLDSCAN[9;77].

Desk research is an analytical method that we position between the participatory and the model-based methods, usually involving the research of a single individual or of a small team of researchers and often based on the analysis of existing literature or on archival research. An example of such a desk study is Bobbitt's[78] The Shield of Achilles, which explores the history and possible futures of the 'market state' based on research of over 300 sources on warfare, international relations, and international and constitutional law. Others include Schwartz et al.'s[130] The Long Boom and McRae's[79] global scenario, described in The World in 2020.

Group composition describes the people involved in a scenario development process and is addressed in a number of manners in scenario literature. Schoemaker[55], among others, stresses the need for management involvement in scenario exercises, if they are to have an effect on decision-making. Schwartz[32] and Van der Heijden[21] describe the idea of 'remarkable people', or unconventional thinkers, whose role in scenario processes is to enable other participants to conceive novel ideas. Van der Heijden[21] also discusses group composition in terms of the law of requisite variety. Drawn from biology, the law of requisite variety states that in the regulation of biological systems only variety can destroy variety[131]. In the context of scenario development, the law is interpreted as a requirement to match the variety of events and processes related to the issue of investigation with a variety of interpretations among scenario participants[21;88].

Civic scenarios studies such as Mont Fleur[37;38] and Destino Colombia[39] typify the use of requisite variety as a leading principle. Efforts were made to draw in wide sections of South African and Colombian society in the scenario workshops, including guerrillas, clergymen, and trade unionists. Barbanente et al.[132] also aimed to gather a heterogeneous group for a scenario study in Tunis. Such groups prove difficult to mobilise, which Barbanente et al. attribute to political and cultural inhibitions.

We distinguish between *inclusive* and *exclusive* groups. Inclusive groups involve a wide range of participants in order to draw on as many perspectives as possible. The VISIONS study is an example of a scenario exercise that aimed to gather such a group[56;73]. Its participants included representatives from governmental institutions, NGOs, companies, and universities as well as citizens and artists from a variety of EU-member states. The participants' expertise included transport, energy, telecommunication, environmental science, ICT, automotives, and water.

Exclusive groups are limited in variety, often as a result of a conscious decision. Commercial organisations, for example, tend not to draw on outsiders in their scenario studies for fear of informing their competitors. To illustrate, an outsider involved in the Telecom study[133] had to sign a confidentiality statement and the outputs of both the Telecom and Nutrition[03;04] scenario studies were strictly for insiders only.

5.3 Scenario content characteristics

A scenario's **temporal nature** can be described in two ways: the developmental or *chain* variety on the one hand, and the end-state or *snapshot* variety on the other[17]. Chain scenarios, such as those developed in the Scenarios Europe 2010 study[9;94;134;135], describe the path or chain of developments to a particular end-state, rather like a film. Snapshot scenarios are like photos. They describe the end-state of a particular path of development and only implicitly address the processes that produced that end-state. Examples of snapshot scenarios are those developed in the NIVE scenarios on leadership in the 21st century[80].

Another characteristic is the nature of the **factors** or issues described in a scenario. Factors refer to the issues and developments a scenario might contain. There are various classifications of factors that a scenario study addresses. One classification distinguishes between socio-cultural, economic, and environmental factors[136], as well as sometimes an institutional dimension[137]. Another classification, referred to by the acronym STEEP, distinguishes between socio-cultural, technological, economic, ecological, and political developments[4]. The range in this characteristic's dimension is indicated by *heterogeneous* and *homogenous* sets of factors. The developments described in a scenario are heterogeneous when they come from numerous of the above classifications' categories. UNEP's (United Nations Environment Programme) GEO-3 scenarios[34] are examples of scenarios that address a heterogeneous set of factors[11]. In contrast, the KPMG scenarios[71;72] consider only five relatively homogenous factors: employers, employees, 'intermediaries', ICT, and the job market.

A final scenario content characteristic is the level of **interaction** between the factors in a scenario. An *integrated* scenario study unifies in an interdisciplinary[114], transparent manner the action and reaction patterns of relevant factors' spatial scales[56;113][12]. Examples of scenarios with a high level of cross-disciplinary interaction are the Destino Colombia[39] and Mont Fleur scenarios[37;38]. The integration of multiple geographical scales was a key objective in such studies as VISIONS [56;73] and UNEP's GEO-3[34]. Both

	MACRO CHARACTERISTICS		MICRO CHARACTERISTICS
A	Goal:	I	Function: process versus product
	exploration vs	II	Inclusion of norms: descriptive versus normative
	pre-policy research	III	Subject: issue- or area-based versus instructionbased
B	Process design:	I	Input qualitative versus quantiative
	intuitive vs	II	Method: participatory versus model-based
	analytical	III	Group composition: inclusive versus exclusive
C	Scenario content:	I	Temporal nature: chain versus snapshot
	complex vs simple	II	Factors: hetrogeneous versus homogenous
		III	Interconnection: integrated versus isolated

Figure 5 *The scenario typology*

---

[11] The factors include demography, economic integration and liberalisation, social inequality, consumer culture, ICT, biotech, environmental degradation, and political decentralisation.
[12] According to Schneider, interdisciplinarity implies an original combination derived from the integration of multidisciplinary ideas or methods permitting an explanation or assessment not achievable through non-integrated application of the ideas or tools of disciplines in question. See Schneider, S.: Integrated Assessment Modeling of Climate Change: Transparent rational tool for policy making or opaque screen hiding value-laden assumptions?, *Environmental Modelling and Assessment*, 2(4), 229-250 (1997).

scenario studies integrate global, supranational, and regional information through a synthesis of a top-down approach, whereby global developments are input for regional scenarios, and a bottom-up approach whereby regional developments are used to enrich European and global scenarios. The integration of regional scales is a relatively new development, not captured by previous typologies.

The alternative to an integrated scenario is one where the factors are relatively *isolated* from one another, such as in the study Sustained risk: a lasting phenomenon[138] carried out by the Netherlands Scientific Council for Government Policy (WRR). While the study addresses three different sectors – water, food, and energy – the interconnection between them is negligible.

The typology is summarised in Figure 5.

6 Towards an overview of contemporary scenario practice

In this section the results of the comparative review are presented using the typology as an analytical framework. The 30 selected scenario studies were analysed using the micro characteristics as a checklist. The selected studies are summarised in Textbox 1. Tables were made per study in which findings from the comparative review were registered. An example of such a table is presented in Table 1.

The 30 studies were plotted onto the scenario cartwheel. A scenario study's position on the cartwheel is determined by the nature of the micro characteristics. For example, if there is a dominance of micro characteristics on the left side of the table then the scenario study is exploratory and was developed in an intuitive manner, resulting in

MICRO CHARACTERISTICS					
Function:	*process*				*product*
Incl. of norms:	*descriptive*				*normative*
Subject:	*area-/issue-based*[13]				*institution-based*
Input:	*qualitative*				*qualitative*
Method:	*participatory*				*model-based*
Group composit.:	*inclusive*				*exclusive*
Temporal nature:	*chain*				*snapshot*
Factors:	*heterogeneous*				*homogenous*
Interaction:	*integrated*				*isolated*

Table 1 *A table used in the comparative review*

---

[13] Area- and issue-based scenarios have been combined here to make the diagram symmetrical. However, their combination can also be justified on the grounds that in nature they are similar, in comparison to the institution-based scenario. The latter is more closely associated with decision-making than are the area- and issue-based scenarios.

THE 30 STUDIES USED IN THE COMPARATIVE REVIEW

1. Surprising Futures *(1987)*: A scenario exercise designed to experiment with methodology for developing 'surprise-rich' scenarios.
2. Beyond Hunger in Africa *(1990)*: A study that aimed to look beyond the conventional image of Africa as a 'hungry' continent by experimenting with methods for creating surprising scenarios.
3. European security beyond the Cold War *(1991)*: Four scenarios that explore the possible outcomes of change and disorder in European security at the end of the eighties.
4. Mont Fleur *(1992)*: A scenario study designed to stimulate debate about the shape of post-apartheid South African society.
5. British Airways *(1994)*: A 1994 exploratory scenario study that examined societal developments and their implications for the airline industry.
6. ICL *(1995)*: The British computer systems and services company's scenario study on the future of the information markets in 2005.
7. Port of Rotterdam *(1996)*: Scenarios and strategic options for the Port of Rotterdam.
8. The Futures of Women *(1996)*: The question of whether men and women will be equal by the year 2015 is addressed as well as the implications of success or failure in achieving equality.
9. Destino Colombia *(1998)*: A scenario study aiming to define alternative routes for Colombia as a basis for developing a shared vision for drafting long-range policies.
10. KPMG Ebbinge *(1998)*: Scenarios on the future of the Dutch job market and of intermediaries such as job agencies, recruiters and 'headhunters'.
11. Questa *(1998)*: A study on the future of the Netherlands with a focus on mobility issues.
12. Scenarios Europe 2010 *(1999)*: A study on possible futures for Europe.
13. The European Environment at the Turn of the Century *(1999)*: A scenario describing the future of the environment in Europe.
14. Which World? *(1998)*: Three global scenarios from the perspective of 2050.
15. Biotechnology Scenarios *(2000)*: A study in which three scenarios were developed on the role of biotechnology in society.
16. IPCC/SRES *(2000)*: A scenario study that addressed greenhouse gas emissions' impact on climate change on a global and a regional level.
17. NIVE Navigating the Future *(2000)*: A scenario study that addressed the question 'what will leadership look like in the 21st century in view of growth and sustainability?'
18. Norway 2030 *(2000)*: A scenario study describing possible futures for Norway.
19. Nutrition *(2000)*: Scenarios and strategic options for the future of the nutrition market.
20. Possum *(2000)*: Scenarios for achieving sustainable development to assist the European Commission in future decisions about the Common Transport Policy.
21. Telecom *(2000)*: The year 2000 scenarios of a telecommunications company that analysed three futures for mobile phone commerce in 2005.
22. Schooling for Tomorrow *(2001)*: An OECD study that included the development of six scenarios for the future of universities.
23. Shell global scenarios *(2001)*: Two global scenarios centring on the theme of interconnectedness.
24. Finnish aquaculture *(2002)*: Four scenarios for aquaculture that aim to illustrate the importance of contingent developments.
25. Foresight Futures *(2002)*: Four scenarios developed to identify potential opportunities from new science and technologies, and to establish which actions might best realise those opportunities.
26. GEO-3 *(2002)*: A Global Environment Outlook that outlined four global scenarios and their implications on a continental level.
27. The Shield of Achilles *(2002)*: A study on the history and possible futures of the 'market state' with a focus on security, culture, and economics.
28. Tunis *(2002)*: Scenarios for the future of metropolitan Tunis.
29. CPB Netherlands Bureau for Economic Policy Analysis *(2003)*: Four scenarios for Europe focus on the issues of international cooperation and pressure on European public sectors.
30. VISIONS *(2004)*: Three scenarios on the future of Europe and three European regions, as well as outlooks that integrate European and regional developments.

See Appendix 1 for a full list of references.

Textbox 1 *The 30 scenario studies used in the comparative review*

complex scenario or scenarios as output. The cartwheel with the comparative review's results is presented in Figure 6.

We draw several conclusions about contemporary scenario practice from the comparative review, the most general of which regards the spread of scenario types over the cartwheel. The 30 analysed studies were conducted in a variety of organisational contexts: businesses, co-operative efforts, governmental organisations, regional exercises, and academic settings. The studies covered sectoral, regional, and issue-based topics. Institution-based scenarios usually produce simple scenarios. Companies carried out nearly all of the institution-based studies. Of the companies' scenarios only Shell[96] and the World Business Council[139] produced complex scenarios. The relatively simple output might be an indication of the resources allocated for scenario work in commercial settings, but our insights in corporate scenario activities is limited. The spread over the cartwheel was relatively even. To illustrate, area-based studies can be found in four of the eight sections of the cartwheel: pre-policy research/intuitive/complex, pre-policy research/analytical/complex, exploration/analytical/complex, and exploration/intuitive/complex.

Similarly, academically–based scenarios can be found in six of the sections: exploration/intuitive/simple, exploration/analytical/simple, pre-policy research/

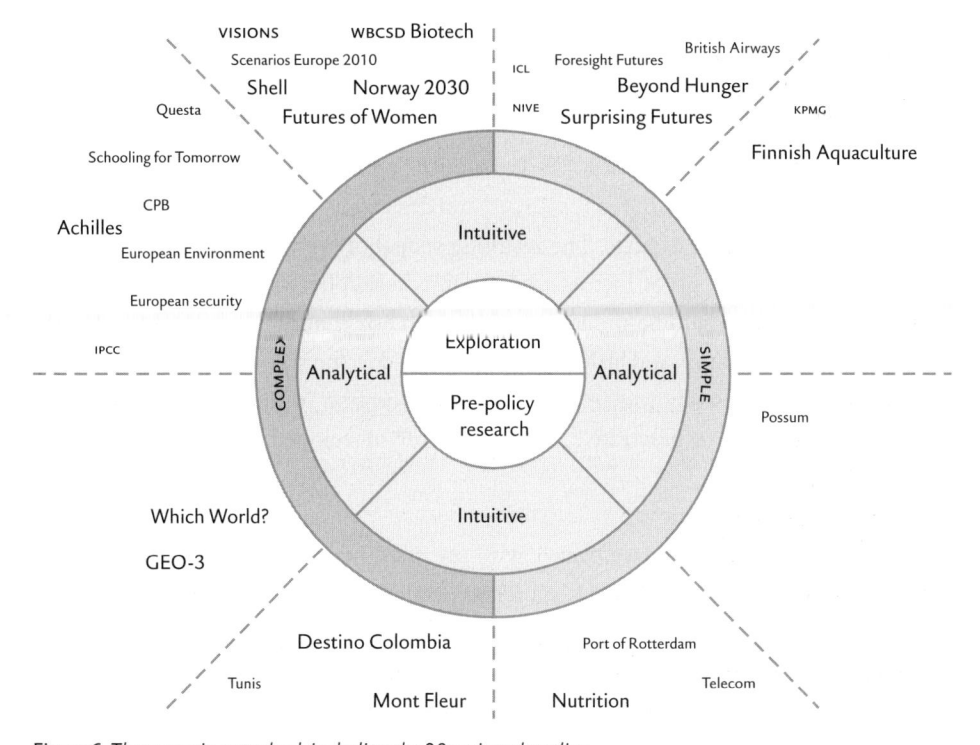

Figure 6 *The scenario cartwheel, including the 30 reviewed studies*

analytical/simple, pre-policy research/analytical/complex, exploration/analytical/complex, and exploration/intuitive/complex.

Twenty-one of 30 studies had an exploratory goal. This statistic is in accordance with the trend toward using scenarios for educational rather than planning purposes. In addition, we noticed that pre-policy research studies are conducted predominantly by using the intuitive approach of scenario workshops as the basis for their research.

With regards to the process design, the comparative review shows that there is more or less a balance of intuitively and analytically developed scenario studies. There is a relatively large category of studies that are hybrids of the two approaches. The VISIONS[56;73;140;141], Shell[96], GEO-3[34], Mont Fleur[1;37;38], Destino Colombia[39], Norway 2030[142], and Questa[49;54;85;143;144] studies are examples of scenario workshops combined with desk research. Also, GEO-3[34] and VISIONS[56;73;140;141] experimented with the modelling of storylines developed in scenario workshops. The difficulties experienced in these studies demonstrate the challenge involved in combining qualitative and quantitative approaches.

There are also a number of conclusions to be drawn regarding the scenario content, particularly in relation to the manner in which scenarios are developed. First, analytically developed scenarios are usually complex in nature. This applies particularly to such model-based studies that are invariably the result of complex arithmetical formulas, whose development requires a considerable investment. Desk-researched studies are also invariably more rigorous than the scenarios developed in scenario workshops. Compare, for example, the output of The Shield of Achilles[78] and Which World?[58] studies with that of NIVE study[80]. The exceptions to the rule that analytical studies produce complex scenarios are the KPMG[71;72], Possum[101], and Finnish Aquaculture[145] studies. The KPMG study had limited resources, and desk research was complemented by a series of interviews with experts. The resulting snapshot scenarios contain a relatively small, homogenous group of factors, and the interaction between them was explored only to a limited degree. The model-based Possum study addressed strategic options arising from the scenarios and little attention was paid to the scenarios themselves. The Finnish Aquaculture study was intended to draw attention to the relevance of contingent developments using illustrative, rather than fully-developed, scenarios.

7 Concluding remarks

In this chapter, we provided an overview of the state of the art of scenario practice. Besides the exploratory goal, there is a relative balance between scenarios developed intuitively and analytically. Combinations between the two are common. However, analytically developed studies are more inclined to produce complex scenarios than the intuitively developed scenarios. The overview that we provided serves as a basis for our investigation of the idea of discontinuity in contemporary scenario practice, described in the following chapters.

3
discontinuity

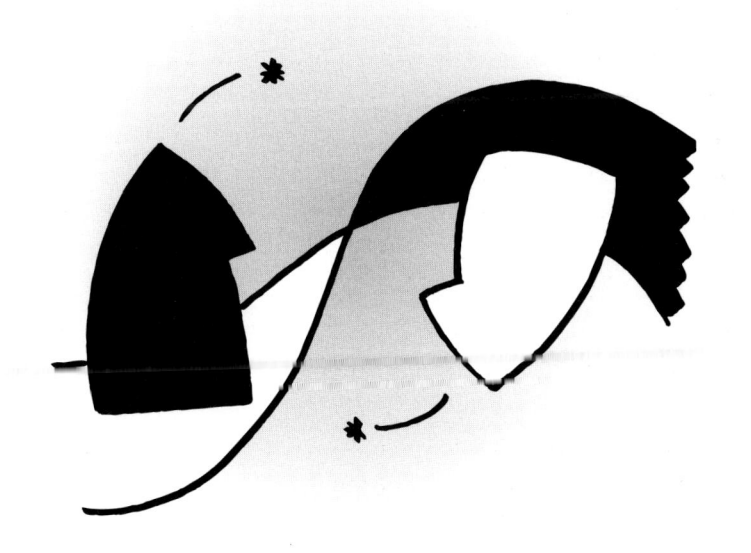

3 DISCONTINUITY

1 Introduction

History does not progress along smooth, incremental trajectories. According to Butterfield[1], the past is littered with "accidents and conjunctures and curious juxtapositions of events". Such discontinuities can have a profound effect on society. Brooks[2] argues that "significant changes often occur in abrupt or discontinuous bursts," and he emphasises their role in shaping the world. Wariness of such unexpected developments as terrorism, disease, fraud, and technological advances, have led to a growing interest in the topic of discontinuity in recent years, especially given the September 11th attacks, Severe Acute Respiratory Syndrome (SARS), food crises, the Enron and Parmalat scandals, and GMO debates among others.

Dutch 'futurists' agree that discontinuity is an important aspect in exploratory futures-oriented exercises[1]. Clark[3] argues that, "by leaving out the external shocks, non-linear responses and discontinuous behaviour so typical of social and natural systems", society is "unprepared to interpret a host of not-impossible eventualities". Others argue that the scenario development should be used to identify potential discontinuity[4;5]. In theory, scenarios "embrace the potential for sharp discontinuities"[6], and they are developed to "identify discontinuity [...] [and] thus help [...] to prepare for 'surprising' change"[4]. Besides, scenarios apparently help in responding to discontinuity[7].

Others argue that discontinuity is rarely addressed in the practice of foresight[8], scenario development[9] or policy-making[10], and the same might be said of IA. Brooks[11] states:

Most visions of the future are based on an evolutionary paradigm that involves the gradual incremental unfolding of the world system through time and [...] space.

Most Dutch futurists agree that current methodology for the anticipation of discontinuous developments is insufficient. A comparative study of scenarios[12] developed in the 1990s concluded that many scenarios have a 'business as usual' character insofar as they assume that current conditions will persist for decades. Furthermore, the study's authors argued that, although the more recent scenario studies do not simply extrapolate trends from existing conditions because the changes they incorporate tend to be incremental and thus cannot be said to account for discontinuity. They also argued that scenarios "often ignore the 'wild cards' of low-possibility futures"[13]. Bruun et al.[14] argue that the overwhelming majority of scenarios can be characterised as conventional and trend-based. It is also argued[15] that scenarios are too risk-averse and tend to portray the most likely future, which

---

[1] A survey was conducted among 19 members of the Dutch Network for Futures Researchers. It include scientists, civil servants, and businessmen. The survey was conducted on January 24th, 2003.

are mere variations on a current theme. Discontinuities are eliminated as fantasy. Ayres[16] laments the lack of theorisation in forecasting discontinuities and argues that a theory capable of predicting economic, social, and political discontinuities is not to be expected in the near-future.

In this chapter we ask how discontinuity is interpreted in IA and foresight literature, especially in sources that focus on scenario development. The point of departure is a review of definitions and descriptions of discontinuity and related terms. Observed gaps in the literature's treatment of discontinuity are addressed using concepts from other disciplines. Building upon our investigation, we present a definition of discontinuity in IA and foresight contexts that we can then use as a theoretical framework. The objective of this chapter is not to produce a comprehensive overview of references to discontinuity, due to the large number and variety of the term's interpretation; but rather to select sources related to IA and foresight, and distil from them interesting ideas about the idea of discontinuity.

2 Research approach

Reference searches were conducted in IA and foresight literature in general and scenario-related literature in particular. The sources included scholarly and, to a limited degree, non-scholarly literature. We included non-scholarly material due to its prevalence in the form of project reports and management literature. A focus on scholarly literature would have produced too narrow an account of how discontinuity is addressed in foresight. References were also collected through discussions with European scientists and practitioners of foresight, policy studies, and business administration.

The literature study revealed some confusion regarding the concept of discontinuity. This warranted a broader survey in order to clarify the concept. The idea of discontinuity features in various disciplines, including law, geology, and finance. In order to avoid superficial analysis and digression beyond areas relevant for the discontinuity concept in IA and foresight, we concentrated on sources from our fields of expertise: history, policy sciences, and the natural sciences[2]. References were collected in similar fashion to that of the review of IA and foresight literature.

3 Literature review

Scenario analyst Peter Schwartz[17] refers to Drucker when addressing discontinuity. In The Age of Discontinuity[18] Drucker describes discontinuities as "the unsuspected and apparently insignificant [that] derail the massive and seemingly invincible

---

[2] The author is a historian. Jan Rotmans, the supervisor for this doctoral research is a mathematician specialised in environmental science. The International Centre for Integrative Studies, the organisation where much of the research took place, is specialised in policy studies.

trends of today". Drucker states that discontinuities are not the prominent trends of today but the "shapers of tomorrow's society" and that they are different from "what most of us still perceive as 'today'". Drucker argues that a very different world would appear if the discontinuities were to come together. The author identifies discontinuities that, while still hidden from view at the time of writing in 1968, were already shaping the economy, politics, and society. Four discontinuities are discussed:

- The creation of technological and commercial opportunities as a result of scientific discoveries such as quantum physics, atomic and molecular science, and biochemistry;
- The transformation from an international economy of interacting national markets, to a world economy with a single global market;
- The establishment of a new, pluralist socio-political system that poses various political, philosophical, and spiritual challenges; and,
- The establishment of knowledge as the crucial economic resource.

The inconspicuous and apparently insignificant are central features of Drucker's description of discontinuity. Another key aspect is the notion of breaks in the character of trends. The future society of which Drucker speaks will be shaped by discontinuities that are markedly different from the dominant perception of 'today'. The notion of breaks is consistent with the following definitions of discontinuity found in various dictionaries:

- 1 lack of rational connection or cohesion[19]
  2 break or interruption
- 1 lack of continuity or cohesion[20]
  2 gap
- 1 the quality or state of being discontinuous; want or failure of continuity or uninterrupted sequence; interrupted condition.[21]
  2 a break or gap in a structure

From the examples Drucker provides, we conclude that he regards discontinuity as a social rather than a physical phenomenon. Presumably, Drucker considers breaks in patterns in the physical world to be discontinuous only if they affect society. For example, Drucker does not discuss abrupt physical changes, such as extreme storms or flooding.

Ayres[16] complements Druckers' description and he provides criteria for discontinuity. They are the rate of change, the magnitude and the consequences of change, and the change's irreversibility. However, these criteria only provide a certain measure of clarity. Ayres points out that whether a development can be considered a discontinuity is often a question of time scale. What seems discontinuous in the short term might appear continuous when regarded from a long-term perspective, and vice versa. Ayres notes that the 1992 hurricane Andrew was a discontinuity in the short term, whereas human population growth only appears explosive from a long-term perspective. Interpretations might also differ according to the discipline from which a discontinuity is regarded. Ayres argues that what appears a smooth and steady trend to an economist or a demographer might be a discontinuity to an historian.

Ayres provides an extensive set of examples of discontinuity, a selection of which are listed in Table 1.

Ayres' and Drucker's descriptions of discontinuity are two of a limited number of descriptions of the concept in IA and foresight literature. Contingency is one discontinuity-related term, which Dammers[9] defines as "events that occur by chance, but that have a large influence on policy issues"[3]. Bruun et al.[14] argue that the problem of contingency does not lie in the nature of future developments but in the limitations of the tools with which to contemplate the future. Dammers agrees, stating that the exploration of contingent events requires a lot of imagination, that the necessary methodology is underdeveloped, and that few scenarios take contingent events into account.

Another term is the 'sideswipe'[22], defined as "major surprises that can influence the future strongly -- a world war, 'miracle' technologies, an extreme natural disaster,

---

AYRES' DISCONTINUITIES

- Biochemical evolution: disequilibrium, nonlinearity and fluctuation in the proteins and nucleic acids;
- Disappearance of the dinosaurs: mass extinctions resulting from asteroid explosions, vulcanism, and radiation;
- Climatic discontinuities on shorter time scales: abrupt warmings, interruption of ocean currents, El Niño;
- Violent conflicts in recent history: from world wars to local conflicts;
- Non-violent political changes: quasi-revolutionary political changes;
- Other discontinuities: economic discontinuities such as financial panics, stock market crashes, recessions;
- Potential epidemics: AIDS, Bubonic plague, influenza;
- The next stock market crash;
- The next oil crisis;
- Chaos and the break up of China;
- Technology and human social evolution: from the first use of fire to the printing press, information and communication technology (ICT), and the mechanisation of production.

Table 1 A selection of Ayres' discontinuities

---

[3] Our translation of the original Dutch definition.

a pandemic, breakdown of the climate system"[22]. The notion of discontinuity is referred to in sources such as Davis[23] and Rotmans et al.[24], although from these sources we deduce that there is no consensus regarding what discontinuity means in the context of foresight. Writing on the discontinuity-related concept of wild cards, Mendonça et al.[25] state, "a multiplicity of unconnected contributions to research on this topic has produced a long list of labels."

Other terms include extreme events[2], abrupt, discontinuous bursts[2], *faites porteurs d'avenir*[26], dislocations[27], trend breaches[28], shocks[11;29], and paradigm busters[29]4. Our observation is that many terms are ambiguous. In 1986, Brooks[11] argued that, "our understanding of discontinuities […] is rudimentary and poorly formulated". On the basis of our literature review, we observe that Brooks' statement is still accurate.

However, not all notions referring to discontinuity in IA and foresight literature are ambiguous. The most detailed, the surprise and the wild card, compare to Drucker's and Ayres' descriptions of discontinuity. An analysis of these two notions might provide a better understanding of discontinuity, and we discuss them below.

3.1 Surprise

Surprise is the term used to express the idea of discontinuity in a number of scenario studies[2;30;31;32;33;34;35;36;37], but the term is not always explained. Streets and Glantz[36] argue that the definitions and classifications of surprise show a great variety, as they are tailored to fit the needs of different disciplines. In accordance with Streets and Glantz, we observe that the numerous interpretations of surprise in the scenario literature draw from various treatments of the concept. For example, the studies Beyond Hunger[32], Perspective 2000[2], and Surprising Futures[33] based their interpretation of surprise on work undertaken in the fields of anthropology and environmental science, whereas Ringland et al.[29] draw on military science.

All the definitions of surprise proposed in environmental scientific literature share a common element – the unexpected[36], corresponding to Drucker's reference to the "unsuspected and apparently insignificant" nature of discontinuity. Three definitions of surprise follow:
- Perceived reality that departs qualitatively from expectation[38].
- The condition in which the event, process or outcome is not known or expected[39].
- A gap between one's expectations about a phenomenon and what actually happens[40].

The notion of surprise is strongly related to perception and expectation. It is also related to the events and developments that trigger it, as Brooks'[11] often-quoted classification of surprises in technology, institutions, and development[2;11;16;33;39;40;41] suggest:

---

4   In the opinion of the author, faites porteurs d'avenir translates (poorly) as heavy trends and seed events.

- Unexpected discrete events, such as the oil shocks of 1973 and 1979, political coups or revolutions, and major natural catastrophes.
- Discontinuities in long-term trends, such as the acceleration of USA oil imports between 1966 and 1973, the onset of the stagflation phenomenon in the OECD countries in the 1970s, the decline in the ratio of energy consumption growth to GNP growth in the OECD countries after 1973.
- The sudden emergence into political consciousness of new information, such as material regarding the relation between fluorocarbon production and stratospheric ozone (O_3), the deterioration of central European forests due to air pollution, and the discovery of asbestos-related cancer in industrial workers.

Most environmental scientific classifications interpret the causes of surprise in one of two ways. The first regards surprise as a form of system change that is a result of particular developments in a system. In this context, Myers[42] refers to synergisms, which occur when two or more environmental processes interact to produce a net result greater than the sum of the parts. He also connects surprise with discontinuity by arguing that surprise occurs when "a little more or a little less of something creates a distinctively new situation"[42]5. The second interpretation addresses the perception of surprise as an outcome of developments in a system in relation to preconceived ideas regarding the system in question[11;43;44;45]. For example, Schneider[46] distinguishes between:

- Unimaginable surprise such as Jules Vernes' journey to the centre of the earth;
- Imaginable surprises that are improbable such as a global nuclear war;
- Imaginable surprises that are probable such as an oil price shock or massive migration due to ecological disasters; and,
- Certain surprises or events such as earthquakes.

The majority of the environmental scientific classifications fall under the second interpretation. A minority of classifications emphasise other aspects of surprises, such as impact of[47] and responses to[41].

Holling[38] explains the connection between the first and the second types of causes of surprise. He argues that concepts that humans develop to provide order and understanding to their experiences are inherently incomplete. The incomplete nature of the concepts eventually produces surprises, which, in turn, force the further development of the concepts. To Holling this sequence of events is characterised by discontinuity. The longer one view is held beyond its time, the greater the surprise and the resultant adjustment.

Like the environmental scientific descriptions, the anthropological view provided by Thompson et al.[48] stresses the perceptual aspect of surprise. Thompson et al.

---

5 This idea is further developed in section 3.4.

argue that an event is never surprising in itself; that it is potentially su
in relation to a particular set of convictions; and that an event is actua
only if it is noticed by the holder of those convictions.

Thompson et al. argue that if an individual has a particular view about the world s/he will not be surprised if the world behaves according to that view. On the other hand, if the world acts contravenes that worldview, then the individual will be surprised. In practice, however, the world is constantly changing, so the holders of any kind of belief system will periodically experience some surprise[48]. Glantz et al.[40] agree, claiming that surprise is a subjective concept triggered by such factors as experience, belief, and knowledge. Easterling and Kok[49] argue that the observer might conclude with the luxury of hindsight that s/he need not have been surprised at all.

Ringland et al.[31] draw their interpretation of surprise from military science. Surprise is addressed in several military scientific works, including those of Von Clausewitz[50] and Sun Tzu[51]. O'Leary[52] draws on their respective views in his analysis of military surprise. His conclusion, which is similar to Thompson et al.'s[48], is that surprise is not so much caused by an absence of knowledge as by the presence of knowledge based on flawed assumptions.

We conclude that surprise is strongly dependent on the perception of the observer. Discontinuity might be surprising depending on the observer, and such factors as context and time scale from which s/he observes.

3.2 *Wild card*

'Wild card' is another commonly used term[25;31;53;54;55;56;57]. Wild cards are addressed mostly in non-scholarly literature, which might account for the ambiguity surrounding the term. One definition describes wild cards as "low-probability, high-impact events that happen quickly"[54]. Another definition refers to wild cards as "sudden and unique incidents that can constitute turning points in the evolution of a certain trend or system"[25]. Examples of wildcards include the fall of the Berlin Wall[25] and the September 11th attacks[56]. GBN identifies three types of wild cards[55]:

- A wholly discontinuous event that interrupts our lives, such as natural disasters.
- Catalytic developments so different in degree or scale that they are different in kind and might be distinguished according to their contribution to or hindrance of progress. Respective examples cited are the transformation of Netscape into the World Wide Web and treatment for one type of cancer that leaves the patient with another type.
- Discontinuities that might be anticipated but have significant unintended consequences. The example cited is ERISA, the Employment Retirement Income Security Act in the United States, developed to insure pensions for the elderly which also created institutional investing.

The only consistent factor in all definitions of wildcards is that they have a large impact. Other definitions vary and sometimes contradict one another. For example, Mendonça et al[25] state, "wild cards are, by definition, surprises". However, GBN[55] argues that not all wild cards are surprising. Like Thompson et al.[48], GBN argues the observer's perspective determines whether a wild card is surprising or not[55]. Another point of contradiction involves whether a wild card is an event or incident, as suggested by the above definitions, or a more gradual process, as indicated in GBN's classification.

The concepts of wild card and discontinuity are connected in two ways. First, the high impact of wild cards corresponds to the irreversible nature of discontinuity. Second, the abruptness of discontinuity described by Ayres corresponds to some definitions of wild cards.

4 Reflection on the literature

Earlier, we concluded that the terms used in IA and foresight literature on discontinuity is ambiguous. However, of the sources available, Ayres and Drucker provide the most useful insights into the concept of discontinuity, which we elaborated in our analysis of literature on surprise and wild cards.

Drucker introduces the idea that discontinuity is a break in time or in the character of a dominant condition in society. He also argues that discontinuity tends to be inconspicuous and dependent on perception or perspective. He emphasises the social dimension of discontinuity. Ayres complements Drucker's contributions by offering criteria for discontinuity: the rate of change, the magnitude of change, its consequences, and its irreversibility. We argue that the rate of change is an ambiguous notion. From Ayres' article we infer that the rate of change relates to whether a discontinuity is relatively abrupt or gradual. Interestingly, many of Ayres' examples of discontinuity are more abrupt than is the case with those provided by Drucker. With regards to the irreversibility criterion, we argue that some of Ayres' examples are not irreversible, but rather partially reversible. Therefore, we propose partial reversibility as a complementary aspect to the irreversibility criterion. Ayres also offers the idea that what constitutes a discontinuity depends on the time scale and the discipline from which it is regarded. We agree, but argue that what constitutes a discontinuity can also be dependent on factors other than time scale and discipline. Assumptions or worldviews might also influence the perception of discontinuity. In our view, a multitude of perspectives – spatial, cultural, ideological, et cetera – are relevant in the consideration of discontinuity.

The literature on discontinuity and the related concepts of surprise and wild card provide a basis for a more expansive concept of discontinuity in the context of foresight. However, we also observe various gaps when comparing the aforementioned descriptions of discontinuity with those in other fields such as history, policy science, and the natural sciences. The gaps as well as suggestions for their correction are the subject of discussion in the following paragraphs.

4.1 Beyond events

From our literature study we conclude that IA and foresight literature more often addresses events than long-term processes. While the descriptions of wild cards repeatedly refer to events[25;54;55;56] and incidents[25], little mention is made of underlying processes. Several descriptions[11;39;48;52] of surprise refer to the concept in terms of events, suggesting a focus on the short-term. However, some sources[11;38;58] acknowledge the influence of such underlying processes as shifts in worldviews and beliefs[48] and environmental conditions[44].

We turn to the French historian Fernand Braudel (1902-1985) to investigate this bias towards events in IA and foresight literature. An explanation of Braudel's views on the practice of history is necessary to understand his ideas regarding discontinuity.

Braudel considered the study of discontinuity to be essentially a matter for historical analysis:

> *Who [...] would deny that the great question of the continuity or discontinuity of our social destiny [...] is essentially a question of history? If great rifts break up the destiny of humanity, if everything has been put in a new light the day after they appear, and neither yesterday's tools nor yesterday's thoughts apply any more – the reality of these breaks is for history to decide[59].*

Braudel emphasised the need for an interdisciplinary practice of history[60]. He suggested that historians look to economics, sociology, anthropology, demography, and geography. Braudel argued that no subject of study should be analysed in isolation but rather in the broadest possible context; the temporal and the geographical in particular.

Furthermore, Braudel criticised fellow historians as well as social scientists for their limited appreciation of time in general and long-term developments in particular[60]. He stressed what he called "the plurality of social time"[59] arguing that time is not constant. Developments might be perceived as fast or slow. He stated[59]:

> *Whether you take 1558 or [...] 1958 the problem for anybody tackling the world scene is to define a hierarchy of forces, of currents, of particular movements, and then tackle them as an entire constellation. At each movement of this research, one has to distinguish between long-lasting movements and short bursts, the latter detected from the moment they originate, the former over the course of a distant time [...].*

Braudel is perhaps best remembered for his differentiation between three time scales in his first major publication The Mediterranean[61][6]: geographical time or the *longue*

---

[6] Originally published in French as *La Méditerranée et le monde méditerranéen à l'époque de Philippe II*.

durée; social time; and an individual time or *l'histoire événementielle*[7][61]. The *longue durée* refers to the geographic and climatic processes that influence the human race over hundreds and thousands of years. It is "a history that is almost changeless, the history of man in relation to his surroundings"[61]. The slow moving, long-term processes and cycles of the *longue durée* exert a dominant and stabilising influence over the other levels, thus providing the context in which other developments in society take place. The second category involves what Braudel calls the "history of gentle rhythms, of groups and groupings"[61]. This social time includes socio-economic trends, such as the Industrial revolution, which span decades or hundreds of years. Lastly, Braudel identifies what he refers to as *l'histoire événementielle*, traditional history, or the history of events. He explains[61]:

> It is [...] the history of events: a surface disturbance, the waves stirred up by the powerful movement of the tides. A history of short, sharp nervous vibrations.

L'histoire événementielle is a history "not so much of man in general as of men in particular"[61], describing events, often diplomatic and political, such as battles and elections that span days, weeks, at most a year. Braudel considered the history of events to be fleeting and superficial[62;63;64] and did not believe that events could influence the more important structures of the *longue durée*[59]. He therefore criticised his fellow historians for practicing an events-focused form of history. Braudel argued that it is the task of the historian to move beyond the history of events towards a focus on the context of civilisation as a whole[59]. Only then can the meaning of events be understood.

A similar categorisation as Braudel's is proposed for scenario development by Van der Heijden[65;66]. Van der Heijden's 'iceberg analysis' distinguishes between events, trends and patterns, and systemic structure. The top part of the iceberg is the level of observable events. Immediately below the water surface is the area of the trends and patterns. At the base of the iceberg is a systemic structure that supports the levels above it. The iceberg is a whole and the three levels are interconnected.

Braudel's criticism of the events-focused practice of history is similar to Slaughter's[58] comments regarding the practice of future studies, which we regard as synonymous with foresight[8]. Slaughter states "short-term thinking is one of the most dangerous perceptual defects that we have inherited from the recent past"[67]. Elaborating his opinion, Slaughter distinguishes between three different levels of operation in future studies[58]: 'pop'; problem-oriented; and critical and epistemological futures studies. Slaughter argues that pop 'problems' correspond to the familiar "litany" continuously reproduced in the global media, such as population, resources, pollution, crime. Problem-oriented futures studies involves a more serious, practical approach examining the ways in which societies and organisations respond, or

---

[7] Braudel attributes the term to economist François Simiand
[8] See Chapter 1.2.

should respond, to the near-term future. Lastly, critical and epistemological futures studies probes beneath the surface of social life to examine the deep processes of meaning-making and paradigm formation. Slaughter's categorisation corresponds to Braudel's distinction between the superficial and the structural.

Slaughter argues that future studies tends to address pop and problem-oriented issues, while it should address deep-seated societal patterns. We argue that this short-sightedness might hamper the analysis of discontinuity and we propose that discontinuity should refer not only to events, but also to the medium and long-term processes on which the events are founded.

4.2 Interactions

Despite Braudel's emphasis on the layered nature of societal processes, he tended to present events and processes as isolated concepts[64]. In his later work[59;68] Braudel recognises the fragmented nature of his classification stating:

> *Breaking down the problem in order to understand it more fully, dividing it into three levels or stages, amounts to mutilating and manipulating a much more complex economic and social reality[68].*

Although this statement shows an appreciation of the interconnection between the three levels, Braudel generally fails to elaborate on it in his practice of history[60;64]. The idea of interaction between levels of time and structure is the basis of the concept of emergent properties of scale[49].

Easterling and Kok[49] argue that, within the context of general systems theory, emergence is the result of "the interaction of pattern and process at a smaller, faster scale [that] produces a fundamentally new organization at a larger, slower scale"[9]. They contend that emergent properties are not new to a system, but rather lay embedded in a system, only emerging in the viewer's field of vision when regarded from a higher spatial or temporal scale level. Therefore, to examine a system from larger scale levels might produce generalisations; while to view the same system at fine spatial and temporal levels might yield a chaotic and unpredictable picture. Easterling and Kok assert that properties emerge at different levels of scale – spatial as well as temporal – due to the manner in which the observer interprets the scales at which various systemic forces operate. They argue that, in a stable situation, order at the larger level acts as a buffer on extreme interactions on the smaller level. Nevertheless, "large upwelling singularities or bifurcations" on a small scale can destabilise the whole system and cause a transition to a new state of equilibrium[49]. As an example of such a 'bifurcation' Easterling and Kok[49] cite the reordering of relations in an economic system resulting from radical technological innovation. If we assume that an emergent property can

---

9   According to Easterling and Kok, the description of emergence as a property of scale receives special attention in ecosystem ecology.

be discontinuous, then we can complement Ayres'[16] above-mentioned observations regarding the temporal scale and disciplinary differences in the interpretations of discontinuity, with Easterling and Kok's notion of spatial scales.

4.3 Immaterial influences

Discontinuity is largely discussed in terms of its physical or material nature. Brooks'[11] and GBN's[55] respective classifications of surprises and wild cards fail to fully appreciate such immaterial influences such as ideas, public sentiment, social values, and religion. Nevertheless, some sources do acknowledge the role of the immaterial. Drucker[18] refers to the establishment of knowledge as an economic resource. He also describes the philosophical and spiritual challenges that result from the emergence of a new political system. Ayres[16] addresses the immaterial in a more marginal manner when he refers to financial panics as a loss of confidence in banks.

The potential influence of such immaterial processes as scientific theories in bringing about societal change is illustrated in Mazlish's The Fourth Discontinuity[69]. Mazlish describes a number of historical instances in which "man's naïve self-love", the assumption of his privileged place in the universe, was dealt a blow. The author draws on Freud when arguing that the first discontinuity was the Copernican revolution, the second was Darwin's theory of evolution, and the third was Freud's theory of psychoanalysis. According to Mazlish, these theories brought about a change in scientific thought. Kuhn[70] refers to these traditions in scientific thought as paradigms. He describes them as "universally recognized scientific achievements that for a time provide mental problems and solutions to a community of practitioners"[70]. Kuhn observed that when a scientific community finds that a problem cannot be solved by the known procedures in an existing tradition of scientific practice, a process of investigation takes place that culminates in a new basis for scientific practice. The problems that violate expectations stemming from paradigms are referred to as anomalies[70].

4.4 Steady or instantaneous change?

There are numerous references to sudden discontinuity in the studied literature. They include terms such as shocks[11;29], fast cycle incidents[11] sharp, discontinuous change[38], as well as terms adopted from the natural sciences such as bifurcation[35] and phase transition[16]. One interpretation of discontinuity in the natural sciences asserts that continuous change in quantity can, at certain decisive points, lead to a discontinuity in state[71]. An example of such a discontinuity is the transformation of water to ice or steam. This interpretation corresponds to Myers'[42] aforementioned description of discontinuity: "a little more or a little less of something creates a distinctively new situation".

The concept of bifurcation describes the point of change from a state of stability to instability. Originally a mathematical term, bifurcation describes a situation when a natural system becomes unstable beyond a critical value[72]. This instability can be induced either by fluctuations within the system or small external disturbances that eventually overwhelm it. In physics, the principle of instability beyond a critical value is described by the notion of the phase transition[73]. Such a transition is a point at which a stable, smooth flow suddenly transforms into a turbulent one, such as when a plume of cigarette smoke breaks up when ascending into the air or when a stream of tap water converts from a neat into a disorderly column.

The instantaneous nature of change that is central to bifurcations and phase transitions correspond to Ayres' description of discontinuity and those definitions of wild cards that speak of sudden, high-impact events. However, not all interpretations on the speed with which discontinuity occurs are consistent. Ayres'[16] examples describe discontinuity more in terms of instantaneous change than Drucker's[18]. The same duality is demonstrated in the concepts of wild cards and surprise. GBN addresses certain gradual wild cards and Brooks'[11] classification of surprise refers to discontinuities in long-term trends, whereas other definitions of both concepts concentrate on events.

5 A concept of discontinuity for foresight

In view of our observations from the review of IA, foresight and related literature we propose a broad definition for discontinuity in the context of scenario development:
A temporary or permanent, sometimes unexpected, break in a dominant condition in society caused by the interaction of events and long-term processes.

We underpin this broad definition with several characteristics of discontinuity: its intrinsic difference with established trends, dominant patterns or paradigms; its high impact; its irreversibility or partial reversibility; its interconnection with various types of events and long-term processes; its combination of physical and immaterial processes; and discontinuity's dependence on the perspective from which it is regarded. The role of perspective and perception in discontinuity implies that its occurrence might come unexpectedly. Lastly, in addressing different views on the relative speed of change in the consulted sources, we distinguish between abrupt and gradual discontinuity.

5.1 Abrupt discontinuity

In the context of IA and foresight, abrupt discontinuity is characterised by an instantaneous break with the status quo. Abrupt discontinuity delivers society a jolt, even if only temporarily. Examples of abrupt discontinuity include economic collapse, such as the financial crises in South America and South East Asia[74], and environmental collapse, such as that which might occur in fish stocks[75]. In the case of economic collapse the so-called Noah effect[73;76] is said to occur when prices change in jumps when, for instance, a stock price soars from $15 to $60 without resting on any of the intermittent values.

Although events trigger abrupt discontinuity, such discontinuity is not isolated from underlying processes. For example, the assassination of Archduke Francis Ferdinand in 1914 is generally considered to have started the First World War. However, the attack might have been the trigger for war, but it was arguably not the cause[77]. Numerous other events could have had the same effect. The war might never have taken place, even given the assassination, if it was not for influential underlying processes such as militarism, nationalism, and the forging of strategic alliances in Europe in preceding years. Similarly, the 1989 fall of the Berlin Wall cannot be explained without considering such developments such as Michael Gorbachev's rise to power, the politics of *glasnost* and *perestroika*, and the crippling effects of the arms race on the Soviet economy. In turn, these developments cannot be seen in isolation of the ideological struggle between communism and capitalism in the twentieth century. In summary, although events play a dominant role in the occurrence of abrupt discontinuity, underlying processes are also influential.

5.2 Gradual discontinuity

Discontinuity can also manifest itself in a more gradual manner over a period of many years, according to the concept of transition[78;79]: a gradual, continuous process of change that leads to the transformation of a society, or a complex sub-system of society, over a period of at least one generation. The transition concept has its roots in biology and population dynamics as applied to the demographic transformation in Western societies from high to low birth and death rates. The demographic transition began with improvements in hygiene and health care. These caused the death rate to fall spectacularly, while the birth rate remained high, causing a quick increase in population levels. In most Western societies the birth rate eventually fell, leading to a period of stabilisation. The stabilising forces included education, the inclusion of women in the workforce, economic development, and family planning.

A transition is a self-reinforcing process of societal change whereby diverse developmentsconverge: socio-cultural, technological, economic, environmental, or political[78;79]. A change of paradigm results, new practices and rules are introduced. The speed of change is relative, involving periods of slow and of fast development, which such unexpected or incidental events such as a war, natural disaster, or oil crisis might accelerate. A transition is made up of four different phases, illustrated in Figure 1:
- A predevelopment phase of dynamic equilibrium, of 'invisible' change;
- A take-off phase of initial change in the state of a system;
- A breakthrough phase of marked structural change; and
- A stabilisation phase of decreased change, establishing new dynamic equilibrium.

Examples of transitions include the shift from coal to oil and gas in the Netherlands[78;79], the emancipation of women[80], the Industrial Revolution and its replacement of wind-drive engines, with steam and, finally, electricity[79]. The Industrial Revolution is itself part of a larger transition from agriculture to an industrial economy, and then to a service economy[79] or an information society[80]. Though these examples correspond to Drucker's discontinuities, at the beginning of this chapter, the concept of transitions has yet to be addressed in scenario practice.

Abrupt and gradual discontinuity are not mutually exclusive. The 1929 Wall Street Crash illustrates the interconnection between abrupt and gradual discontinuity. The crash was symptomatic of the transition from the economically inflated American economy of the 'Roaring Twenties', to the depression years of the 1930s with the social welfare schemes of the New Deal. The stock market crash also shows that discontinuities in one area of society can stimulate discontinuities in others since the 1930s depression was also felt in Europe, providing favourable conditions for the rise of fascism. Similarly, discontinuities on one scale level can converge and stimulate a structural discontinuity on another level.

6 Illustrating the concept

In the remaining part of the chapter we illustrate the discontinuity concept through two examples: the September 11th attacks and the emergence of environmental concern in twentieth-century Western society. The former is an example of an abrupt

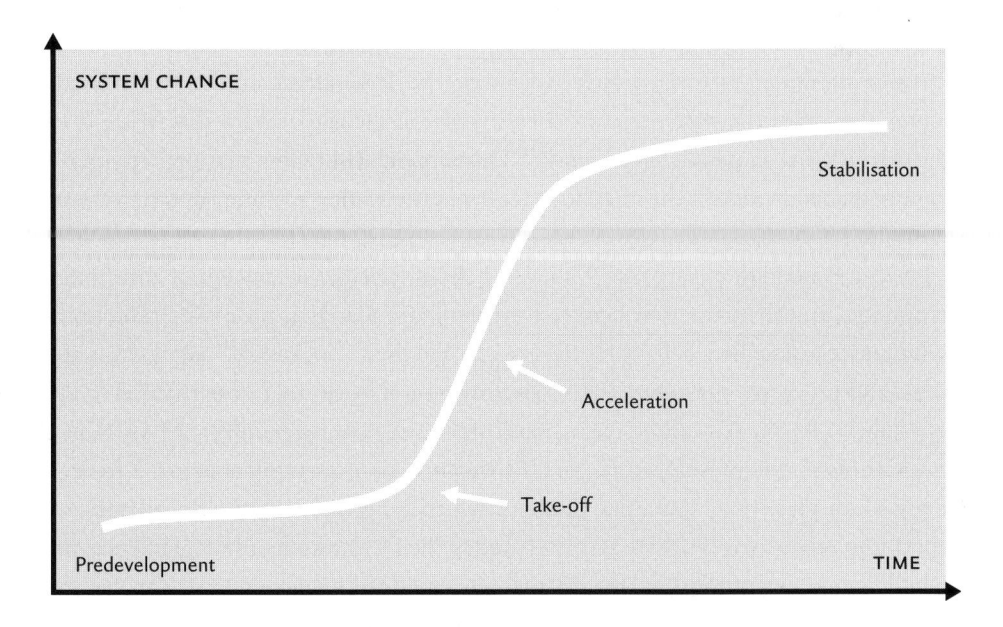

Figure 1 *The phases in a transition*

discontinuity; the latter a gradual discontinuity. We use them to illustrate individual elements of our discontinuity concept rather than to offer a comprehensive overview of the two examples, which is beyond the scope of the current thesis. Furthermore, regarding the September 11th attacks, drawing conclusions about an event that is still so recent and its impacts uncertain is problematic.

6.1 '9/11'

President Bush's claim that "night fell on a different world"[81] after 9/11 was probably more dramatic than accurate. Nevertheless, the 9/11 attacks represent an abrupt discontinuity where events seemed to act as manifestations of underlying processes. The September 11th attacks contained contingent elements that made them impossible to predict, whereby catching society by surprise. US Secretary of State Colin Powell described the difficulty in anticipating the attacks by saying that, although there had been many signs of terrorist activity in the preceding months, "we never got the fidelity and the information that we would have liked to, some warning of what did actually happen"[82]. National Security Advisor Condaleeza Rice reiterated this in testimony to the September 11 Commission in April 2004[83]. However, Schwartz[84], Watkins and Bazerman[85], and the September 11 Commission[86] contend that, even despite the contingencies, the Clinton and Bush administrations might have better anticipated the attacks. Indeed, Schwartz argues that the Hart-Rudman Commission's report on national security strategy, published shortly after Bush's inauguration, pinpointed terrorism as the biggest threat for the US, outlining a scenario in which the World Trade Center towers were attacked by hijacked airliners. Watkins and Bazerman described a host of attempted terrorist attacks, including the 1993 attack on the World Trade Center, deploring the weakness of the U.S. aviation security system that made 9/11 "the surprise that shouldn't have been"[85]. The September 11 Commission[86] points to a failure in imagination in the inability to collate information scattered among various intelligence agencies.

Besides the notion of surprise, 9/11 also helps to clarify the concept of abrupt discontinuity and the interaction between events and underlying processes. The point is illustrated using Braudel's three layers of time and Crockatt's[87] analysis of the events and processes preceding 9/11. On a structural level, the forces that led to the September 11th attacks can be traced back myths of American culture[88] as 'White Man's Burden', 'Manifest Destiny', and 'Providence' so often influential in US foreign policy. These ideas suggest that the values on which American society is based render it superior to other societies. Values formulated in the Declaration of Independence, the United States Constitution and the Bill of Rights, popular images of American patriotism and evangelism echo these suggestions, as do the notions of 'Americanism' and the much touted 'American dream'. Crockatt continues, arguing that another foundation of American culture is the USA's duty to export its cultural values, thereby improving the world. The American economic and military expansion in the 20th century provided the means to such international dominance that allowed for such missionary endeavours. Ronald Reagan expressed the missionary idea when he argued that America had been placed between the oceans according to a "divine plan"[87].

These myths and cultural values shaped the USA's behaviour on the international stage as an investigation of Braudel's intermediate time level shows. Crockatt argues that September 11th should be understood in the light of the interaction between the USA's dominant international position since the end of the Cold War, the rise of political Islam, and globalisation. After the Cold War, the USA became the world's only superpower. Whereas many people were drawn by American popular culture, others increasingly harboured resentment against the values they understood the USA to embody. This hostility is described in terms of a 'clash of civilizations'[89].

US support for Israel arguably played a central role in the rise of anti-American resentment in Islamic communities. Anti-Americanism was a part of a broader movement against the West and modernisation, referred to by Crockatt[87] as political Islam. The most visible manifestation of political Islam was the overthrow of the pro-Western Shah in the Iranian Revolution of 1979 followed by the assassination of the Egyptian President Anwar Saddat in 1981. The foundations for the militant form of political Islamism were laid during the 1979-1988 Russian occupation of Afghanistan. The terrorist networks of Al Qaeda were formed from the mujahadeen that opposed the Russians.

Regarding globalisation, Crockatt argues that September 11th was interpreted by some as an attack by the impoverished and disaffected against the advanced, interconnected, and globally-conscious West. We see this idea reflected in the description of tensions between the forces of globalism and tribalism[90], for example. Similarly, Buruma and Margalit[91] refer to current radical Islamic hatred of the West as 'occidentalism', based on a disdain for the superficial, cosmopolitan Western lifestyle, a soulless machine world personified by the USA.

On Braudel's level of events, the presence of American troops on muslim ground in Saudi Arabia during the 1991 Gulf War served as a catalyst for terrorist activities by such radical Islamists as Osama bin Laden and his deputy, Ayman al Zawahiri. Operation Desert Storm increased American involvement in the Middle East and thereby Islamist hatred. Al Qaeda networks became increasingly active in the 1990s. The attacks on the World Trade Center in 1993, on the US Embassies in Nairobi and Dar-es-Salaam in 1998, and on the USS Cole in Yemen in 2000 were supported, if not engineered by Al Qaeda members. Osama bin Laden had been the US's most wanted man since the Nairobi and Dar-es-Salaam bombings. He was blatant in his anti-Americanism and had given several indications that he intended to attack the American mainland.

3 DISCONTINUITY

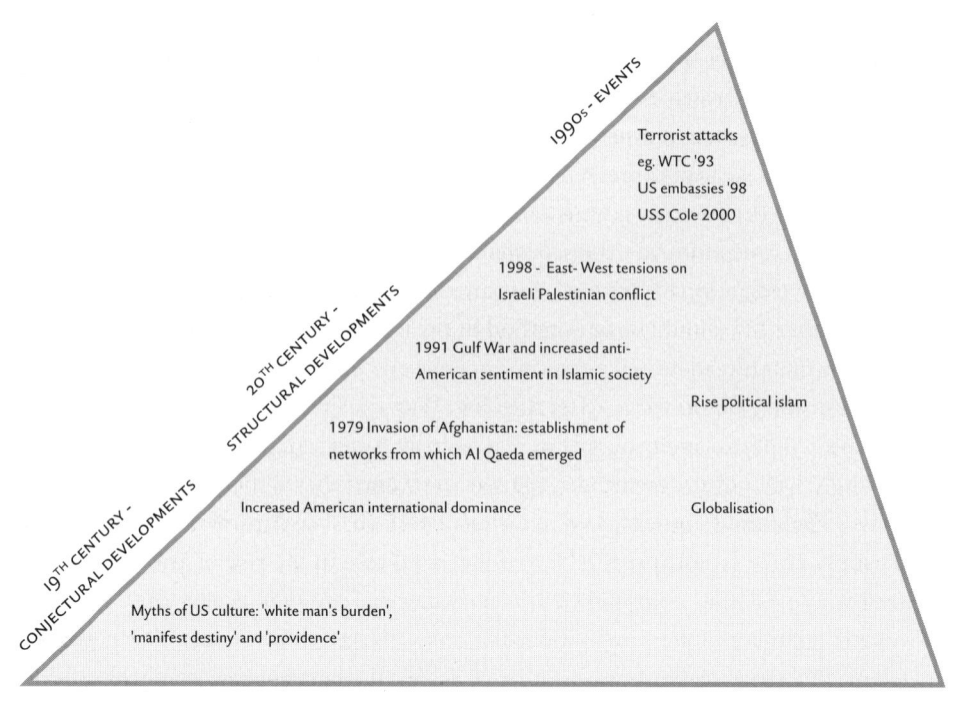

1990s - EVENTS
- Terrorist attacks eg. WTC '93, US embassies '98, USS Cole 2000

20TH CENTURY - STRUCTURAL DEVELOPMENTS
- 1998 - East-West tensions on Israeli Palestinian conflict
- 1991 Gulf War and increased anti-American sentiment in Islamic society
- Rise political islam
- 1979 Invasion of Afghanistan: establishment of networks from which Al Qaeda emerged

19TH CENTURY - CONJECTURAL DEVELOPMENTS
- Increased American international dominance
- Globalisation
- Myths of US culture: 'white man's burden', 'manifest destiny' and 'providence'

Figure 2 *Some processes that contributed to 9/11 to illustrate abrupt discontinuity.*

In Figure 2 some of the events and processes described above are used to illustrate the concept of abrupt discontinuity.

Until here, we have discussed several characteristics of discontinuity: surprise, immaterial influences, and the interaction between events and underlying processes in relation to 9/11. We now turn to the impact of the September 11th attacks. Immediate effects were stock market depreciations, declines in US tourism, increases in the popularity of President Bush and New York Mayor Giuliani, the revival of the Northern Ireland peace talks, and a political swing to the right in many European countries. Also, September 11th arguably provided an impetus for Islamist terrorist movements as suggested by subsequent attacks on Western targets in Asia, Africa, and Europe. The overthrow of the Taliban regime in Afghanistan on December 7th, 2001 and the subsequent efforts to rebuild the country were other effects of 9/11. The Taliban's demise also meant a sharp increase in heroin trafficking[92]. The cultivation of the opium poppy, effectively suppressed by the Taliban, resumed after their removal from power, thus complicating another of the US's on-going wars: the 'war on drugs'. '9/11' had some perhaps unexpected effects, including the revival of New York's commercial-property market and the delay or cancellation of numerous Hollywood films, due to their resemblance to the attacks[93;94]. Also, there was an increase in demand for therapists, security firms, and flag producers[93;94] and there might also have been an upsurge in religious zeal[95] in the US, although the latter is disputed[96].

The costs of 9/11 were high. There were human casualties, immediate and extended, when one considers the resultant military operations. The attacks were also costly in economic terms and Schwartz[84] claims that the West will be paying a "bin Laden surtax" for years to come. A conservative November 2001 estimate of the total losses to insurers from the World Trade Center attacks stood at $40 billion[97]. Furthermore, the attacks accelerated an economic downturn. The airline industry might have felt the effects of '9/11' most acutely, with the bankruptcy of Swiss Air and Sabena within a month after the attacks[81]. By that time commercial airlines had already cut 100 000 jobs[98], and airline manufacturer Boeing had laid off 30 000 employees. Meanwhile, the demand for private jets increased since they were considered a safer alternative to commercial airlines[99].

On a political level, the attacks led to a rapid overhaul of the Bush administration's foreign policy, which quickly became internationalist in orientation. The impact of this change is illustrated by developments in Pakistan in the weeks after the attacks. Before '9/11', Pakistan was considered a pariah state by the international community due to its nuclear weapons programme and its military government[81]. In the weeks after the attacks, Pakistan became an US ally in the 'war on terror'. In the space of two weeks, sanctions were waived and US aid poured into the country according to pledges of about $1 billion in American assistance[100]. A surprising consequence was that the Pakistani rupee, one of the weakest currencies in the world, rather than continuing its rapid depreciation as expected, became so strong that the Pakistani central bank spent $35 million in support of the dollar so as to avoid damaging its export sector[100]. The actions of the Bush administration led Soros[101] to argue that '9/11' changed the course of history, introducing "a discontinuity into American foreign policy", as the president used 9/11 as an excuse for pursuing a radical foreign policy agenda, which included the invasion of Iraq in 2003. The assumptions on which the discontinuity of 9/11 was based predated the event, according to Soros in reference to the aforementioned historical developments.

The least measurable of all impacts of 9/11 was the psychological effect. It might also have been the most profound; another illustration of the role of the immaterial in discontinuity. The irreversible nature of discontinuity is illustrated by the idea of an end of innocence as a result of the attacks[98], and the notion that they dealt the American myth of 'virtuous isolation'[95] such a blow so as to permanently alter US attitudes towards their international position[81;102]. Earlier attacks, such as the Oklahoma bombing in 1995 and on Pearl Harbor in 1941, probably had not instilled a sense of fear and vulnerability to the same degree. Indeed, Larabee[103] argues that the Bush administration purposefully evoked fear in order to return the US to the "militarized citadel culture of the Reagan years". She contends that the Bush administration used 9/11 as an excuse to create an 'empire of fear', in which dissent was stifled and policy disputes were simplified.

3 DISCONTINUITY

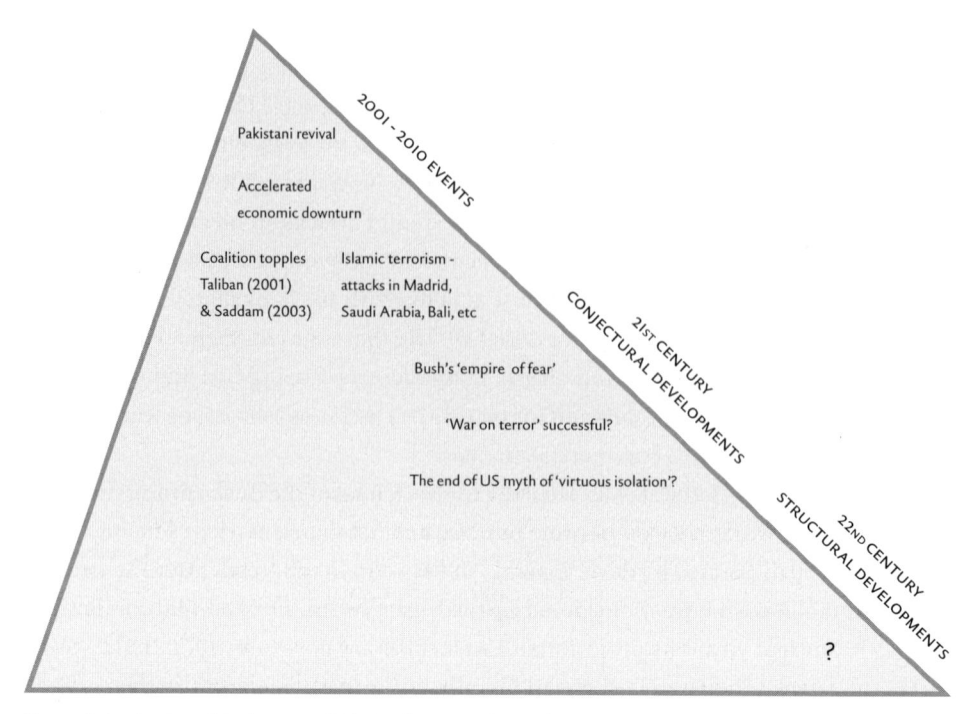

Figure 3 *A selection of the impacts of 9/11 to illustrate abrupt discontinuity.*

The long-term implications of 9/11 are debateable. Perhaps unsurprisingly given his political agenda, President Bush declared the country had fundamentally changed when he announced his decision to create the department of homeland security nine months after the attacks[98]. However, in February 2002, a journalist writing in a local newspaper proclaimed, "Well, shattered nation, good news. September 11 didn't change anything at all"[98]. The patriotic affirmation and the increased religious zeal following 9/11 proved to be temporary[95], and, US party politics in the aftermath of the attacks arguably reaffirmed old attitudes rather than creating new ones. In a similar difference of perspective, Schwartz[84] argued that the attacks changed history irretrievably, due mostly to the economic damage they did, while the Economist contended that 9/11 might prove to be a "bolt of lightning that brightly and briefly illuminated the landscape without changing it"[95]. These different interpretations underscore the idea that discontinuity is subject to the perspective from which it is regarded. A selection of the impacts of 9/11 is presented in Figure 3 to illustrate the concept of abrupt discontinuity.

In summary, using 9/11 we illustrated characteristics of the concept of discontinuity such as its impact, interactions between events and long-term processes, dependence on perspective, and such immaterial influences as religion and cultural values. We also illustrated the prominence of events over underlying processes that is specific to abrupt discontinuity.

6.2 The emergence of the environment as a societal concern

In our second illustration of the concept of discontinuity, we address three examples of abrupt discontinuities and how these led to a gradual discontinuity, namely the emergence of environmental concern. The three examples are fish stock collapse, the damage by chlorofluorocarbons (CFCs) to the ozone layer, and the emergence of 'mad cow disease'. All these cases involve damage by human activity to the environment and environmental health as described in the European Environment Agency's report, Late Lessons from Early Warnings: the Precautionary Principle, 1986-2000[104] and our study on early warnings based on this report[105].

Fisheries and fish stock collapse[75]

Abrupt discontinuities occurred when the Scottish herring stock collapsed in the 19th century, and when the California sardine and Newfoundland cod met with the same fate in the last century. Fish stock collapse illustrates several characteristics of discontinuity: the wide-spread impact of discontinuity, the interactions between various events and processes that produce it, and its sometimes irreversible nature.

Developments leading up to the stock collapses demonstrate the interaction of various processes to produce discontinuity. Twentieth century technological innovation in combination with expanded demand for fish products led to industrialised fishing practices that resulted in centralisation around larger towns and a sharp decline of centuries-old fishing communities. Such new practices nearly caused the collapse of North Sea herring stocks in the 1970s and again in the mid-1990s. The stock nearly collapsed because European policy practices prevent rapid responses to potential crises by distributing control of fisheries among EU Member states making the development of effective policy an arduous process. Global economic and geo-political developments played a role in the Californian sardine stock collapse in 1942. In a long dispute over proposed fishing restrictions, proponents of continued sardine fishing argued that restrictions would hamper one of the few successful industries of the economically depressed 1930s. In 1942, it was even agreed to increase the catch in order to support the war effort. The stock collapsed that same year.

Anticipating fish stock collapse has been complicated because the numbers of many marine fish species fluctuate as a result of natural causes. In the past, policy makers were slow to realise that fishing practices could decimate whole species and, by the time this was understood, several shoals across the world were already eliminated, forcing fishing activity further offshore. By the 1970s there was optimism that past mistakes could be avoided. However, paralysing disputes over the UN Convention on the Law of the Sea failed to stop the collapse of Newfoundland cod, historically the world's largest fish stock, in 1992. The failure of the stock to rebound is an illustration of the irreversible character of some discontinuities.

CFCs and the ozone layer[106]
The case of stratospheric ozone depletion illustrates the potentially unexpected and partially reversible nature, albeit slow, of some discontinuities.

Chlorofluorocarbons (CFCs) are a type of halocarbon used in aerosol containers and refrigerators since the 1930s, and had seen a significant expansion in their production in the 1960s. In 1974, scientists Molina, Rowland,[107] and Creutzen surprised policy makers and scientists alike when they argued that CFCs were so stable that they would reach the stratosphere and release chlorine atoms, initiating an ozone-destroying chain reaction. This, in turn, would allow ultraviolet radiation to reach the Earth, with widespread, damaging effects[41]. Some regulatory bodies moved to prevent potential damage to the ozone layer by banning CFCs in aerosols in the United States, Canada, Norway, and Sweden. However, by the early 1980s, interest in the ozone layer had subsided, and the production of CFCs had reached 1974 levels again[41].

The 1985 discovery of an actual hole in the ozone layer above the Antarctic was the second instance of surprise. This second surprise should arguably not have been so surprising in view of the previous warnings, which justified the monitoring the ozone layer for possible CFC damage. However, NASA's model parameters were based on assumptions that ozone depletion would first be visible at high altitudes in tropical areas and not in the lower stratosphere of the Polar Regions. Therefore, so-called 'outliers' of high and low ozone readings were eliminated because they were considered implausible. Also, monitoring was complicated by the unsophisticated instruments for measuring the effects of CFCs and only taking measurements from airplanes offered the solution.

Ignorance and flawed assumptions have led to a situation where in 2100 the CFC with the longest lifetime will still have a concentration in the atmosphere of at least 37 percent of what it was in 2000.

The 'Mad Cow Disease'[108;109]
Bovine spongiform encephalopathy (BSE, or 'mad cow disease') might serve as a symbol for many recent animal-related diseases in Europe, such as swine fever, chicken fever, and foot and mouth disease. The emergence of BSE illustrates that discontinuity can result from the convergence of various processes over many years. In the case of BSE, the development of various farming practices, in combination with several economic and political pressures, converged to form a crisis in intensive agriculture at the end of the 20th century.

With the intensification of farming practices, it became common practice to use offal in feed. Offal is cheap and has a high nutritional value, but the practice introduced the offal of potentially diseased animals into the human and animal food chain. Also, globalisation turned the human food market into an interconnected international network. Food ingredients, meat products, and livestock were transported over long distances and were processed all over the world. The interconnected global network made the food chain vulnerable to diseases from many more geographical sources than previously.

BSE first emerged in Britain in 1986, with the detection of an infectious protein or prion, which probably got into the food chain through offal originating in carcasses of scrapie-infected sheep or from cattle with a previously unidentified transmissible spongiform encephalopathy (TSE). Scientific evidence suggests that the human ingestion of food products contaminated with BSE might cause variant Creutzfeldt-Jacob (vCJD) disease. The BSE-crisis was therefore caused by an unhappy convergence of various farming practices allowing a discontinuity to creep into the system.

Risky farming practices might also have caused the BSE-crisis, but economic and political interests were important catalysts. The British Ministry of Agriculture, Fisheries, and Food's (MAFF), responsible for British farming interests, initially denied the suggestion that recycling animal slaughterhouse offal into animal feed was potentially dangerous. They did so to diminish the short-term adverse impact of BSE on the profitability of the food industry and to downplay the level of public expenditure needed to combat the disease. MAFF continued to do so even when events proved the dangers of recycling.

Over 180 000 cases of mad cow disease have since been diagnosed worldwide, along with 119 known cases of vCJD, illustrating BSEs high impact. The immediate costs for UK agricultural departments were estimated at GBP 4.2 billion. An estimated loss of value added to the UK economy alone is estimated at GPB 1.15 billion. The crisis has led to an overhaul in intensive farming practices, due partly to the existence of other animal illnesses resembling BSE.

Emergence of environmental concern
In summary, the cases of fish stock collapse, chlorofluorocarbons (CFCs), and the 'mad cow disease' all highlight characteristics of the discontinuity concept. Discontinuity's break with dominant patterns and its large impact is illustrated in all three cases. Large-scale animal and human fatalities in the fish stock and BSE examples illustrate the irreversible nature of some discontinuities. The slow and partially reversible nature of others is illustrated by the CFC case. The interconnection of various events and long-term processes is illustrated by the convergence of political, agricultural, environmental, technological, and socio-economic developments in the fish stock and BSE cases. The influence of immaterial aspects is demonstrated by the political pressures in the BSE case; the notion of surprise in the fish stock and CFC

cases. The sudden nature of fish stock collapse and the gradual development of CFC-induced harm illustrate the distinction between abrupt and gradual discontinuity.

The three cases might be seen as isolated incidents or as connected elements, depending on the perspective from which they are regarded. When the cases are looked at from a long-term point of view, it can be argued that collectively they contributed to the emergence of environmental concern in Western society in the last century. This emergence can be seen as a discontinuity due to the life-threatening nature of ecological problems, which differentiates them from other societal issues[110]. This gradual discontinuity has developed as a result of converging processes and trigger events that, in addition to the examples we discuss, include polluted rivers and the effects of such substances as pesticides, sulpher dioxide, polychlorinated biphenyls (PCBs)[110], and asbestos[111]. Arguably, environmental concern first openly manifested itself in the 1970s in the discussions fuelled by the Club of Rome's report, Limits to Growth[112]. At that time, it was thought that catastrophe would result if problems such as pollution, industrialisation, population growth, food shortages, and the overexploitation of fossil fuels were not solved quickly[110].

Since its emergence, the nature of environmental concern has evolved to affect societal attitudes, international policy agendas, and technological innovations[79]. Following the 1973 oil crisis there developed a growing awareness of the indirect and long-term dangers of environmental degradation, such as stratospheric ozone depletion. The 1990s saw an orientation towards sustainable development, characterised by its focus on the international character of environmental problems and on the interaction between social, economic, and environmental developments.

Environmental concern is strongly driven by immaterial elements such as worldviews and risk perceptions. The emergence and evolution of environmental concern arguably demonstrates a gradual transition from a guilt culture to a risk culture and, ultimately, to a precautionary culture[113]. The 19th century guilt culture maintained that citizens were responsible for their own actions, and thus also for the situations in which they found themselves. In this culture, damage resulting from industrial accidents could not be properly settled. A risk culture emerged. Beck[114] contends that the dilemma for this culture centred on the distribution of the technological risks, produced by the industrial system and the commercial exploitation of scientific knowledge. During the twentieth century, the risk culture became inappropriate, relying too heavily on scientific knowledge. It is argued[113] that the risk society has become more precautionary in nature.

7 Concluding remarks

In this chapter, we explored how the idea of discontinuity is interpreted in IA and foresight. Concepts in other disciplines were used to improve understanding of the concept of discontinuity. The research revealed that a limited number of sources address discontinuity directly. Related concepts in the consulted sources are surprise and the wild card. However, with the exception of several detailed ideas, interpretations of discontinuity in the analysed literature are relatively superficial. We conclude that the literature tends to focus on discontinuous events. The interaction of trends and structural processes that cause these events is acknowledged only to a limited degree. Furthermore, in the literature there is little recognition of immaterial influences such as ideas, paradigms, religion, and cultural values. Lastly, there are conflicting interpretations regarding the speed with which discontinuity occurs.

Our conceptualisation includes an intrinsic difference with established trends, dominant patterns or paradigms; a high impact; irreversibility or partial reversibility; a complex interaction between various events and long-term processes; and a combination of physical and immaterial processes. A dependence on the perspective from which a discontinuity is regarded ensures that it might come as unexpected. We distinguish between abrupt and gradual discontinuity. Abrupt discontinuity is a jolt to society that might be temporary or partially reversible. Gradual discontinuity progresses in a slower, less spectacular manner and it might have a long-term, widespread impact.

We illustrated our conceptualisation of discontinuity with two cases: the September 11th attacks as an example of abrupt discontinuity, and the emergence of environmental concern as a gradual discontinuity. Equipped with a more extensive conceptualisation of discontinuity, we are now in a position to study how discontinuity is addressed in scenario practice.

4
discontinuity and scenario practice

4 DISCONTINUITY AND SCENARIO PRACTICE

1 Introduction

In theory, scenario development is a way to consider future discontinuity. Berkhout et al.[1] argue that, "scenarios provide a response to the problems of discontinuity". They "embrace the potential for sharp discontinuities"[2]. Thus, scenarios help to prepare for "surprising" change[3]. Such scenarios are classified in various sources as unconventional[4], contrast[5], phantom[6] and peripheral[7]. According to the literature[6;8;9;10], these scenarios are developed to raise awareness and understanding about new or uncertain issues, and to challenge existing assumptions.

Scenarios' theoretical promise might not be reflected in scenario practice, however. A comparative study of scenarios[11] developed in the 1990s concluded that many scenarios have a 'business as usual' character and assume that current conditions will persist for decades. This criticism is common. Bruun et al.[4] argue that the overwhelming majority of scenarios can be characterised as conventional and trend-based. Similarly, Marien[12] claims that scenario studies "often ignore the 'wild cards' of low-possibility futures".

In the current chapter we analyse the apparent discrepancy between theory and practice by analysing how discontinuity is addressed in current scenario development[1]. First, we investigate concepts and methods for exploring discontinuity, as proposed in IA and foresight literature. Second, using the thirty scenario studies that are the focus of Chapter 2, we reflect on how recent scenarios actually address discontinuity. In particular, we examine how discontinuity is considered, and the types included in the scenarios. We also address why the idea of discontinuity might have been excluded. We close by considering other factors that might inspire the exploration of the idea of discontinuity, and by suggesting the types of scenarios that are most congenial to the notion's consideration.

2 Concepts for exploring discontinuity in scenario development: are there any?

In Chapter 3 we indicated that factors resulting in a discontinuity are not suggested by the prominent trends of the day. These factors are mostly hidden from view. Therefore, signs of future change are to be found in speculating on potential discontinuity, rather than in focusing on relevant present-day factors[13;14]. In scenario literature, such signs are referred to as signals[15], weak signals[13], and early warnings[14]. Mendonça et al.[13] address weak signals by referring to Ansoff[16], who

---

[1] We acknowledge the contribution of Am Sleegers to this chapter. See 1) Sleegers, A. M. (2003). The Future Shocks: On the role of discontinuity in scenario analysis. *ICIS & Faculty of Economics and Business Administration*. Maastricht University, and 2) Van Notten, Ph. W. F., et al.,The Future Shocks: On Discontinuity and Scenario Development, Technological Forecasting and Social Change, 72(2), 175-194

defines them as "warnings (external or internal), events and developments that are too incomplete to permit an accurate estimation of their impact and/or determine a complete response". They argue that weak signals cannot easily be connected to current trends, but that they can be seen as first symptoms of change. Petersen[14] describes early warnings as indications of an impending event. Van Steenbergen[15] speaks of 'seeds of time', an expression taken from Shakespeare's 'Macbeth', from a line spoken by Banquo to three witches: 'If you can look into the seeds of time and say which grain will grow and which will not, then speak to me'.

The idea of signals suffer from three problems, related respectively to the criteria used to define them, the notions of time and causality on which they are based, and the concepts' simplicity². Harremoës et al.[17] propose scientific credibility as a criterion of weak signals, which they refer to as early warnings, to ensure consistency and to avoid arbitrary use of the term. They make their case using instances in which early warnings are difficult to interpret. For example, in 1952 smog killed more than 2 000 people in London[18]. The measures aimed at mitigating the problem, involving mainly the use of tall chimneys, were slow in coming, and smog killed a further 800 Londoners in 1962. More air quality controls in the UK and other western European countries resulted in the improvement of surface air quality during the 1960s despite increased emissions due to an increase in energy consumption. Experts believed that harmful emissions were being diluted and dispersed to levels that were not harmful. However, several instances of scientific research showed that emissions from the UK and other western European countries were poisoning lakes and damaging buildings on a wide scale in Scandinavia in the form of acid rain. The geographical distance between points of emission and places of damage was a complicating factor, and more than 20 years of persuasion was needed before Western European countries took action. The fact that action was at last taken at all can probably be attributed to the scientific credibility of evidence of damage.

Nonetheless, the precondition of establishing scientific credibility of an early warning in the context of foresight has several drawbacks. First, applying the criterion assumes that there is consensus on what scientific credibility entails. Second, the need to establish scientific credibility implies that early warnings need to occur within an existent scientific frame of reference. Consequently, flawed or absent scientific frames of reference mean that indications of future change are not detected, or are only identified at a relatively late stage. Scientifically credible early warnings might then be considered effectively late warnings. To illustrate, in the

---

² For an extensive discussion of early warnings and risk detection see Van Notten,Ph.W.F, To Learn from Early Warnings, in: Nieuwe Risico's in Zicht (New Risks in Sight),Raad voor Ruimtelijk Milieu- en Natuuronderzoek (Advisory Council for Research on Spatial Planning, Nature, and the Enviroment) (ed.), Lemma, Utrecht (2005)

case of stratospheric ozone depletion, NASA computers were programmed to filter out so-called 'outliers' of high and low O_3 readings, because they were considered implausible. In fact, the low O_3 readings turned out to be evidence of stratospheric ozone depletion in the Antarctic. The model parameters that NASA used exemplify the idea of a dominant flawed paradigm. Here the paradigm delayed the recognition of the hole in the ozone layer until 1985, well after the hole's formation, eleven years after scientists Rowland's, Molina's, and Creutzen's initial warnings. We conclude that the criterion of scientific credibility is not suited for the identification of signals in the context of foresight.

The second problem with signals involves the notions of time and causality. To illustrate, it is possible to wonder whether four American universities' computers in 1969 to form 'Arpanet' (Advanced Research Project Agency) was a weak signal pointing to the Internet's development some 20 years later[19]. Looking back, one would probably conclude that it was, but at the time the meaning of the signal would not have been apparent. Given Molitor's[20] claim that "of every change traces can be found, often in a very early stage", he might disagree. However, the idea of the 'latency lacuna'[17] suggests that, at least in technological cases, 'traces' might become manifest only in a late stage. The lacuna refers to the complication of assessing the effect of a technology when there is a long lag time between first exposure and first measurable impact. Technology and the conditions in which it is used will have changed by the time the impact of the first instance of exposure becomes clear. As a result, only conclusions about older versions of the technology can be drawn at a given point in time; it is impossible to know the effects of the newer version.

The latency lacuna is illustrated by the 10 – 40 year latent period between asbestos exposure and the diseases associated with it[21]. First evidence of the impact of exposure became clear in 1898, twenty years after it was first mined. Not until 100 years later did the European Union ban all forms of asbestos, a delay that Harremoës et al.[17] in part attribute to claims about the improvement of the technology stalling regulatory action. Similarly, it was claimed that low doses of DES in beef could not be as hazardous as the high doses in the DES pill that were prescribed to pregnant women[22]. Harremoës et al. argue that the claim could not be disproved entirely because of the latency lacuna. It is possible that mobile phones and the claimed harm from their electro magnetic fields (EMFs) will prove to be another manifestation of the latency lacuna[23]. The latency lacuna demonstrates a tension between the interpretation of weak signals "in the spirit of the times"[17] and in hindsight. The asbestos and DES cases demonstrate that by the time one interpretation is widely accepted as relevant, the intrinsic natures of the warning, the associated risk, and the societal context have invariably changed. In short, the latency lacuna calls into question the value of weak signals in the context of foresight.

Taken to an extreme, we argue that in certain cases weak signals only gain meaning in hindsight because of the significance of later developments. These are not caused directly by the effects that the early warning refers to, but rather by a convergence of other elements. For example, Mohammed Atta's stay in Hamburg prior to '9/11' is only significant because of the attacks in the United States[24]. His visit to Hamburg in itself does not reveal much about later events. By implication, it is impossible to derive the nature of later effects from the warning, when it first appears. Following this reasoning, even the most scientifically credible weak signals might be flawed, giving little indication of actual future consequences. It is fair to conclude that the idea of signals is an ambiguous point of departure for the exploration of potential discontinuity.

A third problem with signals is their overly simplistic focus on individual events at the expense of the broader context in which they occur. Following Braudel[25;26;27], we argue that an investigation of the interaction between events, conjectural, and structural processes, past and present, might shed light on future development in society. Although ignorance and uncertainty prevent a comprehensive understanding of these patterns, making prediction impossible, we speculate that a partial understanding of such patterns is sometimes sufficient to anticipate possible future development. Although Mohammed Atta's stay in Hamburg was meaningless in itself, could not the September 11th attacks have been better anticipated on the basis of structural developments such as American overseas expansion over the last three centuries, and conjectural developments such as the rise of political Islam and the increased ferocity of the attacks on US targets?

3 Methods for exploring discontinuity in scenario development: are there any?

Given that weak signals do not provide accurate insights about future discontinuity, we turned to investigate possible alternatives. Brooks'[29] observed the lack of such alternatives nearly 20 years ago:

> *The problem is not that analysts have been unaware of the short-comings of surprise-free thinking, but rather that they* LACK USABLE METHODOLOGIES *[our emphasis] to deal with discontinuities and random-events. The multiplicity of conceivable surprises is so large and heterogeneous that the analyst despairs of deciding where to begin, and instead proceeds in the hope that, in the longer sweep of history, surprises and discontinuities will average out, leaving smoother long-term trends as a basis for reasonable approximations of the future.*

Since then, however, several alternatives have been proposed, varying significantly in character, level of sophistication, and scientific basis. Kates and Clark[30;31] propose six techniques: surprise theory, imaging, historic retrodiction, contrary assumptions, asking experts what would surprise them, and simulating surprise using computer models.

Kates and Clark describe surprise theory as the investigation of the principles underlying unexpected events and developments. Imaging involves imagining an unlikely event and then trying to construct a plausible scenario by which it might be realised. Historical retrodiction involves the examination of empirical cases of surprise to determine whether the seeds of those surprises were apparent at the time and, if so, how they might have been recognised as such. This approach is comparable to Neustadt and May's[100] description of history as stimulating the imagination and that, "seeing the past can help one envision alternative futures". A similar method is Van Steenbergen's[32] approach, called comparative prognosis, which involves exploring whether a situation in the past can teach us anything about the future. Kates and Clark also propose introducing contrary assumptions into an analysis. They point out that, in making population projections, analysts usually make several different assumptions about birth and death rates and how they change over time. The authors argue that the assumptions seldom entail such major disruptions as war, economic depression, plague, or a change in deep-seated values. By including such disruptions in the calculations, analysts can get a better idea of extreme cases. A variant of the contrary assumptions-technique that Kates and Clark propose involves asking experts what would surprise them, and how they would define those surprises in probabilistic terms.

Kates and Clark's last approach is the simulation of surprise in system dynamics models that explore how the interaction of current trends produces surprising results. Kieken[33] points out that methodology for introducing surprises into modelling are still lacking. This observation provoked a recent modelling experiment involving the development of a Seine river basin scenario dramatically different from today's vision of the watershed. Recently there has also been experimentation with a different systems dynamic approach called 'chance discovery'[34;35]. It aims to develop computational theory for scenario development in order to enhance the possibility of identifying 'chance events'[34] which are described as entirely new, influential, partly manageable events. Experimentation with the approach has focused on the development of methodology for the early detection of technological risks[35]. However Fontela[96] and Rotmans[97] argue that the majority of prognostic models cannot deal with phenomena at a highly aggregated level, where structural change can be examined. Rotmans argues that model builders struggle with how to express causal relationships of discontinuous patterns in quantitative terms and how to build them into a model.

A proposed IA method is Easterling and Kok's[36] multi-scale approach. Using the concept of emergent properties of scale, they argue that a comparison of developments on different scales might reveal the emergent properties of a system. Those developments that appear incidental or disorderly on a local level might form a new pattern when examined on a regional or national level, for example. The development of the multi-scale approach is in an experimental stage.

Harremoës et al.[17] propose monitoring as a relevant technique for considering potential discontinuity in future-oriented assessments. They argue that lessons from past cases of damage to the environment and human health highlight the value of thorough, long-term monitoring. They point out that for asbestos, benzene, and polychlorinated biphenyls (PCBs) evidence of the adverse health effects was accumulating as early as the 19th century, but that systematic monitoring played no role at the time. Data was either not gathered (benzene), or it became available only in a slow and ad hoc fashion over a period of decades. The authors speculate that systematic monitoring could have prevented harmful effects at an earlier stage, helping identify unusual patterns.

Petersen[14] offers an approach for investigating wild cards. The approach revolves around the questions: which are the most important wild cards? Can we anticipate them? Is there anything we can do about them? Petersen argues that the way to identify the important wild cards is to quantify their relative impact. This can be quantified according to criteria such as resistance and vulnerability to the wild card, the perceived uncertainty of the outcome, and the rate of change. With regards to the anticipation of wild cards, Petersen argues that it involves careful observation, gathering and analysing relevant data, as well as "unusual new methods of accessing information". Besides "traditional" sources, this information might be provided by experts in systems behaviour, by the Internet, or by complexity theory, for example.

Van Steenbergen[15;32] questions the value of such methods as those proposed above, arguing instead that to anticipate discontinuity one needs to develop a type of 'antenna' with which to identify future societal developments. To develop such an antenna, according to Van Steenbergen[32], one has to be alert, to take the time for research in a dedicated manner, to use one's 'sociological imagination', and especially to make mistakes and be willing to admit to them. Maso[37] offers other personal qualities. In addressing the search for technological discoveries, he argues that, one should have keen observational qualities, good powers of abductive reasoning, and an inquisitive mind[3]. Moreover, Maso argues that it is necessary to have a knowledge base or expertise in order to make sense of that which one observes, and to be inspired by unconscious or tacit knowledge triggered as a result of confrontation with new information. A last quality that Maso proposes is a large professional network, exposing one to new ideas. Harremoës and Gee[23] argue that identifying early warnings often involves making sometimes accidental connections among disparate pieces of information. They argue that in order for these 'accidental' connections to occur one must create and nurture an environment of independent 'curiosity-driven'

---

[3] Abductive reasoning is defined by Maso as the inference of the most likely explanation for a particular phenomenon.

research, free of political and institutional constraints as possible. Harremoës and Gee[23], among others, also recommend the use of both theoretical and empirical knowledge in early risk detection. Some scholars[17;38;39;40] suggest using 'lay' and local knowledge. To illustrate, Harremoës et al.[17] draw on examples where people other than specialists raised the alarm in cases of health hazards, citing the example of a factory inspector who is said to have provided the first early warning regarding the dangers of asbestos by reporting deaths in numerous factories[21].

To summarise, signals provide an ambiguous starting point for exploring future discontinuity. We conclude that Brooks'[29] concern about usable methodologies to deal with discontinuities has only been partly addressed in the twenty years or so since he expressed it. Although numerous methods have been proposed, they are still in the experimental phase. Some sources propose alternatives to a strictly methods-oriented approach. These alternatives emphasise personal competences and expertise. Therefore, when investigating contemporary scenario practice and its treatment of discontinuity, our scope should be wider than mere concepts and methods.

4 Discontinuity in contemporary scenario practice

In this section, we further consider how discontinuity is addressed in contemporary scenario practice using the 30 scenario studies from the scenario cartwheel. We first discuss studies that omit discontinuity, followed by the studies in which the idea was addressed. In the latter group of studies, we distinguish between exploratory and pre-policy research studies, in order to evaluate whether the goal of the exercise is a rationale for the investigation of discontinuity.

4.1 Studies that omit discontinuity

European security beyond the Cold War[41]

The four scenarios on the future of Europe's security were written at the time of the collapse of communism, shortly after the fall of the Berlin Wall. Despite this major underling disruption, the scenario study does not explore discontinuity. The author defends his decision to exclude discontinuity by quoting Buchan[42], who argued that scenario building "cannot successfully take account of the element of chance in human affairs, the incidence of wars, economic or social catastrophe, or the emergence of powerful idiosyncratic leaders". The author agrees with Buchan's statement, by pointing out that no study written in the 1970s could have predicted the impact of Gorbachev's *glasnost* and *perestroika* on the international scene.

British Airways[43]

The 1994 British Airways study assumed that the future does not significantly vary from the past. This is highlighted in the study's report, in which it is claimed that to date the scenario team had not experienced any surprises in the external environment. Possible airline regulation and changes in information technology are referred to, but they are not considered to be driving forces powerful enough to cause a significant deviation in current trends.

Port of Rotterdam[44;45]
Staff of the Port of Rotterdam developed two scenarios. Discontinuity is not referred to in the scenarios or the accompanying report. Only desirable scenarios were created in the scenario exercise, which depicted futures of a large, important harbour. The port authority manager responsible for the study indicates that, during the scenario workshops, it was assumed that the port would operate in a stable environment due to the long-term influence of decisions regarding the harbour. The consideration of potential discontinuity was deemed to be a redundant exercise. The manager indicated that organisational resistance to uncertainty and potential disruption was another possible motivation for ignoring discontinuity in the scenario study.

ICL[46]
In the 1995 ICL study, two scenarios were developed on the future of information markets. Ringland addressed discontinuity in reference to wild cards. She pointed out that:
> *The best way of treating these [wild cards] was to identify where in the organization the policy for dealing with these should rest, and discussing them, exploring the processes and responsibilities, and getting policies established, rather than building them into the scenarios.*

Consequently, no discontinuities were incorporated in the scenarios.

Foresight Futures[1;47;48]
The study's four scenarios describe the United Kingdom in 2020. Berkhout and Hertin[47] wrote:
> *The exploratory [...] approach used in these scenarios suggests that change occurs gradually along a single trajectory. Future states are seen as being the outcome of an accumulation of changes over time [...]. But not all change is like this. The direction of change may itself vary over time, with one set of conditions being replaced by a new set. This change in direction may take place slowly [...], or it may happen suddenly as a result of major, surprise external events.*

Berkhout and Hertin appear to distinguish between abrupt and gradual discontinuity, arguing that a directional change might take place slowly or suddenly. However, in the first two sentences the authors indicate that abrupt change is not included in the scenarios. We did not identify other references to discontinuity either.

Questa[49;50;51;52;53]

The Dutch Ministry of Transport's study examined the future of the Netherlands with a particular focus on passenger transport. Four scenarios were developed. The Polderland scenario is described as surprise-free, implying that the others included discontinuous elements. However, there are few references to discontinuity in the other scenarios beyond such occasional examples such as lifestyle changes and far-reaching technological development.

EEA – Environment in the European Union at the turn of the century[54;55]

The European Environment Agency (EEA) developed its baseline or 'business-as-usual' scenario based on three factors: the state of the environment in 2000, projected socio-economic changes, and implementation of existing and proposed EU policies. No reference was made to discontinuity in the scenario.

Scenarios Europe 2010[56;57;58]

No references were made to discontinuity in the explanation of the study's methodology. Also, although the developed scenarios describe paths to differing futures, discontinuity does not feature in them.

IPCC/ SRES[58;59]

The Intergovernmental Panel on Climate Change (IPCC) Special Report on Emissions Scenarios (SRES)[59] explored the impact of greenhouse gas (GHG) emissions on climate change. The SRES authors argue that their scenarios are 'neutral' and that they purposefully exclude catastrophic futures. The authors believed that catastrophic futures typically involve widespread environmental or economic collapse:

> *Many of [...] [these] scenarios suggest that catastrophic developments may draw the world into a state of chaos within one or two decades. In such scenarios GHG emissions might be low because of low or negative economic growth, but it seems unlikely that they would receive much attention in the light of more immediate problems.*

For this reason SRES researchers did not analyse discontinuous futures. Also, due to the worldwide consultative process that the scenarios were subjected to, events and processes considered extreme or politically sensitive by several parties were removed or watered down.

NIVE[60]

No references to or examples of discontinuity were found in the scenarios or the accompanying text of this scenario-study on the future of leadership in the 21st century.

Possum[61]

In this study on transport policy, backcasting methodology was used to develop three scenarios or "images". On the one hand, it is noted in the report that one of the advantages of scenario development over other prognostic methods is the larger emphasis on trend breaks. However, there are no examples of such breaks in the scenarios.

Schooling for Tomorrow[62;63]

Six scenarios for the future of universities were developed in the OECD's Schooling for Tomorrow study. Central questions for the study were: What will schools look like in the future? What big trends are most influential in shaping education and how might these unfold in the coming years? What policy questions need to be addressed today to open desirable pathways to the future? The idea of discontinuity does not play a central role in the study although there is a general acknowledgement that the nature of education is undergoing a transformation. A footnote[63] elaborates as follows:

> *It is worth noting that an assumption is made regarding what tertiary education institutions are about [...].This assumption insists on a certain degree of functional continuity. [...] the explicit aim here is [to] think about how the TES [tertiary education system] might change given relatively constant generic roles but a wide range of potential ways of executing those roles.*

Telecom[64; 65]

The short scenario exercise resulted in three scenarios portraying the future of the mobile telecom sector. There is no indication that discontinuities were addressed. The project coordinator suggests that the reason for the absence of discontinuities was that desirable scenarios had been developed, which left no room in this study for the consideration of radical change.

Tunis[66]

No reference to nor examples of discontinuity were found in the scenarios or the accompanying text of this scenario-study on the future of Metropolitan Tunis.

CPB Netherlands Bureau of Economic Policy Analysis 2003[67;68]

In the 2003 report describing four scenarios for Europe, the CPB indicates four broad policy questions in particular were explored. The CPB argues that the scenarios had therefore to be as broad as the questions around which they were developed. The point is elaborated in a footnote:

> *This implies that we do not develop extreme scenarios, which sometimes appear in studies that have a very long time frame. The emphasis in our study is on the period up to 2020.*

The citation demonstrates the authors' expectation that no extreme events or developments will take place until 2020.

4.2 Analysis of studies that omit discontinuity
Fifteen of the 30 studies that we analysed did not address the idea of discontinuity. This exclusion was the result of methodological decisions in four of the studies: the IPCC/SRES, Questa, ICL, and the European Security scenarios. The IPCC/SRES-authors indicate that they consider discontinuity irrelevant. The authors speak solely of negative discontinuities and argue that, in the event of their occurrence, the issue of emissions would be overshadowed by more immediate problems. In the case of ICL, discontinuities were addressed in a separate process. Ringland[46] explained that the scenario team chose to discuss possible discontinuities with those ICL colleagues who could develop policy to address them, rather than writing them into the scenarios. The author of the publication about the European security scenario studies[41] rejects the relevance of addressing discontinuity in scenario development. In short, not all scenario practitioners consider the combination of the idea of discontinuity and scenario development to be relevant or appropriate.

Numerous studies demonstrate that there are other reasons besides methodological choice for omitting discontinuity. One is a tendency to focus on attractive futures, as demonstrated by the Telecom and the Port of Rotterdam scenario exercises. Here, discontinuity is perceived as negative and threatening, and subsequently ignored to avoid the discomfort of confronting potential problems. This behaviour is referred to by Myers[69] as "ignore-ance". In the case of the Telecom and the Port of Rotterdam studies, the tendency is partly due to organisational resistance to uncertainty and radical change.

Another reason for omitting discontinuity involves institutional feasibility. This played a role during the development of the Questa scenarios at the Dutch Ministry of Transport. Dobbinga[19] argues that at the ministry it is considered taboo to stray beyond the dominant paradigm. This is a likely cause for the general lack of discontinuities in the scenarios. Dobbinga argues that the scenario process was hampered by an organisational culture, in which civil servants believe that they are constantly being watched and controlled. Despite publicly encouraging the scenario team to think the unthinkable, management held tight reins on Questa, and its project team was not allowed to stray beyond established thinking. Consequently, the team opted, albeit unconsciously, for the security of the ministry's dominant mode of thought and behaviour. Therefore, considerations of political and institutional feasibility can impair the exploration of discontinuity.

Concern about institutional feasibility probably also influenced the IPCC/SRES-scenarios. Environmental policy is a politically sensitive issue, and in order for its scenarios to be seen as legitimate, the IPCC needed the approval of countries all over the world. It would have been unacceptable for the IPCC to publish a set of controversial scenarios. The struggle toward a consensus, inherent in the political process, tends to tone down or eliminate eccentric ideas. Similar institutional constraints apply to public organisations such as the CPB and EEA. Like the IPCC, their studies either acknowledged discontinuity, but felt it to be irrelevant, or did not acknowledge discontinuity at all.

De Mooij and Tang's[67] reasoning regarding the exclusion of discontinuity in the CPB study reveals another tendency in contemporary scenario work. They seem to assume that no 'extreme' developments will occur between 2003 and 2005. The underlying assumption in cases such as De Mooij and Tang's study, which we also observed in the British Airways scenario exercise, is that the future will not be radically different to the past. This reasoning suggests that those involved in the scenario study maintain a progressive image of the future[70], which is otherwise referred to as the 'evolutionary paradigm'[29]. The paradigm entails the perception of gradual, incremental unfolding of the world system through time and space[29]. Morgan[70] places the evolutionary pattern in a cultural-historical context, arguing that progressive images of the future connect with the principles of a bourgeois-capitalist society. He argues that:

> *The progressive image of the future contains the idea of continuous and perpetual social change that supposedly 'progresses' due to developments in science, technology and social organization. [...] It does not make a break with the past or the present. It is continuous and more of the same; it does not incorporate the notion of discontinuous change or fundamental reconstruction.*

Therefore, discontinuity is implausible, irrelevant, or undesirable for adherents of the evolutionary paradigm and the progressive image of the future.

Brooks[29] argued in 1986 that most visions of the future are based on the evolutionary paradigm. More than fifteen years later, Kieken[33] argues that in most model-based studies the assumption of incremental progress still dominates. Since discontinuity is inconsistent with the evolutionary paradigm, it is invariably omitted from scenarios.

Internally consistent, conventional, trend-based scenarios are the products of the evolutionary paradigm in combination with what Schooneboom[72] refers to as the 'consistency rule'. The demand that scenarios be consistent can be found in much scenario literature. Reasoning from the evolutionary paradigm, internal consistency means that the elements of the scenario narrative build progressively on one another. Schooneboom contends that the resulting scenarios might then be internally unproblematic as logic becomes a substitute for empirical complexity. The consistency criterion and the explicit decision to exclude discontinuity from the studies might be seen as further instances of evolutionary reasoning.

In conclusion, we observe that there are factors such as the evolutionary paradigm, the perception that discontinuity is an irrelevant, negative or destructive phenomenon, and considerations of institutional feasibility that impair the exploration of the idea of discontinuity through scenario development.

4.3 Discontinuity in exploratory studies

We now turn to the nine examples of exploratory scenario studies that addressed discontinuity. The general aim of these studies was to produce insights into the interaction of societal issues and to stimulate creative thinking about possible future developments.

Surprising Futures[73]

In a five-day workshop, a diverse group of researchers took Kates' and Clark's[30;31] methodology for exploring surprise as their point of departure. Both Kates and Clark attended the workshop. The aim was to develop scenarios that were "not *so* surprising that they were entirely 'science fiction' […]. Thus we were not so much looking for *extreme* surprises, as 'great, but still interesting' ones." Four surprise-rich scenarios and one 'conventional wisdom'- scenario were developed using an imaging-technique. The study also drew from quantitative historical data on issues like demography, energy and food production, and industrial output figures. The function of the data was to help develop a conventional wisdom scenario from which the remainder of the scenarios could break away. In the breakaway lay the surprise. The relationship between the quantitative and qualitative in the scenarios was that the former provided the contours for a creative use of the latter.

Examples of abrupt discontinuities in the scenarios include two Greatpox epidemics, the collapse of the United Nations as a result of unresolved diplomatic wrangling over a hostage crisis, and riots and bloodshed in the Netherlands over tax inequalities. Examples of gradual discontinuities include India's rise to world power, the Great Reversal between 1975 and 2025 involving the end of rapid urbanisation processes begun in the nineteenth century, and a fragmented and ad-hoc lifestyle in Europe as a result of the downfall of science and the end of knowledge accumulation.

Beyond Hunger in Africa[74]

The study took several of the approaches proposed by Kates and Clark[30;31] as its point of departure. In a three-day workshop with 16 African and American researchers, including Kates, extrapolation techniques and expert consultation techniques were used to develop one "surprise-free" scenario as a frame of reference for the development of "surprise-rich" scenarios for Africa, using the imaging technique. The latter techniques involved brainstorming about surprising, alternative end-states in the horizon year 2057. Subsequently, break out groups constructed "credible, coherent, and consistent" pathways to those futures.

The gradual discontinuities featured in the surprise-rich scenarios include a transition from dictatorship to democracy, and sustained economic recovery. Examples of abrupt discontinuity include technological breakthroughs, the collapse of tourism, and a failed experiment with biological weapons, resulting in two million deaths.

The Futures of Women[75]
The approach taken in the development of the scenarios involved an on-line computer conference, which ran from October to December 1993, followed by a face-to-face meeting that same December. The scenarios were developed deductively using the investigation of such so-called pre-determined elements as demographic change, and more women in school and the workforce; and driving forces such as the waxing and waning global economy and tensions between individual and group rights.

The authors used the notion of wild cards, considering such topics as atomic and biological terrorism, climate change, and dramatic new fertility and contraceptive technologies. However, despite acknowledging their relevance, the authors indicate without explanation, that wild cards were only briefly considered in their study. Nor was an explanation as to how the wild cards were conceived and written into the scenarios. Examples of how they are depicted are found in the scenarios entitled 'Backlash' and 'Two Steps Forward, Two Steps Back'. In the first, temporary economic alliances and a large black market lead to "abrupt discontinuities" in employment and wide-swinging currency fluctuations. In the second, another abrupt discontinuity occurs in the shape of the suspension of environmental protective measures. This step is taken to boost a sluggish economy, disrupting the fledgling movement toward global sustainability.

KPMG Ebbinge[76;77]
The study resulted in four scenarios of the Dutch job market with a special focus on the role of recruiters. Two scenarios address abrupt discontinuity. In the 'Survival of the fitting' scenario, large multinationals split into thousands of small businesses as a result of an imagined millennium crisis. In the 'New Worker' scenario talented employees, looking for a balance between professional and private life, leave the multinationals en masse and build networks of like-minded professionals with the help of new information technologies. There are no indications that a specific discontinuity-oriented methodology was applied. Rather, interview material and desk research provided input for the common deductive approach of a 2x2 matrix using two driving forces.

Biotechnology scenarios[64;78]

The study was based on the assumption that in a field like biotechnology "the landscape changes too rapidly, and the cascading developments […] in closely related fields […] make predictions obsolete almost at the moment they are uttered". The scenario development process involved the conduct of over 50 interviews and a series of workshops with 37 participants from 12 companies. Each scenario was developed from three assumptions about biotechnology. First, it is here to stay. Second, in addition to the obvious intended consequences of biotech, there will also be unintended consequences. Third, people are anxious about the unknown. There are no indications of the use of specific discontinuity-oriented methods. The prominence of the idea of discontinuity in the scenarios was conceivably introduced as a result of the awareness among the participants of the potentially discontinuous influence of biotechnology.

In The Domino Effect scenario, biotechnology continues to make steady progress until 2010, when an abrupt discontinuity occurs in the form of the deaths of 25 patients who had been receiving gene therapy. The deaths are given enormous mass media attention, and the biotechnology business ultimately collapses. The other two scenarios portray images of a world of gradual discontinuity over a 50-year period. The 'Hare and the Tortoise' scenario describes a societal transformation movement towards traditional farming techniques and holistic health remedies, and away from biotechnology. The Biotrust scenario describes a transition to a world where biotechnology is a trusted and integral part of human life with many applications in health care, food production, and life sciences.

Norway 2030[79]

Like in the ICL scenario process[46], the Norway 2030 scenario team chose not to include discontinuity in their scenarios because the discontinuities proposed in the creative process either did not conform to the images portrayed in the scenarios, or seemed too violent, too improbable, too provocative, or too negative. In spite of these considerations, the authors of the study's report argued that there is a value in presenting ideas about potential discontinuity. Therefore, they took an approach proposed by Schwartz and Ogilvy[80] involving the development of a so-called wild card scenario that takes a dramatic and relevant surprise into account. The wild card scenario was the product of ideas of discontinuity arising from a series of creative workshops. It resulted in the merger of several discontinuities into one scenario entitled 'Biohazard', involving a global socio-political crisis that occurs after technological breakthroughs in reproductive gene therapy. The cause of the crisis is the political handling of the breakthrough, not in the technology itself. The discontinuities are presented as a cascading series of events triggered by the technological breakthrough at the start of the scenario's trajectory.

4 DISCONTINUITY AND SCENARIO PRACTICE

Shell 2001 global scenarios[81]
Two scenarios are described: Prism and Business Class. The scenarios themselves do not contain abrupt discontinuities. However, in a separate caption the possible impact of the September 11th attacks on the scenarios is considered. Whether the scenarios describe gradual discontinuities is debateable, because the scenarios are presented as snapshots that only implicitly address the events and processes that shape the scenario. It is therefore difficult to assess how discontinuous the scenarios are without knowing their path of development from 2002. The consulted documentation is a 100-page public summary of the scenarios. Few methodological insights into the scenario development process were given, though the scenarios might be discussed more extensively in an internal report.

VISIONS[82;83;84;85;86]
The VISIONS project resulted in three scenarios for Europe; three sets of scenarios for three European regions – Venice, the Dutch Green Heart, and the north-west United Kingdom –; and three visions integrating European and regional outlooks. The idea of discontinuity was addressed in the European scenarios and the integrated visions through the use of bifurcations, complexity syndromes, and multi-scale analysis.

The use of bifurcations is similar to the earlier-described contrary assumptions technique. The bifurcations in VISIONS were conceived by considering possible situations that might lead to paths other than those described in a scenario. The inspiration for the bifurcations can be traced partly to ideas generated in a scenario workshop. Most of the work was carried out in informal meetings and desk research. Bifurcations were used as branch points at which a scenario divides in two. At a branch point, the scenario continues in the direction corresponding to the dominant assumptions underlying the storyline; while the bifurcation represents an alternative trajectory in which some of those assumptions are contravened. The bifurcation is presented as a 'what if?'-caption alongside the scenarios. An example of the use of bifurcations is found in the 'Convulsive Change' scenario. Whereas the main scenario addresses problems of global climate warming, the bifurcation describes a situation of rapid climate cooling due to an abrupt reversal of the Gulf Stream. The ensuing climatic situation causes a domino effect that threatens the European continent.

The syndromes were intended to illustrate the complex interactions of events and processes in cases of structural societal change. The syndromes were written on the basis of ideas in the European and regional scenarios. An example of a syndrome is 'City Chaos' that describes urban transport problems and environmental degradation in a Europe rocked by ecological calamities. The project leader developed the idea of complexity syndromes in 2000, and he elaborated them with members of the European scenario team. The syndromes were written using ideas proposed by the European scenario team on the basis of the completed European and regional scenarios. In contrast to the scenarios, the development of the integrated visions did not include workshop activities. The complexity syndromes in the integrated visions were presented in a similar way to the bifurcations, in the form of short descriptions of the alternative developments placed alongside the main narrative.

In addition, a multi-scale approach similar to that proposed by Easterling and Kok was employed[36]. Similarities and differences between regional and European scenarios were examined to try to identify emergent developments. Four scenarios for Venice were produced, four for the northwest UK, three for the Green Heart, and three for Europe. 144 (4x4x3x3) combinations were possible; the number was reduced to three integrated visions. The process involved the matching of salient similarities between the scenarios and elaborating on interesting tensions between them, which might become prominent issues in the future.

Lastly, the VISIONS scenarios were developed with the intention of depicting surprising and unconventional futures. Some abrupt discontinuities occur within the scenarios, such as unprecedented withdrawal by some countries from the European Union as a result of a political crisis. Also, all three scenarios depict futures of gradual discontinuity. In the scenario entitled 'Knowledge is King', the narrative addresses "societal shifts" towards a healthy, older, and technologically advanced society. The 'Big is Beautiful?' scenario describes such institutional transitions as the increase in scale of European business and government. The 'Convulsive Change' scenario depicts a future in which Europe reels from the effects of a series of environmental calamities.

Finnish Aquaculture[4]
Bruun et al.'s[4] aim was to demonstrate the way in which unconventional approaches can introduce novelty into discourses about the future. To this end, they introduced the idea of unconventional and events-based scenarios focusing on contingency and surprise, although they did not elaborate on the unconventional approaches used to develop them. Such indirect indications as the lack of a reference to a structured scenario process in their peer-reviewed article suggest that the Finnish Aquaculture scenarios might have been developed on the basis of desk research and the authors' expertise. To illustrate their argument Bruun et al. outlined four unconventional trend-based scenarios and conventional events-based scenarios for possible futures of aquaculture in the Finnish archipelago. The scenarios include abrupt discontinuities such as dramatic fluctuations in Value Added Tax (VAT) and the rapid negative effects of new, poisonous algae species in the Baltic Sea. Gradual discontinuities include the transformation of archipelago communities and the gradual erosion of the aquaculture industry as a result of increased oil tanker traffic in the Baltic.

The Shield of Achilles[87]
The Shield of Achilles was a desk study allegedly based on the Shell scenario methodology. First, fundamental choices for the future were inventoried. Second, important driving forces for the future were identified, around which narratives were developed that were subsequently merged to form three scenarios. There are no indications that specific discontinuity-oriented methods were used despite the high number of references to discontinuity in the scenarios. References to discontinuity in the scenarios were presumably based on the author's own expertise and desk research. The scenarios were presented through three different views of the market state: the entrepreneurial, the mercantile, and the managerial. However, the documentation of the study explains only in general terms how these perspectives were used to generate the discontinuities, suggesting that the use of perspectives was more a matter of presentation than of methodology.

The author of the Achilles study on the future of the 'market state' demonstrates a strong awareness of the possibility of "radical [...] discontinuities", "high-impact and low-probability contingencies", and "unexpected futures". In a reference to Shell, the author explains that scenarios help people to look for "signs of [...] unexpected futures". The author lists a series of abrupt discontinuities that feature in the three scenarios: war on the Korean peninsula, nuclear conflict in South Asia, and unprecedented immigration as a result of a Mexican revolution. Some examples of gradual discontinuity are also listed. They include the emergence of new international institutions to manage the effects of globalisation, and the improvement of quality of life and longevity as a result of advances in biotechnology, nanotechnology and the materials sciences. The scenarios themselves contain a host of additional discontinuities: sharp drops in population growth, genetic screening at birth to monitor and contain violence-prone adolescents, weather epidemics, 'virtual holiday' camps for drug addicts, and China's nuclear attack on Taiwan.

4.4 Discontinuity in pre-policy research studies
In pre-policy research exercises, scenarios are developed with a view to informing their audience about policy areas that might shape the future. There are five pre-policy research studies that address discontinuity in the collection of scenarios we analysed.

Mont Fleur[46;88;89]
Three workshops with 22 participants representing a cross section of South African society, along with much desk research, resulted in four so-called 'civic scenarios' on the future of post-apartheid South Africa to 2002. The 'Icarus' scenario, named after the mythic Greek character, describes an abrupt discontinuity where a populist government's unsustainable economic policies collapse, leading to a recession. A

gradual discontinuity is described in the 'Flight of the Flamingos' scenario, describing a responsible post-apartheid government's attempts to steer the country toward prosperity. There are no indications that specific discontinuity-oriented methodology was applied. However, because the workshops were held at a time of upheaval in South Africa, the idea of discontinuity might have been prominent enough enough in the participants' minds to have entered the scenario process as a matter of course.

Destino Colombia[90]
This scenario project is similar to the Mont Fleur study in its design. Four scenarios for the future of Colombia in 2020 were developed. The scenario process involved three workshops of a total of 14 days involving 42 Colombian 'leaders' from a cross section of society, including clergymen, political leaders, and guerillas. There are no indications that specific discontinuity-oriented methodology was applied. Abrupt discontinuity plays a role in two scenarios. In the scenario entitled 'A Bird in the Hand is Worth Two in the Bush', the continuing spiral of decline is broken by the agreement between armed groups, the state, and society to enter into dialogue. In the 'Forward March!' scenario the spiral of decline is broken when a government is elected that proves strong enough to impose order and to put an end to institutional chaos. A gradual discontinuity is described in the 'In Unity Lies Strength' scenario as Colombians' combative mentality changes to one of mutual respect and co-operation.

Which World?[91]
The scenario study produced three possible worlds for the year 2050. There are no indications that specific discontinuity-oriented methods were used. Nonetheless, two of the three scenarios contain a mix of abrupt and gradual discontinuities. The 'Transformed World' scenario describes a fundamental change for the better in a society of prosperity, human welfare, security, and equity. This gradual discontinuity is realised through the adoption of visionary 'green' plans, including drastic cuts in US greenhouse gas emissions, a revolution in industrial efficiency, and an 'urban renaissance' in which urban problems are resolved.

The pessimistic 'Fortress World' scenario contains a series of abrupt discontinuities involving multiple complex environmental disasters. The disasters include the collapse of the major marine fisheries, resulting in the loss of the primary source of protein for three quarters of a billion people; the death of thousands of Mexicans from smog; and violent conflicts in China and between Syria and Turkey over water in the Euphrates. As a consequence civil order collapses, and criminal organisations overtake governments in several developed countries, resulting in an upsurge of violence. 'Fortress World' features a total collapse of Africa, producing huge numbers of refugees and more than five million fatalities per year due to violence, hunger, and disease. We argue that the 'Fortress World' scenario describes a gradual discontinuity, composed of multiple abrupt discontinuities.

Nutrition[92;93]
Three scenarios about the future of the nutrition industry were developed in a two-day workshop with a variety of researchers from a nutrition company wishing to remain anonymous. No specific discontinuity-oriented methodology was used. However, two presentations were given at the start of the workshop that might have inspired thinking about potential discontinuity. The first addressed creative thinking and the potential for future discontinuity in the nutrition sector. The second described the scenario process of the above-mentioned Biotechnology study, highlighting the potentially discontinuous influence of the technology.

Discontinuity is central in the three futures of nutrition described in the study. Two revolve around an abrupt discontinuity and the other addresses a gradual discontinuity. The abrupt discontinuity in the 'Laurel and Hardy' scenario involves a 'slim and slick' craze following the discovery of a weight control drug, which results over several years in fatal side effects, driving the nutrition sector into bankruptcy. The 'Bactocase' scenario describes a deadly epidemic in Europe. The scenario then splits into two branches in a manner similar to the earlier-described approaches of bifurcations and contrary assumptions. One branch describes the cause of the epidemic as a killer virus. The other branch attributes the disease to a bacterium in food supplies. The 'Hy-aat' scenario depicts a gradual transition in the west to Asian dietary patterns and attitudes to health care.

Global Environmental Outlook-3 (GEO-3)[94;95]
The global scenarios in this United Nations study are partly inspired by the VISIONS scenarios[82;83;84;85;86] and those described in 'Which World?'[91]. Two of the four GEO-3 scenarios present worlds based on possible outcomes of current developments. The 'Security First' scenario contains several abrupt discontinuities, including economic crashes and recessions, environmental disasters like folds and droughts, and armed conflict involving the use of chemical and biological weapons. The 'Sustainability First' scenario is unique in its description of a gradual discontinuity involving the transition to a new environment and development paradigm supported by more equitable social values and institutions.

An additional, experimental feature was the use of textboxes outside the main scenarios. Each textbox outlines an unusual event that might occur in the future, and the possible affects of the event on the development of the four scenarios. The events consist of the establishment of an Environmental Protection Commission for Africa, widespread surface and groundwater contamination in Asia and the Pacific, a major food scare in Europe, and the effects of a profound world recession on Latin America and the Caribbean. The use of textboxes was partly inspired by the bifurcations approach used in VISIONS[82;83;84;85;86]. In GEO-3 discontinuities were used to investigate how a discontinuous event in one region might affect developments around the globe. The global scenario team asked each regional team to envision a discontinuity for their region. There are no indications that the regional teams used a specific method to do so. The principle investigator of the global scenario team indicated that the regional discontinuities were probably conceived and developed in informal conversations.

4.5 Analysis of studies that included discontinuity

At the end of Chapter 2, the 30 studies we analysed were classified using a scenario typology. An adapted version of the classification is shown in Figure 1 below. The studies denoted in bold include discontinuity.

In general the studies demonstrate a limited awareness of the notion of discontinuity. Only in the documentation about the 'Shield of Achilles' study is there reference to such concepts as signals, namely the term "signs of unexpected futures".

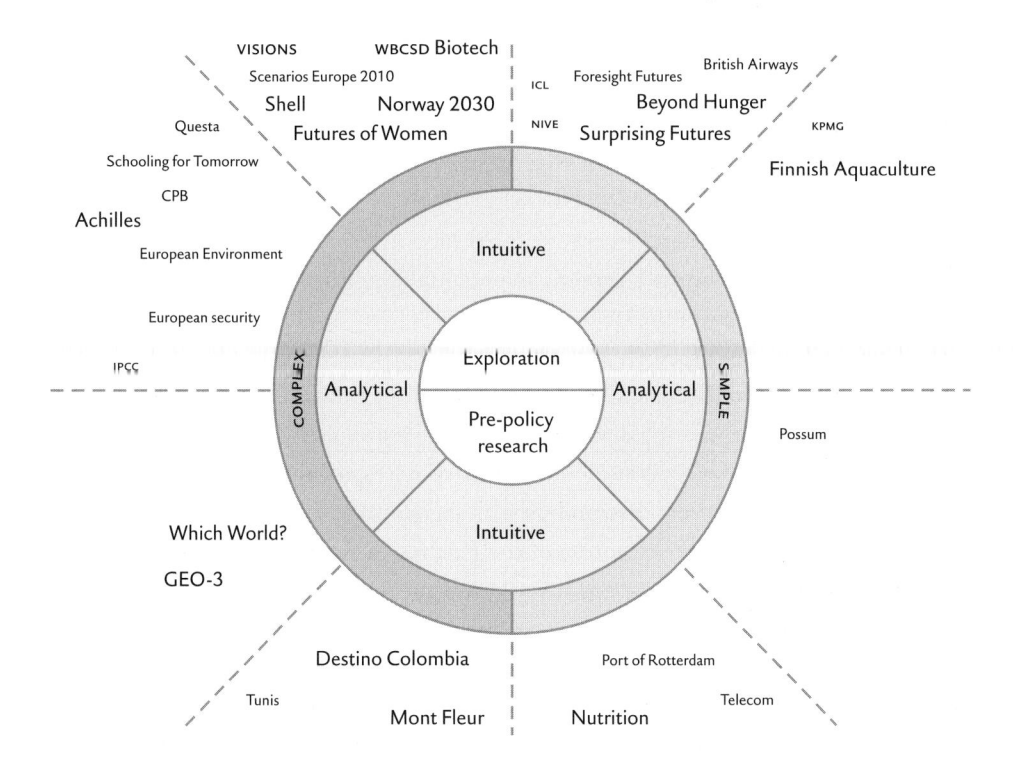

Figure 1 *The scenario cartwheel. Studies that include discontinuity are highlighted.*

Moreover, only in the documentation of the 'VISIONS', 'Beyond Hunger', and 'Surprising Futures' studies is any explanation given of the methods used to explore discontinuity. Some information about the manner in which the idea was explored in the GEO-3 process was obtained through a personal communication[95].

Kates and Clark's[30;31] imaging approach was used to consider discontinuity in the 'Beyond Hunger' and 'Surprising Futures' studies, in which both authors were involved. 'VISIONS' used the concepts of bifurcations and complexity syndromes. Bifurcations were developed through desk research using material from a scenario workshop and informal meetings with scenario team members. Complexity syndromes were developed in much the same way, only they drew from the narratives of the final European and regional scenarios. In addition, a multi-scale approach was taken to form three visions for Europe. A bifurcation-like approach was used in GEO-3 to investigate how a particular discontinuity in one region might affect developments around the globe. Ideas about discontinuity were probably developed in informal meetings with team members. The Shell scenarios were a variation on the bifucations theme, since they used a separate caption to describe the possible implications for the scenarios of an actual discontinuity, namely the September 11th attacks, rather than hypothetical future discontinuities. No explanation of the methods involved in the creation of bifurcation-like constructs was offered. Similarly, discontinuity-oriented methods that might have been used in the Finnish Aquaculture studies were not elaborated. Indirect indications suggest that the Finnish Aquaculture scenarios might have been based solely on the authors' knowledge and inspiration.

Relevant documentation shows that no discontinuity-oriented methods were used in the KPMG, Biotechnology, Nutrition, Norway 2030, Shield of Achilles, and Which World? studies. Therefore, the manner in which discontinuity was addressed can only be explained by such factors as personal qualities and expertise of those involved, and the nature of the scenario study.

In Chapter 3 we discussed various interpretations of the idea of discontinuity. We distinguished between abrupt and gradual discontinuity. Both are addressed frequently in the 15 studies incorporating discontinuity. There is a slight bias towards the former as each of the studies under consideration incorporates abrupt discontinuity. Of the scenario studies that address discontinuity, all incorporate the abrupt type in several of their scenarios. With the exception of the Futures of Women and KPMG studies, gradual discontinuity is addressed in at least one scenario in each of the studies. There are also several examples of a clear interconnection between the two, as demonstrated in Which World?'s 'Fortress World' and VISIONS 'Convulsive Change'. In the latter scenario, a cascade of abrupt environmental discontinuities combine to form a gradual, more structural discontinuity leading to fundamental changes in European society and geography. Most of the abrupt discontinuities in the studies are damaging to human health, the economy, or the environment. Exceptions include such scenarios as 'A Bird in the Hand is Worth Two in the Bush and, 'Forward March!' in the Destino Colombia study in which dialogue between warring parties and a certain election outcome lead to an improvement in Colombian society. The negative tendency is not as strong in cases of gradual discontinuity. On the one hand, there are examples of transitions leading to deterioration such as Which World?'s 'Fortress World' and VISIONS' 'Convulsive Change' scenario. On the other hand, in scenarios such as Mont Fleur's 'Flight of the Flamingos', Destino Colombia's 'In Unity Lies Strength', and Which World?'s 'Transformed World' we find examples of more attractive gradual discontinuity.

5 Reflection

We offer three types of observations regarding the treatment of discontinuity in the 15 studies: the nature of studies in which discontinuity-rich scenarios are likely to be developed, the methods and concepts used to explore the idea, and the manner in which it is presented in scenarios.

An analysis of the 15 discontinuity-oriented studies sheds light on the types of studies that are most congenial to considering the idea of discontinuity. Figure 1 shows that studies that developed discontinuity-rich scenarios are scattered across the scenario cartwheel and that there is not a uniform type of discontinuity-oriented scenario study. It appears as though an investigation on the level of a study's macro-characteristics alone is insufficient when searching for patterns as to how scenario exercises address discontinuity. Nine of the 15 studies that address the idea of discontinuity are exploratory in nature; therefore it is reasonable to conclude that exploratory studies are more congenial to the idea of discontinuity than pre-policy research exercises. Similarly, nine of the 15 studies that addressed discontinuity produced complex scenarios; therefore we conclude that complex scenarios are more likely to include references to discontinuity than simple ones. Only the discontinuity-rich Nutrition study was neither exploratory nor complex.

Our analysis indicates that whether a study is developed intuitively or analytically has a strong bearing on the likelihood of its addressing discontinuity. With the exception of the Finnish Aquaculture, the Which World?, and the Shield of Achilles studies, those that addressed discontinuity were developed in an intuitive manner. The combination of studies with a pre-policy research goal, an analytical process design, and a simple output are likely to exclude the idea of discontinuity. In contrast, our review demonstrates that studies with an exploratory goal, an intuitive process design, and a complex output are most congenial to the idea of discontinuity.

The review suggests that the intuitive process design has a particularly strong influence on the discontinuity-richness of the output. According to our typology of scenarios, intuitive designs typically involve the use of qualitative information, participatory techniques, and a broad, inclusive group of people. All 15 studies that address discontinuity were developed using predominantly qualitative information drawn from diverse sources[5]. The fact that there were no examples of model-based studies including discontinuity seems to highlight the problems with models addressed by Kieken[33], among others.

All but the Sword of Achilles and Finnish Aquaculture studies involved participatory activities. Of those studies, all but the KPMG Ebbinge case involved workshops. Instead, the KPMG scenarios strongly drew from a series of interviews. Interviews and workshops were combined in cases such as the Biotechnology study. On the basis of literature on Shell scenario methods[6;98;99], we speculate that interviews were also used in the development of the Shell 2001 scenarios, but the relevant source does not describe the methodology used. In addition to a workshop, the Futures of Women study conducted a three-month on-line conference. Several studies combined participatory techniques with desk research. These studies are GEO-3, KPMG, Shell, VISIONS, Mont Fleur, The Futures of Women, and Which World?. Two studies appear to have focussed solely on desk research: Finnish Aquaculture and The Shield of Achilles.

The group composition of these studies tended to be inclusive. To illustrate, the Destino Colombia study drew on a workshop group of 43 people, including clergymen, political leaders, and guerrillas. The discontinuity-oriented Beyond Hunger workshop consisted of nineteen prominent scholars, selected according to a nomination procedure. The group was therefore relatively exclusive. On the other hand, the group can also be considered inclusive in its representation of ten sub-Saharan countries, and of a variety of disciplines such as anthropology, medicine, and engineering. Another discontinuity-oriented study, Surprising Futures, involved a weeklong workshop with 22 participants of diverse backgrounds. The humanities, the social sciences, and the natural sciences were all represented. There was also a representation from nine different countries. In the case of the Mont Fleur scenarios a cross section of society was included to ensure that all the important perspectives on the relevant issues were represented, and it is reasonable to assume that similar considerations applied in the other discontinuity-oriented studies.

The idea of discontinuity was addressed in a number of ways within the studies' intuitive methodological frameworks. The Beyond Hunger and Surprising Futures studies were discontinuity-oriented in that they took the exploration of the idea as a point of departure. Others were not driven by the idea of exploring discontinuity but the scenario process involved certain discontinuity-oriented elements.

The lack of references to discontinuity concepts illustrates our observation that they are problematic. One reason for the limited use of discontinuity-oriented methods

---

[5] See Appendix 1 for source details of individual studies.

might be that the available techniques are still relatively underdeveloped. Of the methods described in the previous section only imaging, multi-scale analysis, and variations of the bifurcations technique were used in the analysed studies. All of the methods were in experimental stages of development when they were applied respectively in the Beyond Hunger, Surprising Futures, and VISIONS, and GEO-3 studies. Model-based techniques, historical retrodiction, and monitoring were not used for discontinuity-oriented scenario development in the studies that we investigated.

The limited use or absence of discontinuity-related concepts and approaches focusing on the exploration of discontinuity did not prevent the development of discontinuity-rich scenarios. The resulting scenarios presented the idea of discontinuity in three manners. The Shell, VISIONS, and GEO-3 scenarios used a separate caption or 'shock box' outside the scenarios. There were also two ways in which discontinuity was written into the scenarios themselves. Several studies included scenarios that reason from an abrupt discontinuity at the beginning of the scenario story that sets off a chain of other discontinuous events. Examples include the 'Fortress World' scenario in the Which World? study, and the 'Bactocase' and 'Laurel & Hardy' scenarios in the Nutrition study. A variation on this theme is the slower progress of a gradual discontinuity that follows an initial abrupt discontinuity. Mont Fleur's 'Flight of the Flamingos' scenario is one such example. Another approach is to have the scenario revolve around the description of the causes, the occurrence, and the consequences of an abrupt discontinuity that occurs somewhere in the middle of the scenario story. Examples are the Mont Fleur's 'Icarus' scenario, and the 'Domino Effect' scenario of the WBCSD Biotechnology study. In sum, we identified three ways of writing discontinuity into scenarios: shock boxes, chain reactions, and descriptions of a single discontinuity.

The limited use of discontinuity-oriented methods and concepts in producing discontinuity-rich scenarios underscores the idea that exploring discontinuity is more than just a matter of which techniques to use. Additional methodological issues are relevant as well. These seem to include group composition and the type of information that is used, for example. Sensitivity to discontinuity is another. By definition discontinuity implies change and investigating it means being open to the idea of the unconventional. Harremoës and Gee[23], and Kates and Clark[30;31] agree that the investigation of potential discontinuity sometimes involves going against the grain of conventional scientific practice and such underlying assumptions as the evolutionary paradigm. John Snow's theory of waterborne cholera in 1849 contravened the dominant scientific opinion that the disease was caused by airborne contamination[17] and illustrates of the obstructive nature of paradigm boundaries. Snow's dissenting theory was frowned upon until events proved its accuracy. Therefore, we recommend investigating what methodological steps might be taken to help scenario developers transcend paradigmic boundaries in the exploration of discontinuity.

A related methodological issue that emerged in the research for this chapter is the explicit programming of the idea of discontinuity on the research agenda. The latter occurred in at least five cases: GEO-3, VISIONS, Nutrition, Beyond Hunger, and Surprising Futures. For example, two presentations at the start of the Nutrition scenario workshop emphasised the relevance of considering potential discontinuity. Moreover, interest in experimenting with the idea of discontinuity was the guiding principle in the Beyond Hunger, and Surprising Futures workshops. The Biotechnology, Destino Colombia, Mont Fleur, and Shield of Achilles studies were conducted during times of upheaval, respectively: heated public debates on ethical, medical, and technological implications of a technology; turmoil in Colombia and South Africa; and geo-political disorder in a post-9/11 world. It is possible that media attention and public debates inspired discontinuity-oriented workshop discussions. Consequently, workshop participants perhaps needed little encouragement to think in terms of discontinuity. Therefore, current affairs and 'the spirit of the times'[17] together might be a factor that inspires discontinuity-oriented scenario development.

6 Concluding remarks

In this chapter we analysed methods and concepts for exploring the idea of discontinuity as proposed in IA and foresight literature, and whether they are used in scenario practice. We discussed the concepts of early warnings, seeds, and weak signals, and the difficulty in making them concrete. We concluded that the idea of signals offers an ambiguous point of departure for the exploration of discontinuity. Subsequently, we investigated the claim that discontinuity is seldom addressed in IA and foresight research because of the lack of useable methods. We discussed various, largely underdeveloped methods for exploring discontinuity as proposed in the literature. Besides issues related to concepts and methods, we also found sources that addressed personal qualities such as expertise and inquisitiveness. Several suggestions were also made about the sources of information that might be used in exploring discontinuity. These include a broad variety of theoretical, empirical, and anecdotal evidence.

When investigating whether and how the discussed methods and concepts are used in contemporary scenario practice, we found that half of the analysed studies omitted discontinuity. A small number of those studies did so based on an explicit methodological decision. In the other cases we observed that factors such as the evolutionary paradigm – the assumption of gradual, incremental progress – and considerations of institutional feasibility impaired the exploration of the idea. An inspiring factor for discontinuity-oriented scenario development appeared to be media attention on discontinuous events and the discontinuous 'spirit of the times' in general.

Some scenario studies were designed as methodological experiments to investigate the idea of discontinuity. We found examples of imaging, multi-scale analysis and the bifurcations technique, which can be viewed as an operationalisation of the contrary assumptions approach. We also identified three manners in which the idea of discontinuity is written into scenarios. Although these insights help establish some understanding of the manner in which discontinuity is addressed in scenario development, it is clear that they cannot entirely account for the discontinuity-richness of the studies' output. This observation underscores the idea that exploring discontinuity is more than simply a matter of methods and techniques, and that there are additional factors that inspire thinking about discontinuity through scenario development. However, due to the lack of methodological details presented in the source material, the overview does not provide a sufficient understanding of how discontinuity is addressed in the analysed studies.

In order to establish a further understanding of influential factors for discontinuity-oriented scenario development we consider it worthwhile to reconstruct a scenario study that produced discontinuity-rich scenarios. In selecting such a case we refer to the category of studies that are most congenial to the idea of discontinuity: those with an exploratory goal, an intuitive process design, and which produce complex scenarios.

5
discontinuity in scenario practice
a reconstruction of the VISIONS scenario study

5 DISCONTINUITY IN SCENARIO PRACTICE
A RECONSTRUCTION OF THE VISIONS SCENARIO STUDY

1 Introduction

In Chapter 4 we examined a broad range of scenario studies for their treatment of discontinuity. Due to a lack of methodological detail in the source material, the examination did not provide a sufficient understanding of how discontinuity is addressed in the studies. Sources such as Ayres[1] suggest that discontinuity is context-dependent, and so a deeper analysis of particular cases might help illuminate possible treatments of discontinuity in scenario development. To this end, we now investigate the VISIONS scenario process[1].

The research described in the previous chapter demonstrates that the idea of discontinuity played a prominent role in VISIONS, and we hope that a closer analysis produces relevant insights for how scenario development might result in discontinuity-rich scenarios. As an exploratory, intuitively developed study that produced complex scenarios, the VISIONS scenario process should be most congenial to the investigation of the idea of discontinuity. The decision to examine VISIONS was also motivated by the fact that it was well documented and many of its participants were willing to discuss the process. Through a reconstruction of the process, we aim to gain insights into characteristics of a scenario study that might inspire or impair the consideration of discontinuity in foresight.

2 Research approach

VISIONS involved four studies whose scenarios were integrated to form creative and inspiring VISIONS for the future of Europe. Scenarios were developed for Europe and for three European regions: the North-West United Kingdom, the Green Heart in the Netherlands, and Venice in Italy. For the reconstruction of discontinuity-related aspects of VISIONS we chose to focus on the European scenarios because they were the only part of the study to address discontinuity explicitly.

Two methods were used in the reconstruction. First, we analysed such documentation as papers, correspondence, progress reports, and workshop proceedings. A particularly informative source was a draft version of Van Asselt, Rotmans, and Rothman[2] which provided a comprehensive account of the scenario study. The documentation was used to reconstruct the exploration of discontinuity in VISIONS and its resultant output.

The second method was the conduct of interviews with seven members of the VISIONS European scenario team. Through the interviews we gathered opinions

---

[1] In contrast to what the capital letters might suggest, VISIONS is not an acronym. However, the project's name was written in capitals, which is why we also do so in this chapter.

and interpretations on how discontinuity was addressed in VISIONS, as well as recommendations for discontinuity-oriented scenario development in general. The interviews were semi-structured[3]; they had a basic structure and a standard set of questions, but these left the interviewer considerable freedom. Prompts and follow-up questions were common, and the interviewer modified the format and the order of the questions as necessary. The interviewees and the interview questions are listed in Textbox 1 and Appendix 2 respectively. Each interview lasted 1 – 2.5 hours and resulted in approximately 12 hours of audiotape and 40 pages of edited transcripts. In order to encourage interviewees to be as open as possible, they were informed at the start of the interview that their names would be treated confidentially.

In using these methods, we applied a variation of the research strategy called triangulation[4a,b]. With triangulation different methods and information sources are used so that they might be checked against and complemented by one another. In the original use of the term triangulation a distinction is made between the principal

---

INTERVIEWEES (in alphabetical order)

Dr. Chris Anastasi, MSc: *Consultant to the European scenario study, ICIS Visiting Scientist. Design and facilitation for the major workshops, drafting of scenarios, sparring partner for project team. Interviewed in London, June 13th, 2003.*

Dr. Marjolein van Asselt, MSc: *Acting project leader. Principle investigator of methodological aspects of the European and Green Heart scenario development, and of the integrated visions. Interviewed in Maastricht, October 31st, 2003.*

Sandra Greeuw, MA: *Research assistant for the European scenarios and Green Heart scenario studies. Operational support. Interviewed in The Hague, October 13th, 2003.*

Dr. Bernd Kasemir: *Consultant to the European scenario study. Participant in several workshops. Co-author of two Visions papers including 'Surprises in scenarios'. Interview by telephone from Zurich, August 6th, 2003.*

Dr. Jerry Ravetz, MA: *Project methodologist, trouble-shooter. Co-author of Visions paper 'Surprises in scenarios'. Interviewed in London, June 13th, 2003.*

Dr. Dale Rothman, MA: *ICIS visiting scientist in summer 1999, European scenario team member at ICIS from summer 2000 onwards. Design and facilitation of workshops, first author of European scenarios, co-author of integrated visions. Interviewed in Maastricht, May 15th and 16th, 2003.*

Prof. Dr. Jan Rotmans, MSc: *Project leader. Responsible for overall co-ordination of project. Principle investigator of thematic and conceptual aspects of the project, especially European scenarios and integrated visions. Interviewed in Maastricht, September 26th, 2003.*

Textbox 1 *The people interviewed for the reconstruction of* VISIONS

source of study and the supporting source. The latter is used to support the observations of the former. We used the idea of triangulation in a more flexible manner whereby we sometimes switched between different types of sources and methods. Moreover, we sometimes used sources simultaneously rather than sequentially, as the original concept of triangulation dictates. While the document analysis and interviews often produced insights that were complementary, there were times when they appeared to contradict each other. Rather than viewing these apparent inconsistencies as problematic, we considered them to be potentially insightful, making them explicit in the reconstruction below.

The material from the documentation and the interviews was collated, compared, and used to provide an account of the VISIONS study. The account is divided into five sections: an introduction to VISIONS, the project's approach to discontinuity, a chronological description of the study in terms of its exploration of discontinuity, VISIONS in hindsight, and lessons for discontinuity-oriented scenario development. In accordance with confidentiality agreements, interviewees are named only when necessary. In most cases, references to the interviews are made using words such as 'the interviewee' and 's/he'.

3 An introduction to VISIONS[2]

The decision to draft a proposal for a scenario study called VISIONS was made in the autumn of 1996. At an October 1996 Integrated Environmental Assessment (IEA) conference in Toulouse, the question was raised of what IEA could do for the European Commission. A panellist's response was that the IA community should help the Commission creatove 'visons'. Subsequently, Rotmans and Van Asselt took the lead in drafting a research proposal[5] that was submitted to Directorate General Science, Research, and Sustainable Development (DG XII) of the European Commission[3]. The proposal outlined a number of methodological experiments, including the integration of various spatial and temporal scales and the combining of qualitative and quantitative approaches.

The scenario study 'VISIONS for a Sustainable Europe' was conducted from 1998 – 2001 in a collaborative effort between nine European research institutes[4]. It was funded by DG XII under the 4th Framework Programme of the European Union.

---

[2] The primary source for this section is Van Asselt, Rotmans and Rothman (2005).
[3] DG XII is now called the Research, Technology and Innovation Directorate General.
[4] The Dutch partners were the International Centre for Integrative Studies (ICIS)(co-ordinator) and the Research Institute for Knowledge Systems (RIKS) of Maastricht University, and the National Institute of Public Health and the Environment (RIVM). The British partners were Research Methods Consultancy (RMC) and the Department of Planning and Landscape, University of Manchester (UMIST). Other partners were the Institute for Systems, Informatics and Safety (JRC/ISIS, Italy), Centre Economie Espace Environment (C3E, France), and the Swiss Federal Institute for Environment and Technology (EAWAG).

VISIONS addressed the question of how to design and structure an envisioning process with a sustainable development focus. The study served as an experimental arena for analytical and intuitive foresight methods.

A different team of VISIONS partners conducted each of the four scenario studies: Venice, the Green Heart, the North West-UK, and Europe. Some common methodology was developed for the sake of consistency and comparability. For example, all teams worked with the so-called 'factor, actor, sector' framework which identified important issues and relevant parties. Beyond that, each team was encouraged to develop scenarios as it felt appropriate. The four scenario sets were eventually brought together in integrated VISIONS, describing European futures that might emerge from the interactions between the regions and Europe.

The VISIONS team decided that the study's time horizon should span two generations. The year 2050 was chosen because it was far enough in the future for the impact of today's developments to become visible and close enough to the present for participants to relate to possible societal developments under concern.

Transdisciplinary research was considered a prerequisite for conducting the study. Therefore, the VISIONS team decided to involve a highly heterogeneous group of participants in the scenario development process. A wide variety of over 200 participants took part in VISIONS. The group included representatives from regional, national and international companies, governmental institutions, NGOs, and academia from a variety of EU-member states. The participants' areas of expertise included transport, energy, environmental science, urban development, ICT, automotives, chemicals, and water.

4 VISIONS and discontinuity[5]

The motivation to experiment with discontinuity lay in the past experience of the Integrated Assessment community. It had developed mainly model-based scenarios analysing interactions of social, economic, and environmental variables as related to environmental and climate change in particular[7]. Experience with these scenarios left some IA-scientists, including a number of the interviewees, with the impression that scenarios were generally boring, predictable, conventional, and unrealistically linear. They observed that scenarios rarely led to surprising insights and that they were incapable of addressing shocks and structural change. A few IA-scientists lamented the omission of discontinuity or such related ideas as surprise. They argued that in situations of complexity the unexpected will occur, and that consideration of potential disruption helps to challenge often deep-seated assumptions about the future. Several IA-scientists argued that thinking about potential discontinuity helps one become

---

[5] Unless otherwise stated this section is based on interview material with the seven aforementioned interviewees.

more aware of the possible interactions of societal events and processes by looking at the present and the future in manners different to one's assumptions.

As a result of the IA scientists' concern, an experiment to incorporate discontinuous developments in quantitative, model-based scenarios was conducted as part of an IA-project entitled TARGETS (Tool to Assess Regional and Global Environmental and Health Targets for Sustainability)[5]. This idea of discontinuity as a means to consider different angles proved even more difficult to introduce in modelling than was previously assumed. The decision to develop qualitative scenarios in VISIONS was strongly influenced by the difficulties the TARGETS modellers encountered in the experiment, some of which are described in Janssen's 'Meeting Targets'[8]. The experience also strengthened VISIONS' project leader Rotmans' interest in further experimenting with the idea of discontinuity. Rotmans resolved that models would play a supportive role in the development of scenarios in which quantitative and qualitative information was to be integrated. The decision was a momentous one because the IA community was relatively inexperienced in qualitative scenario development.

The limited knowledge of qualitative scenario development among the project team members was one of the motivations for conducting a review of scenarios[10]. The study reaffirmed the IA-scientists' impression that many scenarios portray unrealistically linear progress in the future. The VISIONS team therefore decided that their scenarios had to be surprising and would try to break with the tradition of developing linear scenarios. VISIONS did not address the idea of discontinuity directly but through the idea of surprise, described in the proposal as follows[5]:

> *In many long-term scenario studies, surprises and bifurcations are not taken into account. However, the inclusion of surprises is important since history shows us that historical trends are characterised by strong fluctuations rather than smooth curves, often triggered by unexpected changes, thus surprises.[...] The idea is that the integrated VISIONS for a sustainable Europe are structured around surprises. [...] Different types of surprises will be introduced: (I) ecological surprises: for example, climate change, where the observed global mean temperature increase is masked by an additional cooling effect, or natural disasters; (ii) economic surprises: such as an energy crisis due to political tensions which will [make] the prices of fossil fuels [soar] in the near-term; and (iii) social surprises: such as massive migration of environmental refugees to Europe [and] political instability in developing countries intensified by environmental change.*

The assessment of European scenario studies, a first step in the project, also addressed discontinuity in terms of surprise[10]. Inspired by Schneider[9], the authors of the assessment report identified several types of surprise: unimaginable surprises like a journey to the Earth's centre in the time of Jules Verne; imaginable but improbable surprises such as a global nuclear war; imaginable and probable surprises like an oil price shock; and certain surprises such as earthquakes.

It was the general idea of discontinuity, rather than a precise definition, that served as the point of departure for the development of surprising scenarios. By the time VISIONS was completed, the concept of surprise had evolved considerably. In order to understand the nature of the evolution it is necessary to analyse the chronology of the VISIONS process in relation to the manner in which that process addressed surprise.

5 Chronology

The development of the European scenarios followed an iterative process of workshops, VISIONS partner meetings, European scenario team meetings, and desk research. This process is summarised in Figure 1 and described in more detail in the following paragraphs. Particular attention is paid to how the idea of discontinuity featured in the scenario process.

5.1 Storylines

The European scenario process began in January 1999 with a two-day participatory workshop in Maastricht. The European scenario team had recruited so-called 'free spirits', unconventional thinkers, to stimulate the generation of 'unthinkable' ideas with the other participants. One such free spirit was an artist whose recent work had included sculptures that expressed unconventional ideas about the future of medical technology. Another free spirit was a journalist. An intensive effort had been made to recruit a greatly varied group of 23 participants – different cultures, disciplines, countries, professions, organisations and ages – in the hope that the mixture of different perspectives would lead to imaginative and unconventional ideas about future developments. The workshop's participants represented various professional backgrounds: policy, business, academia, and NGOs. Seven European Union countries were represented: Belgium, Germany, Greece, France, Spain, the Netherlands, and the UK.

The workshop's structure was inspired by a team members' experience of developing scenarios at Shell. In the VISIONS workshop this approach combined expert lectures

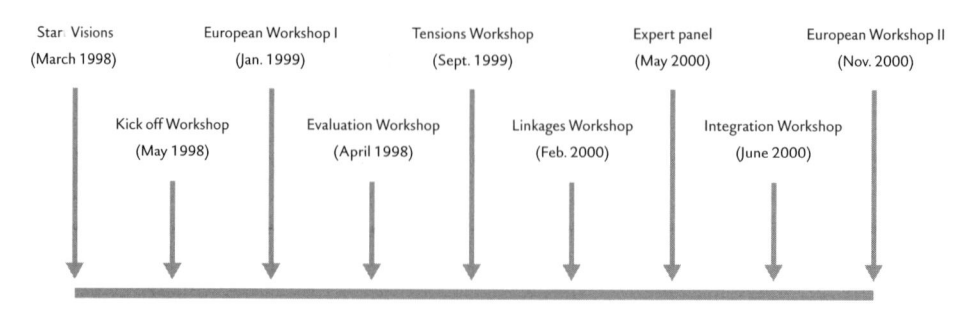

Figure 1 *The European scenario development process. Adapted from:*[2]

with participants 'brainwriting' about the future[2], referred to as brainstorming during the study. Whereas brainstorming involves calling out ideas, brainwriting involves writing them down on slips of paper[11]. Presentations were given on changes that might affect Europe's: environment, economy, culture, institutions, businesses, NGOs, water, transport, and energy. Afterwards, participants were asked to consider

STORYLINE	NAME	CHARACTERISTICS	MAIN DRIVER
1	Survival of the Weak	Empowerment of unskilled labour Locally oriented Environmentally optimistic	Social-cultural
2	Methuselah on Drugs	Ageing/de-greening Artificial life extension Impacts on lifestyle and work Individualistic tendency	Technology
3	Conflict and Calamity	Climate change (Desertification or Ice Age) Mitigation policies fail 'Doom Monger'	Environment
4	Fragmentation and Dematerialisation	Social dependence on ICT Implications of ageing for leisure Localisation vs. globalisation	Technology Social-cultural
5	Benign Technology	Technological solutions for environmental problems Rapid uptake of renewables Increase in energy efficiency 'Green Thinker'	Technology
6 a b c	Tension and Release A Tortuous Path 'Freeze' 'Secession' 'Accession'	Relationship regions and EU Social unrest Failure of EU enlargement for financial reasons EU Enlargement	Regional tensions
7	Regional Tension	Regional economic decline EU agricultural funding reduced Regional protests Export of food outside EU (due to climate change)	Regional tensions
8	Environmental Rupture	Climate change (gulf stream reversal) Mass migration Social conflicts Collapse of EU 'Doom Monger'	Environmental
9	Cultural Variables	Business mergers Social disrespect of institutions Changes in democracy	Economy
10	Economic Change	Mergers into clusters of companies Decreasing power of Goverments Social conflict and inequality	Economy

Table 1 *A summary of the storylines*[2]

107

important issues for the future of Europe. Participants were explicitly encouraged to 'think the unthinkable' and to 'think out of the box' in order to produce an array of eccentric ideas. The participants were given a large amount of freedom in the ideas that they could propose. The only constraint was the 'factor, actor, sector' framework, provided as a structure for the type of ideas that could be proposed.

The workshop participants developed ten storylines, sequences of events, linked in a logical, consistent manner[12]. The 10 storylines are summarised in Table 1.

The storylines contained several discontinuities[12]. The environmentally driven storylines called *Environmental Rupture* and *Conflict and Calamity* include an elaboration of many events and processes, such as a southward migration due to 'ice ages' in northern Europe, the acquisition of the EU by African countries, and the build up to World War III. The storylines *Tension and Release* and *Regional Tension* describe various discontinuous events, including the secession of such regions as Corsica and Scotland. Technological breakthroughs were particularly evident in the technology-driven storylines *Methuselah on Drugs* and *Benign Technology*, which included such events as the invention and use of life-extending drugs, the legalisation of euthanasia in a first step toward its possible compulsory enforcement, and the development of renewable energy technologies. The social implications of a technology driven society were explored in the *Fragmentation and Dematerialisation* storyline with 50 percent unemployment, and the marginalisation of the physical world as society increasingly operates in a virtual one. The economically driven storylines *Cultural Variables* and *Economic Change* also addressed such discontinuous events as the burning down of Euro-Disney and McDonalds by religious fundamentalists and the merger of all European Union banks, as well as such gradual changes as the realisation of an environmental and cultural Utopia.

5.2 From storylines to scenarios

After the workshop the storylines that shared important components were combined to form four clusters of storylines. These were elaborated to produce three draft scenarios using research material from various sources[10,13]. The draft scenarios were reviewed at an evaluation workshop in Paris in April 1999, which was attended by several VISIONS partners and participants of the first European workshop. The meeting helped to put the idea of surprise on the agenda again, as one of the two participants from the European workshop commented that the draft scenarios appeared less surprising, compared to the original storylines. After reflecting on the draft scenarios, a brainstorming session took place to enrich the scenarios with more surprising ideas. Further enrichment took place after the meeting when the European scenario team reviewed the material from the first European workshop for surprising ideas, omitted in preparing the draft scenarios.

Weak signals were introduced to the scenario process in an attempt to make the scenarios more surprising. Outlined in the September 1999 Global Format position paper[13], weak signals were defined as developments that might play an emerging role in the next 50 years; might have a profound impact on society; or might affect Europe indirectly on a "secondary" level. Cited examples of weak signals include the potentially positive effect of the introduction of the Euro on the European tourist industry, and the increase in single parent families as a sign of changing values in European society.

At a September/October 1999 Tensions workshop in Ispra, Italy, the idea of surprise again came to the fore when the importance of so-called action-reaction patterns in the scenarios was stressed. A classification for these patterns, developed after the workshop, distinguished between 'givens', which were developments in line with the dominant expectation, and countervailing responses, which were signals of developments that contradicted 'givens'[2]. The action-reaction patterns are relevant to discontinuity because the reactions to 'givens' might lead to discontinuous behaviour.

In light of the VISIONS team's aim to experiment with the integration of qualitative and quantitative information, efforts were also made to model the scenario narratives using the CPB Netherlands Bureau for Economic Policy Analysis's WORLDSCAN model[14]. However, WORLDSCAN proved incapable of coping with structural changes and other surprises described in the narratives.

The partner meetings and European workshops produced much of the material used to write the European scenarios. The scenarios were written in an iterative process in which they were continuously refined. The scenarios are summarised in Textbox 2.

There are several references to discontinuity in the scenarios. For example, the *Big is Beautiful?* scenario describes transitions of a more institutional kind. The transformation is far from smooth as an excerpt from the scenario shows:

> *The transition to a more stable situation in Europe after the previous decades moves into the take-off and acceleration phase as the EU, regional authorities and NGOs increasingly work together to address the political, economic, social and environmental concerns. There remain many forces pulling in different directions, though, so the outcome of this process remains unclear*[15].

Central to the *Convulsive Change* scenario is a series of environmental calamities. Other features that suggest discontinuous change are shifts in attitudes and lifestyles, as well as in European identity and governance. A number of these aspects are illustrated in the following excerpt:

> *The general mood of optimism that characterised the start of the century has been replaced with a hopeful but more reflective and cautious attitude. Recent maps of the region [Europe] capture some of this change. These show large areas abandoned to the harsh elements of nature and safe havens. These are densely populated and heavily protected from the harsh climate conditions. The almost meaningless markings of national*

borders within the EU and the appearance of the UK, Denmark, and Sweden outside the EU borders serve as reminders of the fundamental political shifts that have taken place. [...] The harsh climate and other crises of recent years have transformed general values and lifestyles in ways that were only hinted at in the first years of the century. Prosperity means much more than economic development, with social and environmental health more often taking centre stage [15].

In the scenario entitled *Knowledge is King*, the narrative speaks of 'societal shifts':

As the middle of the century approaches, the societal shifts of the past 50 years have reshaped Europe. It is a more technologically advanced, connected, and older, yet healthier society. Two societies, one focused on the local and the other on the global, exist intertwined in a dynamic harmony[15].

The scenarios also contain a limited number of abrupt discontinuities, including floods, droughts, and arson attacks on 'Big Business' headquarters and gated communities[12].

5.3 Bifurcations

Inspired by the work of Gallopin and the Global Scenario Group and their idea of sideswipes[16], Rotmans and Van Asselt wrote a memorandum[17] in which they introduced the concept of bifurcations[18], defining it as "a radical change in world view or management style". Bifurcations were developed to explore potential discontinuity, proposing alternatives to a scenario and preventing audiences from choosing a

---

A SUMMARY OF THE EUROPEAN SCENARIOS

Big is Beautiful? describes a world in which 'big business' grows ever stronger. European integration leads to a similar consolidation of power in Brussels. Some groups in society suffer from these developments and social unrest grows as the divide between the haves and have-nots increases.

In *Convulsive Change* environmental problems turn out to be just as detrimental and disruptive as some today predict. Migration from the worst hit areas adds social tension to the mounting economic and ecological problems. The unified effort by European nations to combat the problems, however, leads to stronger integration as the crisis gradually subsides.

Knowledge is King describes a world in which ICT is the driving force of change with far reaching implications for the economy, society, institutions and environment. The resulting unemployment and the continuing ageing of society are problems too large for European governments to deal with. Instead, community-based initiatives supported by NGOs partly succeed in relieving the problem. The gap between the 'connected' and the 'unconnected' is never fully bridged, however.

Textbox 2 *A summary of the European scenarios*[15]

favourite scenario. Another practical function of bifurcations was to posit possible future developments that the team could not explore due to time constraints. The bifurcations were conceived by considering possible situations that might lead to futures other than those described in a scenario. They were partly inspired by material from the first European workshop. Seven bifurcations were included in the final scenarios. They described in brief several alternative developments, placed alongside the main scenario narrative. The bifurcations and the dominant assumptions from which they depart are listed in Table 2.

The full narrative of one of the bifurcations is shown in Textbox 3, presented as an example of how the concept was used in VISIONS. A source of inspiration for the bifurcation might have been a presentation on the changing role of NGOs, delivered in the first European workshop. The presenter speculated on the possibility of partnerships between NGOs and businesses. A variation of the latter idea was proposed in the ensuing brainstorm and discussed in the development of the *Methuselah on Drugs* storyline. Inspiration for some of the bifurcations was probably found in sources other than the first European workshop because there are few or no traces of them in the workshop output. For example, of the 220 ideas of the workshop's brainstorm session carbon emissions were addressed only twice, and once in the *Conflict and Calamity* storyline. Presumably, inspiration for these bifurcations was found in partner meetings and discussions among the European scenario team members, as one interviewee suggested.

SCENARIO	DOMINANT ASSUMPTION IN SCENARIO	BIFURCATIONS
KNOWLEDGE IS KING	New technologies enhance freedom and democracy	New technologies are used to centralise control
	Social stabilisation (empowerment of local level)	The social empowerment expected from establishing self sufficient communities never materialises
CONVULSIVE CHANGE	Climate warms globally and in Europe	Climate cooling occurs at a rapid rate in Europe
	Technology provides 'solution' to climate change	Technology cannot solve environmental problems - it exacerbates them
	Carbon emissions redused through increase in renewables and energy efficiency	Carbon emissions redused through increasing nuclear capacity
BIG IS BEAUTIFUL?	EU political integration from which superstate emerges	EU political fragmentation from which a power vacuum opens up
	Businesses become unregulated and irresponsible	Businesses become socially responsible

Table 2 *Bifurcations used in the European scenarios*

BIG IS BEAUTIFUL?
Imagine instead that …businesses become socially responsible
Over recent years NGOs and society are [sic.] successful in encouraging businesses to set standards for themselves that exceed those set by governmental bodies. There is an increase in the number of companies seeking certification of voluntary standards. This is achieved through a combination of factors, including the influence of NGOs on the non-executive boards of Big Businesses (BB), through employing consumer power and by strong encouragement from the World Businesses Council for Sustainable Development. NGOs have an improved knowledge of the internal operations of BB and highlight issues of ethical concern. This knowledge is disseminated to society in a manner that stimulates boycotts of the products concerned. In addition, the media publicity that follows is a vital tool used to shame the BB into co-operating with the demands of the NGOs and society in general.

Many businesses that cannot afford the change in practices are no longer competitive and go out of business. BB recognise the importance of taking society seriously as it can 'make or break' a company. As a result, business standards for behaviour become less determined by the law and more determined by the need to avoid negative publicity. Over time, businesses demonstrate high standards that go beyond written laws to soft laws (morals and principles). The most notable difference is seen in developing countries where standards concerning labour, exploitation of natural resources and pollution maintained by businesses are higher than those that the governments set. In the EU there are also high standards demonstrated with regard to the treatment of the low waged and the environment. The role of the EU regulatory bodies becomes almost obsolete; there is little need for law reinforcement.

Will this development continue to clean up the practices of businesses or will businesses become more skilled at hiding what is socially unacceptable? What are the consequences for developing countries?

Textbox 3 *Socially responsible businesses – an example of a bifurcation*[15]

5.4 From scenarios to visons

The last meeting in the European scenario process was the second European workshop, held in Maastricht in November 2000, at which the refined scenarios were reviewed. VISIONS did not end with the completion of the European scenarios, but continued until 2001 with the integration of European and regional scenarios to develop so-called 'integrated visions'. The process involved the matching of salient similarities between the scenarios and elaborating on interesting tensions between them, which might become prominent issues in the future. The integrated visions are summarised in Textbox 4.

> **A SUMMARY OF THE INTEGRATED VISIONS**
>
> Living on the Edge: *"The events of the last fifty years have strongly affected the map of Europe. With hindsight it is clear that profound impacts of climate change were evident at the dawn of the 21st century. The whole of Europe was severely hit by the changes, but there has been great variability in patterns."*
>
> Europe in Transition: *"The last fifty years have seen significant transformation in European society. Taken as a whole, these can be described as a true transition. This European transition was a gradual, persistent, but not always smooth transformation of European society, where substantial changes in different domains, i.e. economy, lifestyles, labour, governance, demography and technology, supported each other at both the broad European and more local levels."*
>
> Shadows of Europe Ltd: *"Efficiency – in business, in government, in everything – that was the rallying cry at the dawn of the new millennium. Privatisation moved many services from the public to the private sector. Mergers created huge conglomerates. Big business became Big Business, or simply BB. Smaller companies were gobbled up by larger ones and the local economy in most regions experienced large declines. Governments streamlined themselves domestically by privatising many traditionally public services."*

Textbox 4 *A summary of the integrated VISIONS*[19]

A discontinuity-related component of the integrated visions was the so-called complexity syndrome[2]. According to Van Asselt, Rotmans, et al.[2] the syndromes were intended to illustrate the complex interactions of events and processes in cases of structural societal change. The complexity syndromes in the integrated VISIONS were presented like the bifurcations, in the form of short descriptions of alternative developments, placed alongside the main narrative. An example of a complexity syndrome is presented in Textbox 5. The syndrome, entitled 'City Chaos', is part of the vision called 'Living on the Edge', characterised by the earlier than expected impact of climate change that is at least as severe as 20th century doom thinkers had predicted. The syndrome appears to have been inspired by such transport problems as are also described in the 'Big is Beautiful?' scenario.

6 VISIONS in hindsight

In this section, we reflect on how methodological factors relating to discontinuity influenced the VISIONS process. We do so through a retrospective look at the study through the eyes of the seven European scenario team members whom we interviewed. We focus on the European scenario development process, since the integration of the European and regional scenarios was undertaken separately and it did not involve the same team of people. The interviews were conducted from May

COMPLEXITY SYNDROME: CITY CHAOS

'City Chaos' refers to the ever more common chaotic circumstances which disrupt day-to-day life in many of Europe's big cities. Although urban life had always been considered somewhat chaotic, a number of factors led to increasingly unworkable and unfavourable conditions. As in the US, this led to an exodus from the city to suburban and rural areas by many of those who could afford to do so. However, this in many ways only increased the problem.

A key factor underlying the city chaos was the increasing vulnerability of the transportation systems. Traffic frequently ended up in a mess, often coming to a standstill. What were the reasons for these deadlock situations? Although different perceptions on this city chaos problem arose, an in-depth inquiry showed that a concatenation of interrelated small events and accidents were causing the increasing series of calamities.

Many people pointed to the failure [...] of the privatisation of the public transport system in most European countries. Spokesmen from the European Commission put the blame on European citizens who refused to pay either higher taxes or fares for the high-tech and high-quality public transport systems they demanded. It was admitted, though, that the transnational European transport ideas had failed so far, because most European governments still considered transport as a national or regional problem. Furthermore, investments in most public and private transportation systems, be they railways, underground systems, or roads, had lagged behind for years. Those investments that had been made were offset by the enormous increase in mobility of people.

As a consequence, reserves in capacity were lacking and any small change in demand or supply could cause a serious distortion. The generic pattern was that a small, seemingly innocent incident would cause a chain of reactions that blocked the mobility of hundreds of thousands. Examples included: autumn leaves on the line and winter storms, floods, train accidents, suicides, iciness, strikes, and petrol crises. Weather extremes, attributed to a changed climate, played an important role; they would lead to stranded trains, which in turn lead commuters to seek alternatives, causing congestion on roads and disturbing underground traffic. As there were no possible alternative routes, everybody was locked in. Although the economic damage of these calamities mounted to billions of Euros, the social damage was considered even larger. These occurred almost daily in one or more European cities.

Thus, the deeper causes for this city chaos were privatisation on the one hand and climate change on the other. The market did not seem to provide solutions. Private companies sought quick-and-dirty solutions, such as buying housing capacity for their employees in the neighbourhood of their locations, but this did not provide a structural solution. It was only later, as the transportation systems gradually underwent a transformation, that the chaotic situations began to ease.

Textbox 5 *City Chaos- An example of a complexity syndrome*[2]

to October 2003. Our analysis is divided into three categories: people, methods and concepts, and procedural issues.

Each category is described in terms of inspiring and impairing factors. Factors that inspire are those that stimulate the exploration of discontinuity. In contrast impairing factors hinder discontinuity-thinking. Where appropriate, we also address 'double-edged' factors, which are those that might be both inspirational and impairing, depending on other issues. In addition, we discuss recommendations for discontinuity-oriented studies proposed by the interviewees.

6.1 People: partners, participants, and team members

The people involved in the discontinuity-related elements of VISIONS can be divided into three groups: the participants of the two European workshops, the members of the European scenario team, and the researchers of the nine partner institutes which organised the study.

The January 1999 European workshop featured a varied, inclusive group of participants and was the first important step in the VISIONS process, one that proved influential for the development of discontinuity-rich scenarios. Three interviewees noted that a varied group of workshop participants was considered necessary to realise the creative ambitions of the European scenario team. However, this variety turned out to be a delicate matter, as illustrated by the conduct of one free spirit who did not contribute in the novel manner that the organisers hoped, in the opinion of some interviewees.

A source of inspiration for the European scenario team was project leader Rotmans' drive to do something different, including a focus on discontinuity, and the synergy between him and Van Asselt, according to one interviewee. Another such source was the group dynamic in the European scenario team, based on a balance between those who offered ideas and those who elaborated them. The importance of these group dynamics was emphasised by one interviewee in a reference to Shell International:

> I really think the team is it. If you want [...] to take people outside the box you need the right people, the right qualities. Shell [does] that. If you look at the enthusiasm of the team last October [Shell scenario meeting, October 2002] you can see that they had bonded [sic.]. They supported each other. They were enthusiastic, keen, emotional even. That's very important [...].

The members of the European scenario team and all VISIONS partners shared expertise and skills: conceptual and methodological, as well as knowledge of such important issues as energy, water, and climate change. According to one interviewee, this high level of expertise offered the possibility of considering discontinuity in a rigorous manner. It meant also that the VISIONS team was well positioned to draw on other high-level expertise when necessary, one interviewee claimed. For example, the experts panel of May 2000 included such people as the former Dutch Prime Minister Ruud Lubbers. However, one interviewee pointed out that academic knowledge might be a hindrance in discontinuity-oriented scenario development, insofar as some experts are reluctant to look beyond their respective disciplines.

Three interviewees commented that certain pitfalls of group work can obstruct the exploration of discontinuity. In the words of one interviewee:

I assumed that if people are bright that they would be able to develop good scenarios in a participatory process. It turned out not to be the case [in VISIONS].

The explanation given was that partners did not come to the VISIONS meetings with an open mind and that they failed to "leave their baggage at the door." Another interviewee expressed surprise at the high level of conventional thinking among the partners, and the inability to think in terms of discontinuity and complexity. A third interviewee indicated that although partners were able to contribute interesting ideas, they were not good listeners. S/he argued that several partners were uncompromising in advocating their own ideas.

Two interviewees indicated that much obstructive behaviour could be attributed to the narrow-mindedness of some of those involved in VISIONS . One lamented that narrow-mindedness is common to scenario development in general:

[Ideally in a scenario workshop,] if you say something and I violently disagree with you, I will tell you but you won't take it personally. But you can't do that with certain groups of people, and academics [are] one of those. Academics won't be challenged in that kind of way, they'll defend their patch, they won't keep an open mind necessarily, which is what you need […].

Several interviewees referred to the obstructive effect of some partners' intransigence. These partners felt that the project coordinating team was trying to impose its ideas, including those regarding discontinuity. The partners apparently suspected that the project leader had a hidden agenda. In response, several partners started to resist any apparent interference. The European scenario team in turn felt frustrated, believing that their enthusiasm for the study was misinterpreted. One interviewee argued that the intransigence of some partners was the primary reason why the idea of discontinuity was not explored by the regional teams. However, the socio-psychological nature of group dynamics makes the claimed intransigence difficult to evaluate in the context of the current thesis.

Two interviewees suggested that there was a 'right' or ideal group composition for discontinuity-oriented scenario development. One interviewee argued that such exercises should involve not just experts but also widely read, broad-thinking participants. She argued that the latter is needed to provide eccentric ideas, which experts then refine. Another interviewee expressed the wish to work more with 'non-academics', with journalists, science fiction writers, 'free spirits', and 'visionaries'. She added that complex systems thinkers were should have been recruited to counter the tendency to dismiss discontinuities on the basis of their supposed implausibility. Another interviewee argued that a group needs a relatively high level of "sophistication" in order to be sensitive to the idea of discontinuity, although s/he did not elaborate on what this might mean in practice. Lastly, one interviewee advocated a mix of ages when recruiting participants for a scenario study because narrow-mindedness might increase with age.

In summary, interviewees corroborated our research from Chapter 4 that a varied group of participants is an inspiring and even a necessary factor for discontinuity-oriented scenario development. Interviewees recommended the involvement of a variety of participants. Besides narrow-mindedness, intransigence was an impairing factor in group work. Knowledge and expertise were double-edged factors, sometimes inspiring, sometimes impairing.

6.2 Methods and concepts

Most interviewees were particularly enthusiastic about the design of the first European workshop. One interviewee believed that the horizon of 50 years enhanced the exploratory character of the workshop and that a shorter time frame would have made participants more conservative in their ideas. Furthermore, s/he argued that the exploratory nature of the exercises created an environment in which the consideration of the novel and unusual was not only legitimate, but desirable. It was argued that had the workshop been constrained by the need to model the scenarios, for example, it is likely that some ideas would have been dismissed due to limits on the types of data that can be modelled. Another interviewee suggested that at first participants probably had to be pushed into thinking 'the unthinkable' and 'out of the box', but that participants generally were comfortable in thinking about unconventional developments. Although such developments need not be discontinuities, it was argued that encouraging participants to take an imaginative look at the future meant that participants at least entertained the idea that discontinuous change might occur.

There were also some critical comments about the workshop. One interviewee recalled a free spirit arguing that the session did not go far enough in thinking imaginatively about the future, thus limiting the scope for discontinuous ideas. This allegedly led to some exasperation among other participants, some of whom dismissed the workshop as a science fiction exercise, far removed from their own frame of reference; others questioned its scientific validity. Another interviewee pointed out that some participants did not appreciate the open approach taken in the workshop design. The freedom enjoyed by participants apparently made some of them uncertain and insecure.

On the basis of experiences with the structure of the workshop, one interviewee recommended limiting the eccentricity of the ideas that participants could offer; but s/he acknowledged that this might also have drawbacks. Another interviewee concluded that the combination of an open format and a varied group of participants made the workshop difficult to facilitate, resulting in a high risk of failure. However, two interviewees indicated that the facilitation problems were partly the result of the varied quality of the VISIONS facilitators. The quality of the facilitation is relevant, so stated one interviewee, because the crux in thinking about discontinuity is combining the proper process with the appropriate facilitator and the right group of people.

A number of the interviewees' comments suggest that there was not a systematic development of discontinuity in VISIONS . Efforts were made to address the idea of discontinuity in the form of commentary in the proposal[5] and the paper entitled 'Surprises in scenarios"[20]. However, the process of inserting surprises and bifurcations in the scenarios seemed pragmatic and at times even arbitrary, according to one interviewee. To illustrate, it was argued that circumstance played an influential role in the creative process, where inspiration for the discontinuities in the scenarios was found in current affairs and events in team members' lives. Rather than pragmatic, another interviewee described the process as inductive, explaining that steps were taken with the help of "experienced-based insights". A third interviewee argued that some methodological issues were evaded, such as the question of the importance of plausibility when considering the possibility of particular discontinuities. In any event, the unsystematic approach that was taken was not detrimental to the discontinuity-richness of the scenarios.

Interviewees also commented on how the concept of discontinuity was introduced, and how it evolved. Many interviewees complained that the operative term for discontinuity, surprise, was a difficult concept and that it was never explicitly defined in VISIONS . This is corroborated by the variety of interpretations of surprise that the interviewees offered. One interviewee argued that two types of surprise existed: external and internal. An external influence might force change, such as environmental pressures might cause the reversal of the Gulf Stream, whereas 'internal surprise' occurs due to the interaction of several developments within a system. When asked about the essence of surprise, one interviewee answered by saying it was an unexpected event, whereas another suggested it was a break in established patterns. A third interviewee proposed a combination of the two: a sudden event that changes everything. A fourth emphasised that a surprise to one person might not be as surprising to another, and that surprises distinguish themselves on the basis of likelihood and visibility, among other factors. In summary, numerous interpretations of the idea of discontinuity were used by those involved in VISIONS . This observation is similar to that of the scenario studies examined in Chapter 4.

Two interviewees indicated that, in spite of the various definitions, there was a general understanding of discontinuity among the partners and participants and that few had difficulty addressing it. If there was initial confusion about the concept, so stated one interviewee, then by the end of the study, the idea of surprise had become shared knowledge among the partners thanks in part to a document on bifurcations[17] and the paper 'Surprises in scenarios'[20]. Another interviewee argued that all partners perceived bifurcations to be a powerful, logical, and manageable interpretation of discontinuity. Yet another indicated that the definition of discontinuity was always clear to those who introduced it, although general familiarity with it increased over time. This increased familiarity translated into a slight transformation of the idea, according to one interviewee. S/he argued that such evolution is typical of participatory processes in which definitions become somewhat fluid. In any event, the absence or fluidity of definitions did not prove an obstacle to the development of discontinuity-rich scenarios.

One interviewee indicated that a predefined concept might have kindled an interest with partners and participants to further investigate the concept. In contrast, another interviewee speculated that by leaving the definition open, partners and participants were drawn to the idea of discontinuity more than they might have been if presented with a predefined concept. The differing opinions raise the question which strategy is more constructive, the use of a predefined concept of discontinuity or leaving the development of the concept to the creativity of participants in a scenario process. We therefore consider the use of a predefined concept a double-edged factor for discontinuity-oriented scenario development.

The interviewees proposed some recommendations for structures, methods, and concepts involved in discontinuity-oriented scenario development. Regarding the methodological structure needed for working with a varied group, one interviewee argued that many of the "eccentric" people needed for discontinuity-oriented scenario development would rebel if they had to work "within the structure of a planned and tidy process." Another interviewee stated that the point is not to create the ultimate method for investigating or even anticipating discontinuity through scenarios. As one interviewee speculated, "You cannot go looking for happiness and expect to find it. The same is probably true of surprise."

Rather, as another interviewee put it, the aim should be to create and foster the conditions that inspire the exploration of discontinuity so that ideas might emerge serendipitously. S/he acknowledged, however, that this might be an unattainable ideal:

> There are lots of little elements that you need to make the optimal environment [for dealing with discontinuity]. Maybe you can never get the optimal environment that includes all these facets.

The interviewee added that, in any event, the creative environment necessary for discontinuity-oriented scenario development requires a methodological framework of some kind; a freewheeling approach is inappropriate. To this end, several interviewees offered as suggestions several features common to exploratory and intuitive scenario development. One interviewee argued that the process should have a mix between group activities, in which the integration of ideas takes place, and time for participants to come up with ideas on their own. Gestation time and the iteration of activities was also considered influential to discontinuity-rich scenario development, since the required creativity cannot be triggered on command.

With regards to discontinuity-oriented methods, one interviewee indicated that the drawing of analogies might be effective in helping participants to look beyond their own discipline. Two interviewees noted the importance of looking to the past, arguing that history shows that events and processes develop in a much less logical manner than one is normally inclined to believe. Another interviewee suggested the possibility of thinking of 'nice discontinuities', as opposed to the more common unpleasant discontinuities. Yet another interviewee indicated that a useful approach might be to mix forecasting and backcasting techniques, posing both the question 'what if?' (forecasting) and the question 'how could?'(backcasting) are asked[6]. An additional suggestion was that an emphasis be placed on discontinuities *in* scenarios rather than simply on discontinuous scenarios in order to encourage a more explicit treatment of the idea. The use of models was dismissed out of hand by two interviewees, one of them arguing that a rigorous, analytical approach is inappropriate when exploring discontinuity.

In summary, our VISIONS reconstruction underscores the inspiring nature of an intuitive process design, as suggested in the comparative review in Chapter 4. The seemingly pragmatic approach to discontinuity did not prevent the development of discontinuity-rich scenarios. However, this observation underscores Brooks'[29] and Dammers'[30] claims that methodology for discontinuity-oriented scenario development is underdeveloped. Consequently, we conclude that underdeveloped methodology is a double-edged factor for discontinuity-oriented scenario development.

6.3 *Procedural issues*
Discontinuity "was always looked at as a strategic issue and not a technical detail", according to two interviewees. Several interviewees indicated that, even in the European scenario team, the idea was overshadowed by the attention that was given to the VISIONS experiments, such as the integration of scales and of quantitative and qualitative information. However, these experiments had been identified as focal issues from the beginning of the VISIONS process. It is understandable that the idea of

---

[6] The interviewee explained that the manner in which s/he used backcasting involves the positing of a particular future event and then considering what developments might lead to the occurrence of that event. This is a variation on the original approach for backcasting. See Chapter 2 for further details.

discontinuity was given a second priority in the study. Nonetheless, from the start the idea of discontinuity featured regularly in the scenario process. A factor that allegedly stimulated thinking about discontinuity in the first European workshop was that the goal of developing surprising scenarios was made clear to all participants at the start of the meeting.

Nonetheless, ensuring the consistent presence of discontinuity in the minds of those involved in VISIONS proved to be a challenge because of the tendency for the idea of discontinuity to occasionally and inadvertently slip from the research agenda, according to three interviewees. In the words of one interviewee:

Surprise is something that disappears from the research agenda surprisingly quickly. The reason for this is that people do not naturally think in terms of surprise. In fact, people would prefer to ignore it. It is not an issue that is placed on the agenda as a matter of course.

Another interviewee suggested that surprise was rarely discussed beyond the team sessions and the first European workshop. S/he argued that surprises were hardly addressed in such sessions as European scenario workshops and partner meetings because the scenarios were apparently considered surprising in themselves and no further discussion of surprise was deemed necessary. Even at the European scenario team meetings, there was an inclination to forget about the discontinuity experiment at these meetings, according to one interviewee. Three others indicated that the project leader intermittently returned the idea of surprise to the research agenda, when it slipped from team members' attention. On such occasions, the European scenario team went back to the storyline material to see if and why ideas had been excluded in the scenarios. In any event, the European scenario team made sure that there were different types of surprising elements in each scenario, so argued an interviewee.

The ideas about discontinuity that were proposed often evolved during the course of the scenario process. This occurred with the idea about the destruction of a McDonald's restaurant, incorporated into the general theme of anti-globalisation and anti-capitalism. The scenario team therefore considered it ironic that seven months after the workshop, anti-globalist José Bové demolished part of a McDonalds restaurant in Millau, France. The Bové incident was seen by some interviewees as an illustration of a tendency in VISIONS to water or tone down ideas about discontinuity either as a result of the writing process or the negotiation process aimed at achieving broad agreement on the scenarios. Other interviewees argued that rather than being toned down, the ideas about discontinuity became subtler and more sophisticated as the scenarios were refined. The development of the bifurcations and complexity syndromes are illustrations of this elaboration. It is therefore unclear what role the writing and negotiating process played in developing the discontinuity-rich scenarios, and so we categorise it as a double-edged factor.

To summarise, with regards to the procedural issues raised by the interviewees, an inspiring factor for exploring the idea of discontinuity is the idea's explicit programming. A related factor is the presence of a 'discontinuity guardian', who ensures that the idea remains in the forefront of people's minds during the scenario process. We identified the writing process as a double-edged factor.

7 Reflections

The VISIONS study is one of a small group of studies in recent years that produced discontinuity-rich scenarios[24]. Here, we summarise what factors inspired the development of discontinuity-rich scenarios in VISIONS, as well as those that had an impairing affect. We also address double-edged factors, where appropriate.

7.1 Inspiring factors

From our reconstruction we distil four factors with inspirational effects on the exploration of discontinuity: group variety, teamwork and team spirit, discontinuity guardianship, and an open and intuitive process design.

Group variety in VISIONS was highest during the first European workshop. The workshop clearly contributed many ideas about discontinuity for the scenarios. We cannot provide conclusive evidence of a relationship between group composition and the quality of discontinuity thinking, but we argue that the VISIONS reconstruction provides strong indications that group variety has an inspirational effect on discontinuity-oriented scenario development. Although group variety is recommended for all successful scenario exercises[25;26], the fact that so many interviewees emphasised its importance suggests its relevance to discontinuity-oriented processes. According to several interviewees, group variety should be sought through variations in age, gender, nationality, professional context, and academic discipline. This corroborates Van Steenbergen's[23;31] suggestions, as well as Maso's[27], presented in Chapter 4.

So-called 'free spirits' played a special role in the context of group variety. In VISIONS, free spirits were recruited as participants for the first European workshop in the hope that they would provide novel insights and inspire others to consider and propose unconventional ideas. The idea of free spirits is analogous to the idea of 'remarkable people'[26;28]. The free spirits were probably not briefed on the kind of contribution expected of them. Such a briefing might ensure that free spirits are attuned to their role. In any event, the use of free spirits appears promising for discontinuity-oriented scenario development.

The potential offered by a varied group composition might be enhanced by a synergy within the scenario team. The interview material suggests that good teamwork and team spirit contributed to the discontinuity-rich output in the European scenarios and the integrated visions. Similarly, there are indications that thinking about discontinuity was obstructed in cases where synergy was absent and teamwork was problematic. Therefore, although synergy is an asset for any type of teamwork, we consider it to be sufficiently relevant to adopt it as an inspiring factor for discontinuity-oriented scenario development.

The reason that the European team developed discontinuity-rich scenarios can largely be attributed to the fact that its members included champions of the idea of discontinuity. The interview material shows that what we call 'discontinuity guardianship' or the effort to keep the idea of discontinuity in people's minds was an influential factor in the VISIONS process. The effect was an iterative process in which novel ideas proposed earlier in the VISIONS process were regularly revisited. Furthermore, discontinuity guardianship gave the development of the idea an impetus resulting in the paper 'Surprises in scenarios'[20] as well as in the concepts of bifurcations and complexity syndromes. We therefore conclude that regular prompts to remind participants of the idea of discontinuity are needed to ensure that it remains a focal issue throughout a scenario process. In view of the apparent tendency of people to think in terms of gradual, incremental progress, we argue that a scenario study would benefit from experimenting with 'discontinuity guardians' who ensure that the idea is kept on the research agenda throughout the process.

Another inspiring factor was the open character of the first European workshop. Such openness allows workshop participants freedom and flexibility to consider a range of possible future developments rather than merely probable or preferable futures. Judging by the VISIONS experience, an open structure also involves taking a long-term view. These conditions compare to intuitive designs of exploratory studies described in Chapter 2. Interviewees' comments about the uneasiness of some participants regarding the freedom that they were given suggests that openness has potential drawbacks as well. Furthermore, a total lack of structure is inappropriate, as one of the interviewees argued, because of the risk that the process might not lead to a product. A balance therefore needs to be struck between structure and freedom. We argue that the seemingly paradoxical idea of a structured yet open, intuitive discontinuity-oriented design is worthy of further investigation.

7.2 Impairing factors

We identified two factors that appeared to impair the exploration of discontinuity in VISIONS. They were: obstructive behaviour and the evolutionary paradigm. Here, we consider to what extent these factors might be impairing to discontinuity-oriented scenario development in general.

An impairing factor in VISIONS was the obstructive influence of intransigence and narrow-minded thinking on creative processes. Several interviewees suggested that this might have been avoided if the 'right' participant group had been assembled.

However, the participating group in VISIONS was larger and more varied than in most scenario studies. Is achieving the 'right' group therefore an attainable ideal? And would a 'better' group have been more discontinuity-minded? Unfortunately it is not possible to answer these questions. Ours is not an anthropological or social psychological study, nor is it possible to draw on an extensive body of research on the intricacies of group scenario processes.

Secondly, in Chapter 4, we offered the evolutionary paradigm[29] as an explanation for the absence of discontinuity in scenario development. The evolutionary paradigm was referred to in the VISIONS proposal[5]. It was argued that in many long-term scenario studies surprises and bifurcations were not taken into account even if, "history shows us that historical trends are characterised by strong fluctuations rather than smooth curves, often triggered by unexpected changes, thus surprises." This was the motivation for addressing the idea of discontinuity in the VISIONS study in an explicitly 'anti-evolutionary' way. However, some evidence exists of its impairing influence in VISIONS, namely the comments about partners' thinking in conventional terms. The VISIONS teams' awareness of the evolutionary paradigm and efforts to avoid it probably ensured that its influence was tempered in comparison to many studies discussed in Chapter 4.

7.3 Double-edged factors

Double-edged factors might have both inspiring and impairing effects, depending on other factors. We identified three double-edged factors in the VISIONS study: the role of knowledge and expertise, underdeveloped methodology, and the writing process.

Comments from the interviewees revealed an ambiguous assessment of the role of knowledge and expertise in VISIONS. Some interviewees' comments indicate that, on the one hand, the absence of knowledge and expertise in a scenario process might result in bland, if not flawed, scenarios. Moreover, the participation of recognised experts might increase the profile and credibility of the scenario study. On the other hand, some comments suggest that knowledge and expertise can also impair discontinuity-oriented scenario development, if a group of participants choose to stay within the boundaries of existing knowledge.

The VISIONS reconstruction demonstrates that methodology for discontinuity-oriented scenario development is underdeveloped. The process of exploring the idea of discontinuity and incorporating it in the scenarios was carried out pragmatically and, at times, even in an arbitrary manner. Nevertheless, the resulting scenarios were discontinuity-rich. With regards to the definition of discontinuity, the concept was not predefined but was gradually made concrete during the course of the study. The disappointment that some interviewees felt regarding the development of the concept of discontinuity raises the question whether more progress would have been made if a predefined concept had been used. In view of these comments, we argue that leaving the definition of discontinuity open might kindle interest with participants in developing the idea and thus instil a sense of ownership. However, in the absence of a definition, extra effort should be made to programme discontinuity to ensure that it remains a prominent feature in the scenario process.

In the opinion of some interviewees, the evolution of ideas about discontinuity resulted in their dilution. A different interpretation was that the ideas became subtler and more sophisticated as the scenarios advanced through the writing phase. It is unclear exactly what the nature of the writing and negotiating process was and so we categorise it as a double-edged factor[7].

We provide a summary in Table 3 of the inspiring, impairing, and double-edged factors for exploring the idea of discontinuity, based on the VISIONS reconstruction and the comparative review in Chapter 4.

8 Concluding remarks

In this chapter, we reconstructed the VISIONS scenario process in order to understand how the discontinuity-rich scenarios that resulted from the project were developed. In doing so, the chapter built on provisional insights from the comparative review of scenario studies (Chapter 4) in which factors that inspire and those that impair the exploration of discontinuity were discussed.

Our research shows that discontinuity-oriented scenario development is a challenging practice, more complicated than we anticipated at the start of the research. The VISIONS reconstruction demonstrated that discontinuity-oriented

	INSPIRING FACTORS	DOUBLE-EDGED FACTORS	IMPAIRING FACTORS
SCENARIO TEAM AND PARTICIPANTS	Group variety	Knowledge & expertise	Obstructive behaviour
	Team synergy		
METHODS AND CONCEPTS	Open structure	Underdeveloped methods and concepts	
PROCEDURAL ISSUES	Discontinuity guardianship	Writing process	Evolutionary paradigm
	Current affairs, spirit of the times		*Institutional barriers*

Table 3 *A summary of inspiring, impairing, and double-edged factors for discontinuity-oriented thinking on the basis of the comparative review (in italics when only addressed in Chapter 4) and the reconstruction of VISIONS.*

[7] Ethnographic research of these processes in foresight, as undertaken by Van Asselt and Van 't Klooster, might provide relevant insights for discontinuity-oriented scenario development. This research is part of the same research programme on foresight methodology as the current..

scenario development involves the careful combination of various factors rather than the simple use of a particular method. On the basis of our research, we argue that exploring discontinuity is unconventional and innovative. It should therefore be given extra attention in a scenario process, if the development of discontinuity-rich scenarios is the objective.

The analysis of inspiring, impairing, and double-edged factors led to a number of issues for further research, of which four in particular are interesting and sufficiently manageable to investigate in the context of the current thesis. First, group variety was inspirational for the development of discontinuity-rich scenarios. Was the apparent correlation between group variety and the exploration of discontinuity in VISIONS coincidental; or is it possible to find evidence of a constructive relationship? Second, VISIONS struck a good balance between a free format and a structured process in its exploratory phase. Is the balance struck in VISIONS reproducible? Another potentially interesting insight that requires further investigation is the idea of programming of discontinuity. Might more intense programming in the absence of a definition kindle an interest and an on-going awareness of the idea during a scenario study? Lastly, although the VISIONS scenarios were relatively discontinuity-rich, the idea was not subject to one of the methodological experiments formulated at the start of the study. The challenge therefore remains to see what happens when a discontinuity-oriented process design is used. We provide an account of experimentation with such a design in the following chapter.

6
exploring discontinuity
an experiment

6 EXPLORING DISCONTINUITY: AN EXPERIMENT

1 Introduction

Our research has demonstrated that, despite claims to the contrary, many scenario studies do not address the idea of future discontinuity. The sources of those studies that produced discontinuity-rich scenarios provide little indication of the use of discontinuity-oriented concepts and methods. Conceptual vagueness and the lack of established methods appear to underscore the idea that exploring discontinuity involves more methods alone, and that there are additional factors such as personal skills and professional qualities that inspire thinking about the idea. A deeper methodological understanding of the exploration of discontinuity is therefore needed in order to understand how discontinuity-rich scenarios can be developed.

The VISIONS reconstruction in the previous chapter helped to establish a better understanding of discontinuity-oriented scenario development. VISIONS reinforced some of the earlier identified factors influential in the exploration of discontinuity, and it revealed several new ones. In this chapter, we elaborate on these methodological insights in the form of an experiment in discontinuity-oriented process design. By conducting an experiment we aimed to gain insights into the process in a way that a reconstruction of VISIONS could not offer. So far, we had not worked from a hypothesis about the idea of discontinuity in the context of scenario development. However, the body of knowledge collected in the research described in the previous chapters allowed for the formulation and testing of a hypothesis in the experiment. The hypothesis was:

Discontinuity-oriented scenario development involves fostering the interplay of influential factors whereby inspiring ones are mobilised and impairing ones are quashed.

The degree to which the experiment's output was discontinuity-rich was the measure for our hypothesis. Therefore, the interplay of influencing factors was more relevant than the workings of individual factors.

The subject of the experiment was the future of European salmon aquaculture. After a brief overview of aquaculture today, we describe the reasoning behind the design of the discontinuity-oriented process for the experiment. Finally, we reflect on the process and its output.

2 Salmon aquaculture

We chose salmon aquaculture as the subject of the experiment because it is a current example of a persistent and wicked problem with the potential for discontinuous change[1]. Salmon aquaculture is a relatively new and thriving industry, the activities

---

[1] See Chapter 1 for a description of persistent and wicked problems.

of which have large implications: ecological, economic, and socio-cultural. Salmon aquaculture is a controversial industry, its activities having large local and global effects. There are many competing interests as well as uncertainties regarding the impact of farming activities on the physical and socio-economic environment. Moreover, improvements in farming practice are constrained by economic pressures and the still experimental nature of certain technology. Remedies to aspects of salmon aquaculture pose problems in other areas. Aquaculture's potential for discontinuous development lays in the stress it places on livelihoods, food safety, and wild fish stocks.

A more elaborate explanation of the current situation in salmon aquaculture is desirable in order to understand the experiment's output. Unless otherwise indicated the source used in the below account is Vellema and Van Notten[1].

2.1 Driving forces behind European salmon aquaculture

The consumption of fish in Europe is increasing in relation to meat[2]. This is due partly to fear of such diseases as salmonella and BSE, but it has also to do with the image of fish as a healthy food source. FAO projections for 2010 place demand for fish at 30-40 million tonnes more than can be produced. Changes in the structure of the population might have important implications for food demand in the future[2]. These changes include more single person households, decreased fertility, decline in marriage, a greater incidence of divorce, and an ageing population.

Increased consumer demand and government subsidies in the last 20 years have ensured that the global fishing fleet has grown twice as quickly as the size of fish stocks[3]. Between 1970 and 1990 the number of fishing vessels doubled from 585 000 to 1.2 million. It is argued[3] that the global fishing fleet is more than 30 percent larger than necessary. Moreover, technological innovation has made fishing considerably more efficient. This results in the depletion of many fish stocks.

In 2000 the FAO[4] estimated that, among the major marine fish stocks, only 25 to 27 percent are underfished. The remaining part is either fished to capacity (47-50 percent) or overfished (15-18 percent). A remaining 9-10 percent of stocks has been depleted or is recovering from depletion. The threat of overfishing has led to the prohibition of wild catch of some species, such as cod, in selected seas. New fishing areas are sought, including the open ocean where illegal fishing has become common[3].

Fish farming or aquaculture is seen as the solution to the problems of traditional fisheries. The farming of fish is an old practice, but the scale of past farming practices does not compare to the current production of farmed fish, which has grown spectacularly since in the last decades of the 20th century. Indeed, the fish farming sector became the fastest growing provider of food in the 1990s[5]. In 2002, more than 20 percent of the total global fish production came from aquaculture[3]. Aquaculture normally results in higher yields than conventional fisheries[6]. The potential higher yields in aquaculture make it possible to meet the rising demand for fish by consumers. Yet, aquaculture raises numerous concerns about its ecological, economic, and socio-cultural impacts. The developments that drive the expansion of salmon aquaculture are presented in Figure 1.

2.2 Ecological impacts[7]

Salmon farming does not take place in a closed system. It often occurs in inland waters and on migratory routes of wild salmon. Much uncertainty surrounds the exact nature and scale of aquaculture's impacts, but there are fears that salmon farming might harm the environment, as described below.

Dependence on wild catch
One of the chief criticisms of fish farming is that species such as salmon, trout and cod need to be fed large amounts of wild fish[8]. In 2001, for the ten most commonly

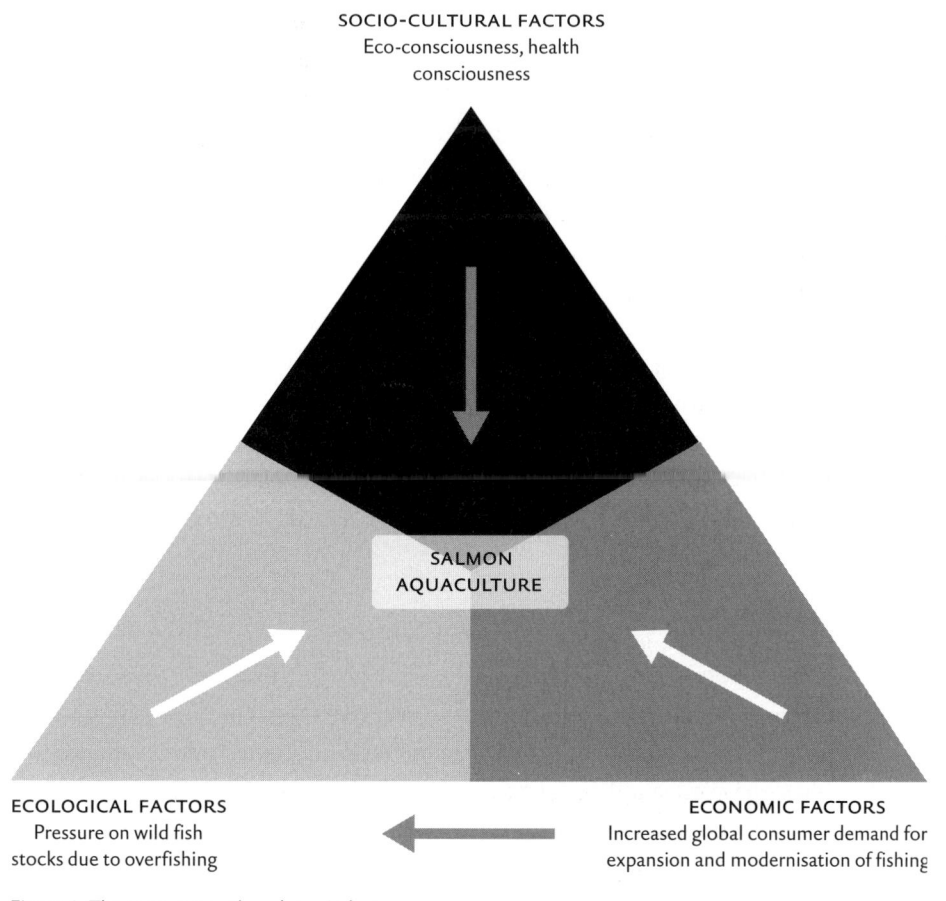

Figure 1 *The pressures on the salmon industry.*

farmed fish, an average of 1.9 kg of wild fish was required for every kilogram of fish raised. It is aquaculture's dependency on feedstocks of wild catch that arguably makes the ecosystem most vulnerable[9;10]. There is a possibility of fish stock collapse if current fishing practices combined with an expansion of the salmon aquaculture industry continue. Such a discontinuity would have enormous impact on the ecosystem as well as on the industries that exploit it.

Disease
Sea lice plague farmed salmon. The densely packed cages in which salmon is farmed contain up to half a million fish and diseases such as lice thrive in densely populated farms and can contaminate local wild fish. Though salmon farmers dispute the claim, there are indications of increased levels of infection of wild salmon by lice since the birth of industrial salmon farming. Norway's marine research institute has calculated that 86 percent of young wild salmon are eaten alive by or are fatally infected with sea lice. A 1998 outbreak of Infectious Salmon Anaemia (ISA) led to the slaughter of four million salmon and the closure of 25 percent of the Scottish industry. The rest was put into quarantine. The Scottish parliament's European Committee claims that ISA cost € 160 million and 200 jobs in Scotland. The threat of the microscopic parasite *gyrodactylus salaris* is also worrying. By 2001, the parasite had already wiped out salmon stock in 42 Norwegian rivers. Combating the parasite in farmed salmon involves an expensive chemical treatment.

Contamination and pollution
Farmed salmon is said to contain high contamination of dioxin and PCBs, mainly caused by a consumption of feed materials of fish origin (up to 75 percent of the total diet) combined with a high level of contamination in these feed materials. Other chemicals include pesticides that are used extensively to combat sea lice. Furthermore, wastewater from salmon farms containing uneaten food, fish faeces, and antibiotics is said to contribute to the spectacular increase of a type of plankton called algal bloom, toxic to shellfish.

Wild salmon species
The salmon varieties used in farming usually originate from extensive breeding programs. Besides such distinct physical differences as the size of the tail and the shape of the jaw, farmed salmon grow faster than wild salmon, and they do not follow the wild salmon's natural cycles, which include the return to spawning grounds. Furthermore, farmed salmon manage only 16 percent of the breeding rate of those that spawn free. This would not be a problem if farmed salmon and wild salmon were kept isolated from one another. However, 'escapes' from salmon farms are common.

Indeed the number of escapes quadrupled in two years, from 95 000 fish in 1998 to 491 000 in 2000. On one occasion in 1999, a farm lost as many as 20 000 salmon.

Escaped salmon interbreed with wild salmon, leading to the contamination of the wild strain. Norwegian scientists claim that the degree of genetic distinction between farmed and wild salmon is being halved every 3.3 generations. According to the World Wildlife Fund, the wild salmon stock in 129 Scottish rivers are now classified as endangered. If interbreeding continues all salmon will eventually be descendants of farmed salmon[11].

2.3 Economic impacts

Salmon farming is a lucrative industry that significantly contributes to the welfare and livelihood of many European communities, mainly in Scotland and Norway. The salmon farming industry provides thousands of jobs in areas that otherwise have few employment opportunities. The industry contributes € 416 million to the Scottish national economy, more than the Highland beef and lamb industries put together. The Norwegian Seafood Export Council (NSCE) reported in 1997 that the industry provides 15 000 jobs.

On the other hand, large-scale aquaculture might lead to the demise of other industries. Shellfish farmers and the tourist industry claim that the environmental damage caused by salmon farming undermines their livelihoods. The threat of toxic algal blooms to shellfish has left the industry with moratoria on shellfish growing along 10 000 square kilometres of Scotland's coastline. Moreover, changes in the ecosystem might have adverse effects on employment in certain regions. Anglers in Scotland are faced with declines in wild salmon catch of up to 40 percent a year, as occurred in 1999. A healthy industry in recreational fishing is worth up to € 640 million.

2.4 Socio-cultural impacts

The environmental impacts of aquaculture have led to increased concern from consumers, the public, interest groups and scientific expert groups[9]. Public awareness about the safety and sustainability of farmed salmon was heightened by the BBC documentary 'Warning from the wild: the price of salmon'[12]. This documentary was followed by several other media items that have shaped public opinion.

Farmed salmon is criticised for its purported dangers to human health. It is argued that the chemicals used to treat and feed farmed salmon are potentially damaging to humans. Claims about contamination from dioxin and PCBs, for example, have alerted regulators[13] to such potential health risks as cancer and learning difficulties in children. Furthermore, farmed salmon are reportedly fed the remains of other farmed fish, a controversial practice in light of the BSE and foot-and-mouth crises.

The salmon industry's vulnerability to public relations crises is a potential source of discontinuity. The public uproar against Monsanto's genetically modified

'Frankenstein food' and Shell during the Brent Spar affair demonstrate the power of public pressure. Both companies suffered from the affairs, and it is conceivable that such a setback might befall the aquaculture industry.

2.5 Possible solutions?

The salmon aquaculture industry invests considerably in the development of technological solutions for the production of healthy and safe food, and the reduction of

LEGEND

Income → Example of driving process

Fish stock collapse ----▶ Example of possible discontinuity

SOCIO-CULTURAL FACTORS
Public anxiety, risks to human health

Negative publicity about farming practices

Salmon aquaculture in disrepute, collapse of the industry

Negative publicity, persistent chemicals

Fish stock collapse, disruption of ecosystems and fishing industries

SALMON AQUACULTURE

Technological breakthrough, relief of pressure on ecosystem

Parasites, chemicals, escapes, wild fish as feed

Income, meeting consumer demand

Calls for measures and (technological) solutions

ECOLOGICAL FACTORS
Pressure on fish stocks, risks to wild salmon, shellfish, and other wildlife

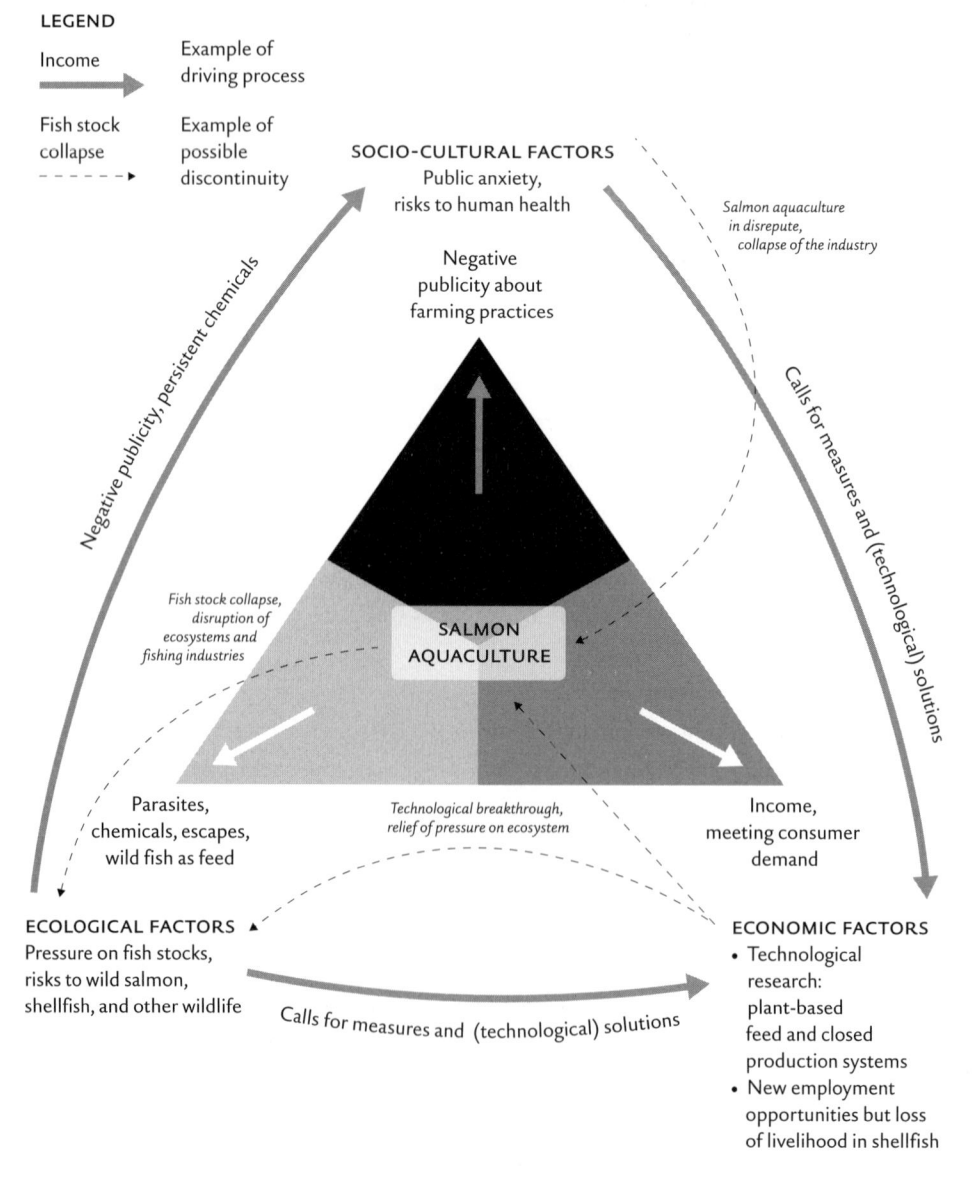

Calls for measures and (technological) solutions

ECONOMIC FACTORS
- Technological research: plant-based feed and closed production systems
- New employment opportunities but loss of livelihood in shellfish

Figure 2 *The impact of salmon aquaculture and examples of possible discontinuities.*

negative environmental impacts. Current research focuses on alternative sources of proteins and oils and alternate technological possibilities contributing to healthy and safe end products. It is still uncertain how and when the results of this research will be implemented on a large scale. Few alternatives are commercially viable at present due to the relatively low number of available products, their high prices, unfamiliarity, and complex legislation.

With respect to the reduction of environmental impacts, an alternative to production of fish in marine environments is land-based fish production, which uses closed recirculation systems. Such systems will help contain environmental pollution and the mixing of farmed and wild fish. Closed system farming is the focus of much current research. Should the research lead to an industry-wide breakthrough then the impact could be significant. Such a discontinuity might ensure that many of the negative impacts of salmon aquaculture on wild fish stocks and other parts of the ecosystem are sizeably reduced.

An illustration of the economic, environmental, and socio-cultural impacts of salmon aquaculture and the discontinuities that might occur as a result thereof are presented in Figure 2.

3 Organisation of the experiment

The experiment was organised over a two-year period. The process began with finding an appropriate context in which to experiment with insights about discontinuity-oriented scenario development. The research had to meet two self-imposed requirements. First, we wanted to work with actual stakeholders in order to approach as real a scenario process as possible. Secondly, we wanted as much freedom as possible in the design of the experiment. Organising an experiment that met these two criteria was difficult because working with stakeholders often involves client-based work where the client has considerable influence over the process and its output. The salmon aquaculture study met both criteria because we were able to conduct an experiment with stakeholders with relatively little constraints imposed by the project's sponsor.

Preparation for the experiment involved six pilot sessions. These acted as rehearsals for the experiment. In the pilot sessions the various parts of the experiment were tested and refined. Each pilot session consisted of a workshop that lasted 3.5 hours. The sessions were conducted September 1 – 15th, 2003. The group that participated in pilot sessions consisted of seven researchers in the age group 25-35 from five European countries, as part of a course on integrated assessment. The writing of a position paper[1] on the state of affairs in the salmon industry was

---

[2] Section 2 of this chapter is an adapted version of the position paper.

another part of the preparations[2]. The aim of the paper was to provide the diverse group of stakeholders an overview of the current issues in aquaculture, and to introduce them to the idea of discontinuity. The desk study was conducted in the period September 2002 - February 2003.

The experiment itself involved two stakeholder workshops held in October and November 2003. The stakeholder workshops lasted for a total of 11 hours. Four observers, an audio recorder and a video camera recorded the workshop proceedings. The experiment was conducted by a team of researchers, including the author, from Maastricht University's International Centre for Integrative Studies (ICIS) and Wageningen University's Agro-technology and Food Innovations (A&F, formerly Agrotechnological Research (ATO)[3].

The steps taken in the organisation of the experiment are summarised in Textbox 1.

4 Discontinuity-oriented process design

The goal of the experiment was to test a process design based on insights about factors that inspire and those that impair the exploration of discontinuity.

4.1 Basic framework

The experiment's basic framework was modelled after the typology for scenarios described in Chapter 2. Several discontinuity-oriented elements were then added to the design. In the typology, scenario studies are classified according to their goal, process design, and the content of the scenarios.

ORGANISATION OF THE EXPERIMENT

Proposal phase:
- *September 2001 – April 2003*

Preparatory phase:
- *Position paper: September 2002 – March 2003*
- *Design of experiment: March – August 2003*
- *Pilot sessions: September 2003*

Conduct of experiment:
- *First stakeholder workshop: October 2003*
- *Drafting of rudimentary storylines,*
  design of second stakeholder workshop: October 2003
- *Second stakeholder workshop: November 2003*

Textbox 1 *The organisation of the experiment*

[3] The research was funded by Supply chains, Logistics, and Information and Communication Technology (in Dutch KLICT) as part of the research programme Strategic transparency in supply chains.

In Chapter 4 we observed that exploratory scenario studies are more congenial to the idea of discontinuity than pre-policy research studies. Therefore, although some attention was paid to strategic options, more attention was given to exploratory features during the experiment[4]. The comparative review described in Chapter 4 showed that most studies address discontinuity in a predominantly intuitive manner. It was decided to adhere to this dominant trend in intuitive studies and focus on qualitative issues in the experiment. Our research demonstrated that most discontinuity-oriented scenario processes produce complex scenarios. Rather than look at the whole scenario development process, we limited our investigation to the systematic facilitation and production of discontinuity-rich material by focussing on two workshops. The processing of these ideas and the scenario writing process was not included in the experiment. No full-fledged scenarios were therefore developed. We limited our time and energy to producing three rudimentary stories that participants had developed in the first workshop. The degree to which the output is discontinuity-rich would provide the measure for testing the above-mentioned hypothesis.

4.2 Discontinuity-oriented design: mobilising inspiring factors

After establishing the basic process design we refined it for the purposes of investigating discontinuity. Of the ten factors of influence in the exploration of discontinuity that we identified in Chapters 4 and 5, four were used in the aquaculture experiment. We chose three of our previously identified inspiring factors: group variety, open structure, discontinuity guardianship and programming. The fourth, underdeveloped methods and concepts, was a double-edged factor. The factors are highlighted in Table 1, which is an adaptation of Table 3 from Chapter 5.

	INSPIRING FACTORS	DOUBLE-EDGED FACTORS	IMPAIRING FACTORS
SCENARIO TEAM AND PARTICIPANTS	Group variety	Knowledge & expertise	Obstructive behaviour
	Team synergy		
METHODS AND CONCEPTS	Open structure	Underdeveloped methods and concepts	
PROCEDURAL ISSUES	Discontinuity guardianship	Writing process	Evolutionary paradigm
	Current affairs, spirit of the times		Institutional barriers

Table 1 *The inspiring and double-edged factors (in bold italics) chosen for the experiment*

[4] The consideration of strategic options was one of the few requirements that were imposed on the study by the sponsor.

The factors were chosen because they contained interesting issues for further investigation and they could be operationalised and tested. Other previously identified factors were excluded for a number of reasons. For example, the explanation of such group dynamic issues as intransigence requires socio-psychological or anthropological research beyond the scope of this thesis. Some impairing factors and double-edged factors were indirectly incorporated in the experiment. The evolutionary paradigm was considered through an active programming of the idea of discontinuity. The knowledge and expertise factor was partially addressed through the group variety factor.

In the following sections we describe each of the chosen factors and how they were incorporated in the experiment. The methods and concepts factor is divided into three sections, each one dedicated to a different technique.

4.2.1 Group composition

The comparative analysis (Chapter 4) and the VISIONS reconstruction (Chapter 5) demonstrate that intuitive scenario development often involves group work. There are indications that group performance can be improved by selecting a heterogeneous group of stakeholders, as demonstrated by psychological research on brainstorming[14], described by Nijstad[15]. We aimed to investigate the influence of group variety in the context of discontinuity-oriented scenario development[5].

We drew on insights from the VISIONS reconstruction for mobilising a varied group of participants. In collating the interviewees' recommendations a picture emerged of a multidisciplinary group that consisted of individuals with a host of qualities, including open-mindedness, and the ability to discuss a broad range of issues. Of interest to our research was whether a varied group has an inspirational influence on discontinuity-oriented scenario development in combination with the other chosen factors.

To achieve group variety for our experiment we recruited a diverse set of people with a stake in salmon aquaculture: public policy, business, non-governmental organisations (NGO), the research community, and hybrid groups such as branch organisations and information services. Participants were recruited using the position paper[1] as a guide. A number of other stakeholders were recruited after considering Internet sources, a television documentary, and newspaper articles. The groups that proved most difficult to recruit were NGOs and businesses. An extra recruitment round therefore took place after the first workshop. This was successful in increasing the number of stakeholders from businesses but not from NGOs. The varied group of stakeholders that eventually participated in the workshops included retailers, a caterer, a farmed salmon producer, an oceanographer, a researcher of alternative food sources, and a specialist in tropical fisheries.

---

5   In doing so, we also connect with the idea of requisite variety described in Chapter 2.

In addition, we recruited two so-called 'free spirits'. They had no specific knowledge of European salmon aquaculture and our expectation was that they would provide new and different perspectives on the issue. The free spirits were recruited through the research team's network. Those that participated in the experiment were a member of the clergy, who was also professor in business ethics, and a former spokesperson for Greenpeace. One of the recommendations from the VISIONS interviewees was the need to recruit broadly read participants. The clergy member was recruited on the basis of his/her expertise in business ethics. S/he had degrees in Law, Economics, Theology, and Business Administration. Moreover, s/he had experience as an academic, a member of the clergy, and as a manager both inside and outside the church and the Netherlands. The former Greenpeace spokesperson was recruited on the basis of his/her experience of the Brent Spar affair, a well known example of confrontation between commercial and environmental interests.

The participants are described in Figure 3. The names and positions of the stakeholders are withheld in the interests of confidentiality. Instead, we describe them in terms of type of organisations or fields they represented. Approximately 25 stakeholders were invited to attend the workshops. Eleven invitees attended the first workshop; 15 attended the second. Nine people declined the invitation, mostly because of scheduling problems. The stakeholders were invited to contribute to the experiment

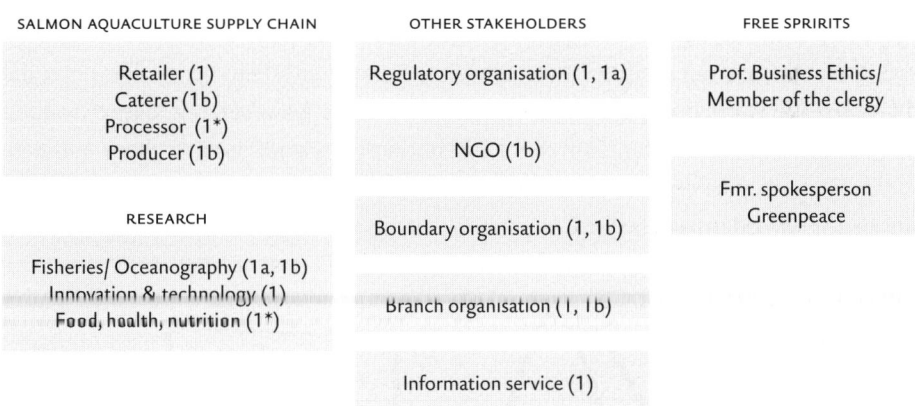

SALMON AQUACULTURE SUPPLY CHAIN	OTHER STAKEHOLDERS	FREE SPIRITS
Retailer (1) Caterer (1b) Processor (1*) Producer (1b)	Regulatory organisation (1, 1a)	Prof. Business Ethics/ Member of the clergy
	NGO (1b)	
RESEARCH		Fmr. spokesperson Greenpeace
Fisheries/ Oceanography (1a, 1b) Innovation & technology (1) Food, health, nutrition (1*)	Boundary organisation (1, 1b)	
	Branch organisation (1, 1b)	
	Information service (1)	

LEGEND
(1) Number of participants from stakeholder group
(a) Attended 1st workshop only
(b) Attended 2st workshop only
*   Participant working for 2 stakeholder organisations

Figure 3 *Workshop participants* [6]

[6] For the sake of clarity, the boundary organisations in the case of our experiment were institutions that provide government-funded incentives for commercial activities. The information service refers to an organisation that provides nutritional information to the public.

on a personal basis rather than as representatives of their respective organisations. The reasoning behind this was the idea that open, exploratory dialogue might be impaired if stakeholders believed that they needed to voice their organisations' opinions. In encouraging the participants to speak openly, we tried to minimise potential institutional or contextual constraints on the experiment.

4.2.2 Discontinuity guardianship
Our research in earlier chapters indicated that people are often inclined to think in evolutionary rather than discontinuous terms, and that efforts should be made to ensure the idea of discontinuity is constantly brought to participants' attention. In the experiment, however, we did not want to be so direct that participants might feel that the idea was imposed on them. The VISIONS reconstruction demonstrated that it is possible to develop an understanding of discontinuity and to make it concrete without introducing an initial concept. The reconstruction also suggested that placing discontinuity on the research agenda without defining it might kindle some partners' and workshop participants' interest in exploring the idea for themselves. In that case, extra effort should be made to programme the idea. In the experiment, no predefined concept of discontinuity was used, but the idea was regularly brought to the stakeholders' attention.

A first step in programming discontinuity was to send a summary of the position paper to the participants two weeks before the first workshop. In the summary, attention was drawn to the vulnerabilities and impacts of the aquaculture industry. The potential discontinuities were not spelled out for the stakeholders, however, because we wanted only to stimulate their thinking about discontinuity, not to provide them concrete ideas. Second, participants were regularly reminded of the idea of discontinuity during the workshops in the facilitator's presentations through such terms as surprise,

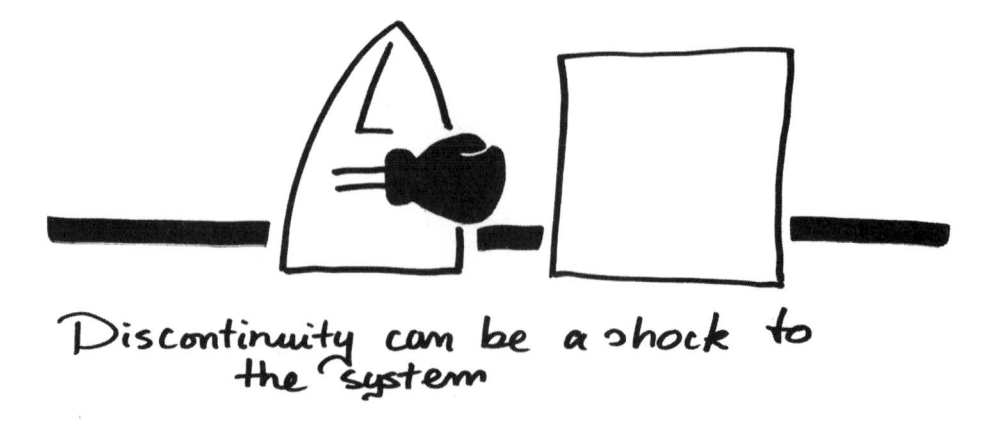

Figure 4 *The artist's drawing* © www.zwaarwater.nl

abrupt, gradual, structural change, and hidden and unexpected developments[7]. The term discontinuity itself was only used in an artist's drawing, presented in Figure 4[8]. The term was not otherwise used because the research team believed that it might appeal less to the imagination of the stakeholders than other terms[9].

The facilitator addressed discontinuity several times in the workshops. It was mentioned through synonyms in the opening presentations of both workshops, when the context and the aim of the study was described. Like in VISIONS' first European workshop, the stakeholders were encouraged to reason from the assumption that anything was possible. Moreover, discontinuity was referred to in the various task descriptions. For example, one task was to consider what lessons might be drawn from analogous cases for the anticipation of surprising developments.

The facilitator also programmed the idea of discontinuity by posing the question, you can think of ideas that might surprise perhaps[...] other stakeholders. What kind of hidden, unexpected developments might [the salmon industry] be confronted with in the future?" In order to encourage stakeholders not to hold back in proposing eccentric ideas, the facilitator added that there was no such thing as a bad idea. The facilitator intervened once during the exercise to encourage stakeholders to come up with issues other than those directly related to salmon. He used a war in Pakistan and the collapse of the European Union as examples, whereby he once again programmed the idea of discontinuity.

4.2.3 Open structure
The research described in previous chapters indicated that it is helpful to create a format that strikes a balance between an unstructured and a highly structured design. We tried to design a process with an open structure that provided conditions for as constructive and exploratory an exercise as possible. A manner in which we sought to achieve openness was through a flexible approach to the exercises, designing them so that they could be conducted independently of one another. In doing so, the exercises were not dependent on a particular ordering and could be run simultaneously, if desired. A design using several exercises would also help the effort to exhaust the participants of their ideas.

Two workshops were considered the minimum possible number, since a second workshop would allow stakeholders some time to consider the ideas of the first workshop and to introduce new ideas, if desired. The design of the second workshop was

---

[7] The discontinuity-related terms used in the presentations were inspired by research described in Chapter 3.
[8] The drawing was made during the pilot sessions and it was used in the second workshop to remind participants of the notion of discontinuity.
[9] In hindsight, the decision not to use the term discontinuity made the analysis of stakeholders' interpretations of the idea of discontinuity more difficult.

not decided until after the first had been conducted, to allow experiences from the first to be considered in the design of the second. A last aspect of the open structure was that stakeholders were given a relatively free rein during the exercises. In accordance with Vennix[16a], facilitation was limited to time management, stimulating group interaction, and providing organisational information. It was agreed that the facilitator would rarely intervene on points of content.

4.2.4 Underdeveloped methods: A general observation

Both the comparative analysis and the VISIONS reconstruction demonstrated that methods for exploring the idea of discontinuity are underdeveloped. Nevertheless, several methods have been proposed, and some have been experimented with, as discussed in Chapter 4. We decided to use methods to provide some sort of framework, but not to apply them in a rigid manner, in view of the wish to keep the process open. This decision had implications for the design of the three methods used in the experiment. We proposed staggered brainwriting, a variation of the more common brainstorming approach, as a potentially effective method for exploring discontinuity. The second method, historical analogy, is one of the approaches that follow directly from our discussion of discontinuity-oriented methods in Chapter 4. Perspective-based imaging is an experimental combination of two of the methods also proposed in Chapter 4.

Method: Staggered brainwriting

Group brainstorming is one of the most popular methods for generating creative ideas[15] and it is a commonly used approach in participatory scenario development. With brainstorming, workshop participants are instructed to generate as many ideas as possible, and to postpone judgement of the ideas. Osborn[16b;17], cited in Nijstad[15], argues that brainstorming in this manner can lead to the generation of many good ideas, and that creativity is enhanced. Moreover, he argues that brainstorming should be done in groups, and that group members generate more ideas than individuals working in isolation. However, some 40 years of controlled research of group brainstorming has shown that, in fact, brainstorming in groups leads to poorer results in both quantitative and qualitative terms when compared to ideas generated by individuals working in isolation[15].

Nijstad cites Lamm and Tromsdorff[18] when proposing that production blocking is the main reason for the relatively poor performance of group brainstorms. Blocking arises from the implicit rule that in group brainstorms people must take turns expressing their ideas. Consequently, ideas cannot always be communicated the moment they arise, which might interfere with a person's train of thought, leading to the forgetting or suppression of ideas.

To avoid blocking in the experiment, it was decided to apply an often-used variation of brainstorming called 'brainwriting'. This approach involves workshop participants communicating their ideas in writing rather than verbally. Although brainwriting helps avoid production blocking, when conducted by individuals in isolation, it lacks a number of benefits of group brainstorming[10]. People tend to enjoy working in groups more than working on their own. Also, people are usually more satisfied with their work when carried out in a group setting. Moreover, group brainstorming can add to the cohesion of a group and create a sense of ownership of the session's output.

In order to see what forms of brainwriting would be most effective in the context of the experiment, three approaches were tested in the pilot sessions: a group, an individual, and a 'paired' approach. Group brainwriting involves individuals simultaneously writing ideas on post-its and subsequently posting them visibly for other participants to use in the generation of their own ideas. In individual brainwriting participants are not offered the opportunity to take account of others' ideas. We did not consider the distinction between verbal and written communication relevant in the case of working in pairs, so we decided to do the paired variation in the form of a brainstorm rather than a brainwriting session.

The primary aim of the brainwriting session was to investigate whether conducting a staggered approach using multiple rounds might deliver more ideas about discontinuity than if only one round was conducted. By disallowing the repetition of ideas, it was assumed that multiple rounds would help exhaust the participants of their ideas. The staggered approach was tested in the pilot sessions. The participant group was not informed of the fact that each round would be followed by another in order to ensure that workshop participants would not withhold any ideas during any of the rounds. The first brainwriting round in the pilot sessions was intended to 'purge' the participants of ideas foremost in their minds. A second round then took place, an individual brainwriting session intended to elicit ideas less prominent in participants' minds. Then a third round of brainwriting took place, a paired brainstorm session intended to exhaust the participants of their remaining ideas. Different coloured post-its were used in each round in order to be able to analyse the quality of the ideas each round produced. Lastly, the group was asked to cluster all the post-its according to major themes.

The individual and group brainwriting sessions produced an abundance of ideas. The exercise with the paired brainstorm in the pilot sessions resulted in extensive dialogue between participants. The resulting ideas were markedly lower in quantity, albeit more developed, than the ideas produced resulting from group and individual brainstorms. Since there would be time for only two rounds of brainwriting during the stakeholder workshops, it was therefore decided to dismiss the paired variation.

---

[10] Compare with Nijstad (2000).

In the experiment's group brainwriting round. the participants' task was to answer the question: "What do you think are currently the important issues for the future of salmon farming?" The participants were not asked specifically to think about discontinuity. The second round involved an individual brainwriting exercise. The question to be answered in that round was: "Are there issues currently hidden from view that might lead to surprises in the future?" The question was an example of programming the idea of discontinuity in the scenario process.

Method: historical analogy
Historical analogy involves the analysis of past situations in the study of present-day situations[20]. There were several reasons for choosing to test historical analogy as a method for discontinuity-oriented exploration: Braudel's claim that history is necessary for understanding discontinuity (Chapter 3), a number of proposed techniques related to historical analysis (Chapter 4), and methodological suggestions proposed in several VISIONS interviews (Chapter 5). Our assumption was that the investigation of past cases of discontinuity might inspire thinking on possible future cases. Furthermore, we assumed that the drawing of analogies would facilitate a creative discussions about the future that might otherwise be lacking. The contexts for historical research might be various. For example, one might investigate past cases of discontinuity in other food sectors such as bovine spongiform encephalopathy (BSE), foot-and-mouth disease, and dioxine.

In the design of the analogy session we drew on several variations on the historical analogy approach such as historical retrodiction[23;24] and comparative prognosis[25], which, to our knowledge, had not yet been tested in the context of scenario development. Two variations of historical analogies were tested in the pilot sessions. The first exercise involved the participating researchers answering the question: "Does the case of salmon farming have parallels with other, analogous cases that you are familiar with? If so, which cases? How do they relate to the case of salmon farming?" Whereas in the first exercise the researchers were not given any support in thinking of analogies, in the second exercise they were presented with many of examples to use as sources of information, if desired. This second exercise included presentations about possible analogies with food scares and public relations crises. Also, a list of 10 –15 suggestions for possible analogous cases was providedas well as a stack of articles and reports related to each proposed analogous case.

The pilot session's first analogy exercise resulted in a more homogeneous set of analogies than the second. The first set of analogies addressed issues related to the dangers of intensive farming and related regulatory issues: BSE, dioxin in chicken, and the pork industry. The more diverse set of analogies from the second exercise consisted of stratospheric ozone depletion, the ban on tobacco advertising in

Formula 1 racing, and the death of native populations in the New World as a result of diseases imported by colonisers. With the exception of the analogy about the death of native populations, all addressed issues that occurred in the last 30 years, and most are still part of contemporary public and policy debate. As a result, we decided that in the experiment analogies need not only be drawn from historic cases.

The analogy session for the experiment was developed on the basis of experiences in the pilot sessions. Considering the time constraint on the stakeholder workshops, we chose not to do two rounds of analogies. Only one round was conducted and, to compensate for the loss of an extra round, we tried to inspire in the participants to draw novel analogies from the very start of the exercise. To that end, the participants were given two examples of possible analogous cases where discontinuous developments took place. Each presentation described a past case that might have parallels with salmon aquaculture. One presentation described the aftermath of the sinking of the Prestige in November 2002, which exposed flaws in legislation and crisis management procedures, and resulted in large economic and ecological impacts. A second presentation described the 1995 Brent Spar affair, which demonstrated the severe impact that public relations crises might have on organisations. After the presentations the stakeholders were asked to propose other possible analogous cases to salmon aquaculture in a short brainstorm round. Subsequently, three analogies were selected for further investigation in break-out groups of up to five people. The stakeholders were free to choose which groups they wished to join. The groups were then asked to consider the possible parallels between salmon farming and the analogous case. Several sub-questions were used to help the stakeholders in completing the exercise. One of the questions directly addressed the idea of discontinuity by referring to lessons that might be drawn from the analogous case in anticipation of surprising developments.

Method: Perspective-based imaging
The idea of perspective-based imaging as a discontinuity-oriented approach was inspired by the imaging technique and perspective-based techniques, described in Chapter 4. Imaging, as proposed by Kates and Clark[23;24], involves the positing of an unlikely event and the construction of a plausible chronology of developments by that event might be realised. Experimentation with the approach took place in the Beyond Hunger[26] and the Surprising Futures[27] studies[11]. In both cases several 'surprise-rich' futures were developed.

The theoretical basis of perspective-based analysis lies in the idea that such factors as norms, values, and experience influence individuals' views of the world. This

---

[11] These studies are described more extensively in Chapters 2 and 4.

CULTURAL THEORY'S TYPOLOGY OF PERSPECTIVES

Cultural Theory describes four, and at times five perspectives: the hierarchist, egalitarian, individualist, fatalist, and hermit. The first three perspectives are often referred to as active perspectives, because they share an action-oriented world-view and management style.

Egalitarians hold that all humans are born 'good', but that they are highly malleable. Just as human nature can be corrupted by bad influences, it can be positively guided by an intimate relationship with nature and other people. Self-realisation lies in spiritual growth rather than in the consumption of goods. The egalitarian world-view implies a risk-averse attitude. The associated management style can therefore be characterised as preventative. With regard to the capitalist economic system, drastic and structural social, cultural, and institutional changes are advocated. The egalitarian believes that nature is fragile. Small disturbances might have catastrophic effects. Any man-made change is likely to be detrimental to the environment. Activities that might harm the environment should be avoided.

For the *individualist*, human nature is based on self-seeking behaviour. Human beings are considered to be rational self-conscious actors seeking to fulfil their ever-increasing materialistic needs. Individualists believe that changes provide opportunities for human ingenuity that will manifest itself through market mechanisms. The individualist is risk seeking, believing that highly unlikely negative consequences of human activity will be resolved by technological solutions. The management style of the individualist is adaptive. Nature is robust, when regarded from an individualist perspective. Anthropogenic disturbances, even if they are large, will merely result in mild and harmless disruptions. The individualist considers humans to be at the centre of the universe, while nature is seen as the provider of resources that can be exploited.

Hierarchists consider humans to have been born in sin, but that they can and should be educated by good institutions. The role of management is to prevent serious problems by careful control so that the system is kept within its limits. This management style of control can be associated with a risk-accepting attitude. Hierarchists believe that nature is robust within certain limits, and that nature can cope with small disturbances. However, once a threshold has been reached, anthropogenic disturbances pose a threat to the functioning of nature. The hierarchist's attitude towards man and emphasises his dependence on nature, and nature's dependency on him. A balance between human and environmental values must be maintained.

Textbox 2 *The Cultural Theory perspectives*   Adapted from: Van Asselt[36]

idea has been presented in various ways in a number of disciplines, including philosophy[28;29;30], cognitive psychology[31], physics[32], and management science[19;33]. Perspective-based scenario development as proposed by Rotmans and Van Asselt[34;35;36;37] uses ideas developed in cultural anthropological and political scientific research contained in what is referred to as Cultural Theory[38;39;40]. The perspectives proposed by the theory are summarised in Textbox 2.

The use of perspectives in scenario development involves investigating possible paths to the future on the basis of different perspectives on how the world works and how it should be managed[36]. The development and comparison of these perspectives might lead to new insights about the progress of current developments not manifested when viewed from a single perspective[36]. Initial experimentation with the perspectives approach took place in the TARGETS study[34;35;41] and a related endeavour[42]; the environmental outlooks of the Dutch National Institute of Public Health and the Environment (RIVM)[36]; and a study for the design of water management strategies for the Rhine and Meuse rivers[43]. The Shield of Achilles[44] and Norway 2030[45] studies also worked with perspectives but the lack of documentation on the their use suggests that their application was not based on a methodological decision, but more a matter of presentation.

Experiences with imaging and perspectives motivated us to further experiment with the techniques. We combined the two so that the imaging approach might stimulate participants to explore the future, and the perspectives technique might encourage them to do so from several vantage points. Perspective-based imaging was tested in the pilot sessions. The pilot's participants were split into three-person groups. In the first exercise the participants worked solely with the imaging technique. They were asked to think of a possible discontinuous future for salmon farming in 2023 and to describe the events and processes that could occur between 2003 and 2023, leading to that future state. The participants were then asked to repeat the exercise from the point of view of a Cultural Theory perspective. Each group was given a different perspective to work with and asked to answer the question: "if hierarchist/ individualist/ egalitarian interests were to be given a 'carte blanche', what would salmon aquaculture look like in 2023?" In a reference to discontinuity, the participants were also asked to consider two disruptive events that would be influential on the break out groups' respective perspectives.

Positive experiences with the perspective-based imaging in the pilot sessions motivated us to use it in the experiment. The participants were asked to develop three extreme images of possible salmon farming futures in 2023 on the basis of perspectives outlined in Cultural Theory. In addition to the 'carte blanche' question asked in the pilot sessions, the participants were asked: "What would the path of development to that future look like? What indications were there in the past 20 years to suggest that such a future might arise? What abrupt or gradual changes might alter the path of development that you envisage?" The participants were grouped according to the perspectives that most closely represented the participant group that they represented. Experience from the above-mentioned water management study[43] suggested that groups containing a strong mix of perspectives might spend a disproportionate amount of time debating the cultural theory perspectives, resulting in an unconstructive group dynamic. The composition of the egalitarian group was different from the rest, in part because of the difficulty in recruiting NGOs who would have been assigned to this perspective. The two free spirits, in addition to a researcher, were assigned to the egalitarian perspective to see whether they would provide the novel ideas expected of them.

DESIGN OF DISCO 1.0

Main factors in the design:
- group variety
- open structure
- discontinuity guardianship
- 3 discontinuity-oriented methods

Preparation
- Drafting of position paper for use as basic information for participants and for programming the idea of discontinuity

Staggered brainwriting *
- Group brainwriting exercise: what are key issues for the future of farmed salmon?
- Individual brainwriting exercise: what hidden developments might have a surprising impact on the future of farmed salmon?
- Clustering of ideas

Analogies *
- Presentation on the sinking of the Prestige (example of discontinuity)
- Presentation on the Brent Spar affair (example of discontinuity)
- Plenary: What analogies can you think of?
            Which would you like to further investigate?
- Group session: 3 groups elaborate on chosen analogy
- Plenary: presentations of analogies for salmon aquaculture

Perspective-based imaging *
- Presentation: Perspectives in Cultural Theory
- Group session:
  o If 'your' perspective had a 'carte blanche' what would salmon aquaculture look like in 2023?
  o What would the path of development to that future look like?
  o What indications were there in the past 20 years to suggest that such a future might arise?
  o What abrupt or gradual changes might alter the path of development that you envisage?
- Plenary: Presentations of perspective-based images

Reflection on process

* = The methods can be applied simultaneously and independently rather than sequentially.

Textbox 3 *Process design for* DISCO *1.0 presented in the order in which the exercises were conducted.*

4.3 DISCO 1.0: *prototype for discontinuity-oriented scenario development*

The four factors described above were the basis of a propotype for discontinuity-oriented exploration in which we tried to ensure that the inspiring aspects were favoured over the impairing ones. We named the prototype DISCO 1.0, taken from the word discontinuity as an expression of the energy, playfulness, and openness that we felt was a feature of discontinuity-oriented thinking. The qualificiation '1.0' signifies that a first version of the prototype was being used. DISCO 1.0 is outlined in Textbox 3.

Our research was not a socio-psychological analysis, and the experimental nature of the research made a systematic comparison of observations problematic. One related problem was the lack of a satisfactory manner in which to measure or benchmark the results through a control group. The group of researchers that participated in the pilot sessions was too dissimilar to the experiment's participants for it to be used as a control group. Furthermore, the concept of a control group was in itself problematic for the experiment, since various of it's aspects could not be controlled. Examples of these aspects include the moods and personalities of the participants.

In summary, the research described in this chapter concerned a first experiment with discontinuity-oriented methodology. Conclusions were not definite, but provisional.

5 Output of the DISCO 1.0 experiment

In the following paragraphs we present the output from the various exercises, whereby we focus on the three methods we tested. The other factors are largely addressed in the subsequent section 6, in which the output is analysed.

5.1 *Staggered brainwriting*

The primary aim of the brainwriting session was to investigate whether conducting multiple rounds might help to exhaust the participants of ideas about discontinuity. The result of the brainwriting and clustering process is presented in Figure 5. The ideas from the second brainwriting round are presented in italics.

Forty ideas were proposed in the first round, a small number of which might qualify as discontinuous, including such incidents as food scares, the discovery of dangerous substances in farmed salmon, and the collapse of the aquaculture market. The 21 ideas that resulted from the second round were arguably more novel and discontinuity-oriented than those produced in the first round. Examples of the ideas proposed by stakeholders include such discontinuities as the collapse and bankruptcy of the aquaculture industry, the demise of edible fish, the realisation of a closed aquaculture system, and salmon becoming herbivorous.

The discontinuous ideas from the brainwriting exercise can be grouped in three categories: environmental impacts, technological breakthroughs, and commercial

6 EXPLORING DISCONTINUITY: AN EXPERIMENT

and consumer developments. Both positive and negative discontinuities were named in the first two categories. Environmental calamities included contamination of wild fish stocks and disease, endangering the existence of wild salmon. Positive environmental developments include the closing of the salmon aquaculture system, eliminating the burden on the environment.

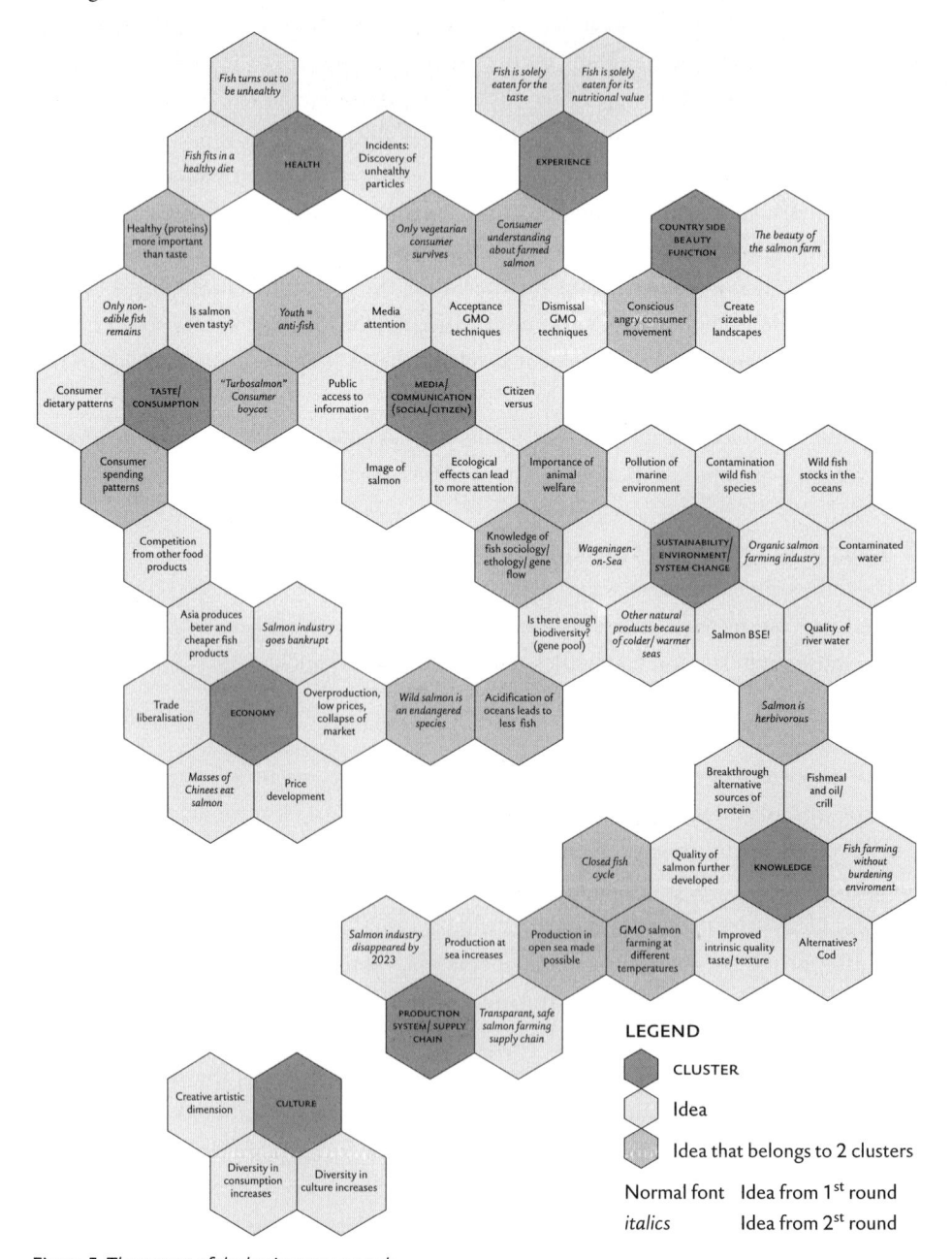

Figure 5 *The output of the brainstorm rounds.*

150

Discontinuity in commercial and consumer developments show a similar distribution of positive and negative outcomes. On the one hand, ideas proposed included the general turning away from eating fish by consumers, and the bankruptcy of the industry. On the other hand, one proposed idea speculated on the possibility of a massive expansion of the Chinese market for salmon.

Proposed technological breakthroughs included the discovery of alternative protein sources for fish feed and the earlier-mentioned closing of the aquaculture system. Salmon becoming herbivorous was a positive discontinuity from a technological and commerical perspective, but perhaps not from an ethical or environmental viewpoint.

Besides individual discontinuity-oriented ideas, there was also an entire cluster of ideas that addressed discontinuity under the name, 'system change', conceived by the participants. This cluster contained ideas such as pollution, organic salmon farming, and the creation of new products and production systems as a result of warming or cooling of the seas.

We conclude that the staggered brainwriting exercise produced a discontinuity-rich output.

5.2 Analogies

The aim of the analogy exercise was to investigate whether an examination of discontinuity in cases other than aquaculture might shed new light on possible future

---

PROPOSED ANALOGIES

- Intensive pig farming: ethical, and environmental issues and poor communication thereof. Also pricing issues.
- Ecological calamities
- CFCs and stratospheric ozone depletion
- Genetically modified organisms (GMOs): influential roles of NGOs and public sentiment in the UK
- Radiation of food: many potentially positive effects but the possible negative effects are given more attention in public debate.
- Air travel: Concorde crash in Paris, Challenger and Columbia disasters
- Corporate social responsibility and its communication
- Fur industry: from status symbol to taboo and banning of the industry
- Feed and food ingredients: traceability thereof
- Public debate about nuclear energy
- Salmonella and legionnaires disease: sporadic incidents but very scary and people die
- Fireworks disaster in Enschede (NL)

Textbox 4 *The analogies proposed by the stakeholders*

changes in the salmon farming industry. At the beginning of the exercise participants were asked to consider whether there were other, analogous cases that might provide an interesting vantage point from which to consider the issue of salmon farming. In a brief group brainstorm, the participants proposed 13 possible analogies, listed in Textbox 4.

Three analogies were selected for further investigation in break-out groups of up to five people. The selected analogies were 1) genetically modified organisms (GMOs); 2) chlorofluorocarbons (CFCs) and the ozone layer; and 3) sustainable development, corporate social responsibility (CSR) and public relations.

In contrast to that of the other two exercises, little of the groups' output in the analogy exercise referred to the idea of discontinuity. Instead, groups tended to present lessons for future strategy on the basis of the examined analogies. The idea of discontinuity was more conspicuous in the group discussions. The CSR discussion addressed in part the salmon industry's vulnerability to public criticism and the potentially devastating impact of food crises such as dioxin in chicken. One participant from the industry argued that they had a potential Brent Spar on their hands, because aquaculture companies are not taking heeding sufficiently public sensitivities with regards to animal welfare. S/he indicated that increased consumer knowledge about aquaculture's unsavoury production processes might significantly change dietary patterns. Group members mentioned the need to try to anticipate unexpected, abrupt discontinuity.

The GMO group addressed public relations issues in the context of the failed introduction of the GMO technology in Europe in the early 1990s. However, the group did not address the discontinuous nature of the debacle directly. An indirect indication of the group's awareness of the idea of discontinuity was the reference by one participant to, "the potential for gigantic problems" for the salmon industry.

The CFC group discussed the factors that contributed to a gradual discontinuity involving the termination of the CFC industry over a 20 year period in an effort to stop stratospheric ozone depletion, and the growing societal awareness of the impact of human activity on the environment. Factors included the interaction between environmental processes, scientific discoveries, technological innovation, public pressure, and regulation.

In conclusion, the output of the analogy exercise was not distinctly discontinuity-rich but an examination of the group discussions revealed several instances where the idea was discussed albeit it implicitly.

5.3 Perspective-based imaging

The perspective-based imaging exercise aimed to explore different perspectives on salmon aquaculture. The image of the future in 2023 created by the hierarchist group featured a less intensive, differentiated, locally-based salmon farming industry. This development was the consequence of a series of abrupt "Chernobyl-like" calamities. They included the discovery that wild salmon was no longer able to find its way back to their spawning grounds as a result of interbreeding with farmed salmon, and, later, the presentation of evidence by a renowned fish authority that wild salmon was nearly extinct. According to the hierarchist group, these events would breathe new life into the decaying European Union as it becomes the facilitator of a public debate on how to create 'honest salmon', a certified label for farmed salmon. The EU would also become the enforcer of subsequent legislation.

The future in 2023 as envisaged by the individualist group featured a blossoming fishing industry with a variety of healthy products. Technological innovation, such as widespread, closed-system fish farming and mobile fish farms at sea, would contribute significantly to the realisation of the individualist's image of the future. The group described abrupt discontinuities such as a BSE-type food scare, and the damaging health effects of poisonous chemicals in farmed fish.

The egalitarian group developed an image of the future based on the assumption that by 2023 there would be no more fishing industry and salmon aquaculture in Europe. Such a future would be a discontinuity in itself, given the large expansion of the industry in recent decades. Abrupt discontinuities that the group suggested would contribute to this future are health scares, European famine, fish stock collapse, the disruption of the fishing and aquaculture industries after bombings in traditional fishing villages, and a Greenpeace protest involving the dumping of farmed salmon in front of a supermarket. Gradual discontinuities in the egalitarian image, other than the decline of the industry include continued pollution, leading to a deep mistrust of sea-based products, a taboo on fish and meat products across society and the socio-economic impact thereof, as well as an emerging stigma on associated industries, much like the fur and the tobacco industries in recent decades.

As with the staggered brainwriting exercise, we conclude that the perspective-based imaging sessions produced discontinuity-rich output.

6 Analysis of the DISCO 1.0 experiment

In this section we reflect on the lessons that might be drawn from the DISCO 1.0 experiment. In particular we look at the experiment in terms of the inspiring, impairing, and double-edged factors for exploring discontinuity. We first discuss the methods used and then we reflect on the process from the point of view of group composition, open structure, and discontinuity guardianship.

6.1 Methods: Staggered brainwriting

From the staggered brainwriting exercise we conclude that the aim of progressively exhausting the stakeholders of ideas about discontinuity was achieved by conducting multiple rounds. A second contributing factor was the explicit programming of discontinuity in the second round and guardianship over the idea during the brainwriting session by prompting workshop participants during the exercises.

Did the interaction between stakeholders through the sharing of ideas stimulate thinking in terms of discontinuity? The interaction between the stakeholders in the group brainstorm was supposed to take place as they posted their post-its on flipover charts. However, despite encouragement by the facilitator, participant interaction did not materialise. Stakeholders remained seated until they had written down all their ideas. The fact that the brainwriting exercise was the first activity of the experiment and that participants still had to get accustomed to the process might have contributed to the lack of interaction. Another influencing factor might have been the awkward lay-out of the room. The flipover charts were poorly visible to the participants. The question remains whether a group session would have produced more and/or better ideas[12]. In any event, interaction turned out not to be a pre-requisite for the production of discontinuity-rich output.

6.2 Methods: Analogies

Although the output hardly reflected ideas about discontinuity in an explicit manner, all three discussions in the analogy session addressed discontinuity-related aspects. All groups addressed discontinuity from the point of view of its high impact and the influential role of such immaterial processes as public sentiment. Moreover, the CFC group used terms such as transition, surprise, structural change, and long-term societal change; all references to discontinuity. The recordings of the discussions between participants show a relatively large degree of talk about discontinuity.

There are indications that the drawing of analogies is a inspirational approach for exploring discontinuity. The drawing of analogies came easily to the participants. They had already drawn several analogies in the brainwriting and the perspective-based imaging exercise of their own accord. In the brainwriting session, for example, an analogy was drawn with hunting. In the perspective-based imaging exercise, analogies were drawn with social taboos and stigmas on tobacco, whaling, and fur. Several of these analogous cases might be considered discontinuous. In scenario literature, there is little reference to the use of analogies in contemplating the future. Therefore, in the absence of theoretical and empirical understanding of the analogies, we merely observe that in the DISCO 1.0 experiment analogies were drawn almost instinctively by the participants in all three of the sessions.

---

[12] The question of the effectiveness of group work versus individual work is investigated by Nijstad (2000).

6.3 Methods: Perspective-based imaging

In the perspective-based imaging exercise, the break-out groups considered a large variety of discontinuous events and processes, including socio-cultural changes, health and disease, environmental disaster, economic progress and decline, and technological mishaps and breakthroughs.

A proportionally higher number of abrupt, as opposed to gradual, discontinuities was proposed, suggesting that participants regarded discontinuity more in terms of events than of processes. The perspective-based imaging exercise allowed for a more elaborate description of the discontinuities than did the brainwriting exercise. There are indications that the comparison of perspectives led to new insights on potential discontinuities with at least a few participants, as stated by two of them in their feedback afterwards.

Numerous participants expressed their approval of the approach as a creative way to consider future possibilities and to make contrasting interpretations explicit. Although one participant experienced working within the boundaries of a perspective as a constraint, overall the Cultural Theory perspectives succeeded in producing alternative outlooks. Therefore, as with the brainwriting exercise, we conclude that perspective-based imaging was inspirational for thinking in terms of discontinuity.

6.4 Open structure

There were three design aspects in the open structure: organising the exercises as a set of independent exercises that could be conducted in any order; leaving the design of a second workshop open until after the first had taken place; and giving the participants considerable freedom.

The participants did not perceive the process to consist of a stepwise approach. For instance, the postponement of the analogy session as a result of a presenter's illness did not disrupt the process. This finding supports our idea that 'independent' exercises add to the flexibility of the process design. However, one participant suggested that a brainstorm or brainwriting exercise should always be taken as a first step. That way participants might propose their initial ideas and establish some common understanding, which then serves as a point of departure for other exercises. Another aspect that proved effective was designing the second workshop using experiences of the first.

The participants were generally positive about the structure of the workshops. There were no signs that the structure acted as a straightjacket, save one comment regarding the constraint of working within the boundaries of a perspective. There were no signs that participants felt lost in too freewheeling an approach. Therefore, it appears as though the DISCO 1.0 design of an open structure struck an adequate balance between a regimented and an uncontrolled approach.

6.5 Group variety

The aim of experimenting with group composition was to further investigate the relationship between group variety and discontinuity-richness of output. The stakeholder group represented a host of different affiliations with salmon aquaculture and related issues. The group at the second workshop was not only larger but also more diverse than the set at the first. The business community was better represented in the second workshop.

Numerous sources described in Chapters 4 and 5 argue that maintaining a broad overview and keeping an open mind to new ideas are necessary for thinking about discontinuity. The participants' feedback supported this argument, as well as the correlation between group diversity and thinking about discontinuity. Numerous participants voiced their appreciation of the group variety, indicating that it ensured that discussions addressed the "big picture" and that it made them open their eyes to new ideas and interpretations.

The value of group variety was highlighted by the constructive roles of the two free spirits. This was illustrated in the discussions of the egalitarian group during the perspective-based imaging exercise, in which a free-spirit expressed the need to posit "the extreme perspective" so as to ensure that the output of the break-out groups as a whole was highly divergent. S/he argued:

If one wants to posit an ecological [egalitarian] perspective [...] then we should develop an extreme image [of the future]. Otherwise it's no fun! Otherwise it would be like the council of EU ministers of agriculture; you end up with a compromise.

S/he consciously took an extreme position to stimulate and challenge the rest of the group to come up with eccentric and novel ideas. S/he did so by inviting participants to look beyond current salmon aquaculture and to draw on analogous cases of social taboo and the downfall of industries such as fur and tobacco. Also, the free spirit posited the idea that commercial fishing would no longer exist in Europe in 20 years time, which would be a discontinuous development.

The free spirits' contribution was also demonstrated in the analogy exercise in which the Brent Spar analogy was presented and which strongly inspired the subsequent discussions. Their role was also manifest in the analogy's break-out group exercise when a free spirit tried to counter the tendency by two stakeholders to focus solely on salmon, science, and policy, by offering more far-fetched analogies about the education of children, public awareness and appreciation of animal welfare. It is debateable whether the free spirit's input was effective here, because there are no indications that these suggestions were adopted in the output of that particular group's discussion. It demonstrates perhaps that the role of the free spirits might be beneficial to discontinuity-oriented exercises but that it sometimes is a difficult and demanding role. Nonetheless, free spirits' ability to challenge conventional thinking is related to ideas about personal qualities described in Chapter 4.

We conclude that the diversity of the group and its ability to keep a broad scope in combination with the novel input of the free-spirits contributed to an environment where the thinking about discontinuity was stimulated.

6.6 Discontinuity guardianship

There are indications that the participants' interest in discontinuity was kindled by the experiment, although they were probably not conscious of the prominent role it had played in the process design. In a debriefing session, even a project team member appeared unaware of the degree to which discontinuity had been weaved into the process design. Some participants were more attuned to the idea than others, which might be attributable to such differences in personal qualities as inquisitiveness and abductive powers, described in Chapter 4.

In Chapter 4 we found that a negative association with discontinuity is common and that it is a motivation for ignoring the idea. Given the frequent references to crises and calamities, we observe that the stakeholders generally regarded discontinuity as negative. This is all the more noteworthy because the facilitator pointed out to the group that the analogies might also describe positive situations. Only the CFC group discussed a topic that had a positive connotation. The same negative tendency is also apparent when looking at the analogies proposed in all three exercises: environmental and health disasters, crashes and other accidents, and discontinuity as a result of changing social norms and values. The tendency to see discontinuity in negative terms is common to many studies of the future, as demonstrated in the comparative review of Chapter 4.

The partial awareness of the role of discontinuity in the experiment's design corresponds to such consciousness in the VISIONS study. However, the VISIONS experience also demonstrated that discontinuity does not need to be prominent in the minds of stakeholders at all times in order for it to feature in the process and its output. There is evidence that the same phenomenon occurred in the DISCO 1.0 experiment because, despite only a partial appreciation of the prominence of discontinuity, the exercises produced a relatively large number of various discontinuities. To improve the process design one might emphasise and elaborate the idea of discontinuity in presentations to support stakeholders during discontinuity-oriented exercises, bearing in mind that participants should not feel that the idea is forced upon them. However, the question remains whether more intensive programming would lead to a keener interest in the idea of discontinuity and whether that would be reflected in the richness of the output. In any event, we conclude that discontinuity, guardianship and programming worked in an inspirational manner in the experiment.

7 Concluding remarks

In this chapter, we described the methodology of an experiment for discontinuity-oriented scenario development referred to as DISCO 1.0. In conducting the experiment, we aimed to test the hypothesis that discontinuity-oriented scenario development involves fostering the interplay of influential factors whereby inspiring ones are mobilised and impairing ones quashed. The experiment involved the design and conduct of an exploratory process in a workshop setting in order to observe participant behaviour under conditions intended to inspire discontinuity-oriented thinking. These conditions were created using insights from the comparative review (Chapter 4) and the VISIONS reconstruction (Chapter 5). The four influential factors on which DISCO 1.0 was based were group variety, an open structure, discontinuity guardianship, and a set of three methods.

On the basis of the generally discontinuity-rich output, we conclude that the interplay between the four inspiring factors in experimenting with DISCO 1.0 was a valuable step in developing procedures for discontinuity-oriented scenario methodology. The variety in the participant group, including the role of the free spirits, ensured that the future of aquaculture was discussed in broad terms, helping to open participants' eyes to different interpretations and new ideas about possible future developments. The open structure allowed the participants to explore the idea of discontinuity within the loose format of the three methods. The regular programming and guardianship of the idea of discontinuity led to an interest in investigating the idea, even if it was partial and unconscious at times. A virtue was made of the double-edged factor of underdeveloped methods by adopting an open and flexible approach.

It is conceivable that other factors also influenced the discontinuity-richness of the output. Facilitation, group dynamics, and the influence of current affairs and public sentiment, for example, might also have played a role. However, they were not investigated in the DISCO 1.0 experiment.

7
towards discontinuity-oriented scenario development

7 TOWARDS DISCONTINUITY-ORIENTED SCENARIO DEVELOPMENT

Societal developments do not solely progress in an evolutionary, linear manner but also in a discontinuous manner. Events in recent years such as the September 11th attacks and the collaps of communism are proposed illustrations of discontinuous developments. One would expect the idea of discontinuity to play a central role in scenario studies. We investigated this assumption by exploring the idea of discontinuity in the context of foresight and Integrated Assessment. Here we present a summary of findings, then an overview of hurdles for discontinuity-oriented scenario development, and we conclude with proposed challenges for future research on discontinuity.

1 Summary of findings

A typology for scenarios

Scenarios are coherent descriptions of alternative hypothetical futures that reflect different perspectives on past, present, and future developments, which can serve as a basis for action. In this thesis we presented our analysis of how the idea of discontinuity is addressed in scenario development. In order to develop an understanding of how the notion of discontinuity is addressed in scenario practice, we first established an overview of contemporary scenario studies. We examined approximately 100 studies carried out in the past 20 years. The development of a typology allowed us to organise the variety of studies into a framework in order to establish an overview of contemporary scenario practice. The 'macro' methodological characteristics of the typology were summarised in the 'scenario cartwheel' (Figure 1).

Broadly speaking, scenario exercises can be classified according to the studies' goal, the manner in which they are conducted, and the output that they deliver. Two basic categories of goals can be distinguished: exploration and pre-policy research. We also distinguished between two manners in which scenarios might be developed. On the one hand, there are intuitive approaches that typically involve elements of participatory work, workshops and interviews, for example. On the other hand, there is the more analytical approach that regards scenario development as a rigorous and systematic exercise. The resulting scenarios vary according to their complexity.

Discontinuity

We proposed the following definition of discontinuity in the context of scenario development on the basis of a literature review: a temporary or permanent, sometimes unexpected, break in a dominant condition in society caused by the interaction of events and long-term processes. We underpin this broad definition with several characteristics of discontinuity: its intrinsic difference with established trends, dominant patterns or paradigms; its high impact; its irreversibility or partial reversibility; its interconnection with various types of events and long-term processes; its combination of physical and immaterial processes; and discontinuity's dependence on the perspective from which it is regarded. The role of perspective and perception in discontinuity implies that its occurrence might come unexpectedly. Lastly, in addressing different views on the relative speed of change in the consulted sources, we distinguish between abrupt and gradual discontinuity. Abrupt discontinuity is characterised by a relatively instantaneous break with the status quo. Abrupt discontinuity gives society a jolt, even if it is of a temporary and partly reversible nature. Although events play a dominant role in the occurrence of abrupt discontinuity, underlying processes are also influential. Drawing on the concept of transitions, we describe gradual discontinuity as a steady, continuous process of change that leads to the transformation of a society, or a complex sub-system of society, over a period of at least one generation. Events play a role, but slower moving processes dominate gradual discontinuity.

Discontinuity-rich and discontinuity-poor scenarios

The typology was used in a comparative review of 30 studies representing a cross-section of contemporary scenario processes. The review aimed to provide insights in the types of scenario studies that are congenial to the notion of discontinuity. The results from the review are presented in the scenario cartwheel in Figure 1. Our research revealed that discontinuity is not addressed in scenario development as a matter of course. Approximately half of the examined studies omitted the idea of discontinuity. Of those studies that did address the notion, most were exploratory in nature and produced complex scenarios. Two thirds of the discontinuity-rich scenarios were developed in an intuitive manner.

Influential factors in discontinuity-oriented scenario development

The sources of the studies that developed discontinuity-rich scenarios provided little information about how they were developed. In order to establish a more detailed understanding of relevant factors for the exploration of discontinuity we reconstructed the VISIONS scenario study, which we identified in our comparative review as one of the studies that produced discontinuity-rich scenarios. Using the reconstruction we analysed whether the scenario process that produced discontinuity-rich scenarios was discontinuity-oriented. The reconstruction addressed three types of issues: people involved in the study, methods and concepts, and procedural issues.

The VISIONS reconstruction did not result in the identification of a single success factor for the exploration of discontinuity. Instead, it revealed that an interplay of inspiring, impairing, and double-edged factors resulted in discontinuity-rich output. Examples of these factors include group variety, team synergy, knowledge and expertise, open structure, and discontinuity guardianship. The reconstruction allowed us to formulate the following research hypothesis: discontinuity-oriented scenario development involves fostering the interplay of influential factors wherby inspiring ones are mobilised and impairing ones are quashed. The degree to which output was discontinuity-rich was the measure for our hypothesis and therefore the interplay of influencing factors was considered more relevant than the workings of individual inspiring factors.

Prototype for discontinuity-oriented scenario development
In order to test the hypothesis, we developed a prototype for a discontinuity-oriented experiment, named DISCO 1.0. The prototype was based on four factors selected from the VISIONS reconstruction: group variety, open structure, discontinuity guardianship, and underdeveloped methods and concepts. The experiment allowed us to observe a discontinuity-oriented exploratory process in a natural setting. Observations of the process indicated that the experiment's design provided a framework for discontinuity-oriented thinking in which the influence of impairing factors is reduced. The design is summarised in Textbox 1.

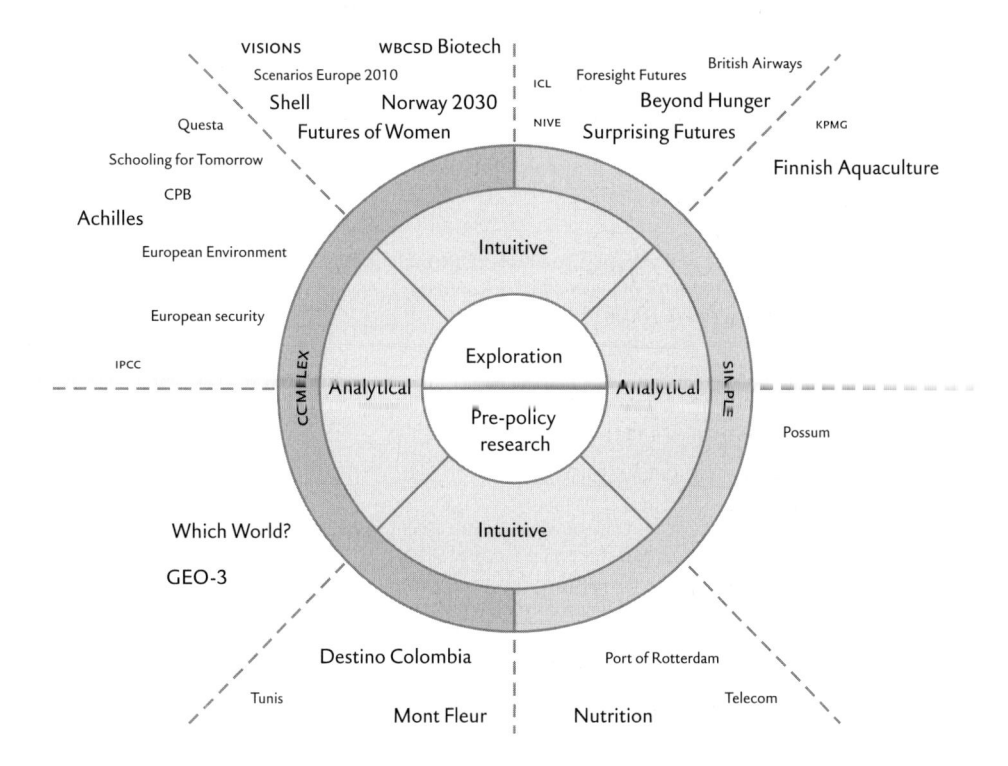

Figure 1 *The scenario cartwheel. Studies that include discontinuity are highlighted.*

There is not one single success factor for discontinuity-oriented scenario development. Like the VISIONS reconstruction, the DISCO 1.0. experiment demonstrated that several interacting factors contributed to the development of discontinuity-rich output. The experiment showed that it was possible to design a systematic and reproducable discontinuity-oriented process. We therefore conclude that the hypothesis withstood the first intellectual challenge.

Does discontinuity-oriented scenario development have a future?
In our research we came across various reasons why scenario developers might ignore the notion of discontinuity, such as methodological difficulties, institutional

---

DESIGN OF DISCO 1.0

Main factors in the design:
- group variety
- open structure
- discontinuity guardianship
- 3 discontinuity-oriented methods

Preparation
- Drafting of position paper for use as basic information for participants and for programming the idea of discontinuity

Staggered brainwriting *
- Group brainwriting exercise: what are key issues for the future of farmed salmon?
- Individual brainwriting exercise: what hidden developments might have a surprising impact on the future of farmed salmon?
- Clustering of ideas

Analogies *
- Presentation on the sinking of the Prestige (example of discontinuity)
- Presentation on the Brent Spar affair (example of discontinuity)
- Plenary: What analogies can you think of?
            Which would you like to further investigate?
- Group session: 3 groups elaborate on chosen analogy
- Plenary: presentations of analogies for salmon aquaculture

Perspective-based imaging *
- Presentation: Perspectives in Cultural Theory
- Group session:
   o If 'your' perspective had a 'carte blanche' what would salmon aquaculture look like in 2023?
   o What would the path of development to that future look like?
   o What indications were there in the past 20 years to suggest that such a future might arise?
   o What abrupt or gradual changes might alter the path of development that you envisage?
- Plenary: Presentations of perspective-based images

Reflection on process

* = The methods can be applied simultaneously and independently rather than sequentially.

Textbox 1   *The DISCO 1.0 design*

barriers and a failure to see the idea's relevance. It is reasonable to ask whether we are content to continue to be surprised, given the complications involved in trying to anticipate discontinuity. Discontinuity need not be a negative phenomenon. Moreover, we do not contend that all scenario studies need consider it. The decision to address discontinuity should be dependent on the goal and context of a study. To illustrate, the idea of discontinuity might not be given a high priority for the development of simple scenarios for assessing the short-term impact of a new product introduction in a stable market. The level of uncertainty in the issue might be judged to be so low that a focus on discontinuity would be irrelevant. Is it therefore worth the investment in trying to pre-empt it? Perhaps not! However, if the objective is to conduct an exploratory study of future societal developments then further research is beneficial in view of both the possibility of discontinuity and the relatively sparse research on the idea to date in the context of foresight and integrated assessment.

2 Hurdles for discontinuity-oriented scenario development

Our research demonstrated that many scenarios do not address the concept of discontinuity as a matter of course. Indeed, we found that discontinuity-oriented scenario development is more complicated than we anticipated. If we deconstruct the complications involved in discontinuity-oriented scenario development we learn that they manifest themselves on four interconnected levels: epistemological, analytical, contextual, and procedural.

Epistemological hurdles

On an epistemological level, the idea of discontinuity is difficult to grasp in scenarios because it describes events and processes in an uncertain, unknowable future. It is difficult to accommodate future discontinuity in present-day frames of reference. Instead, there is the tendency to reason from some evolutionary development whereby the future is considered to be a logical consequence of causal patterns in the past and present.

In Chapter 4 we indicated that a possible underlying reason for omitting the idea of discontinuity is that the evolutionary paradigm or the progressive image of the future is dominant in many visions. This paradigm reasons from the idea of incremental progress to the future, whereby excluding the idea of discontinuity. Herman Kahn[1] draws our attention to the dominant tendency to think in conventional terms:

> *History is likely to write scenarios that most observers would find implausible not only prospectively but sometimes, even in retrospect. Many sequences of events seem plausible now only because they have actually occurred; a man who knew no history might not believe any. Future events may not be drawn from the restricted list of those we have learned are possible; we should expect to go on being surprised.*

Evolutionary thinking is not limited to a particular type of scenario study. Even the more exploratory studies suffer from the natural tendency to reason in terms of evolutionary development. Despite efforts to produce discontinuity-rich scenarios, there is evidence that the evolutionary paradigm played a role in VISIONS, in some of the work to make the scenarios plausible and consistent. This was manifest in the attempts to make the scenarios 'realistic', the discontinuities became less pronounced.

Analytical hurdles

Discontinuity is analytically complicated because it is difficult to define and conceptualise. It is inherently ambiguous. This ambiguity arises because discontinuity is subject to the perspective from which it is regarded: spatial, temporal, and disciplinary, for example. What seems discontinuous in the short term might appear continuous when regarded from a long-term perspective, and vice versa. An added complication in the analysis of the idea of discontinuity is that its manifestations can take a variety of forms, from abrupt environmental calamities and technological breakthroughs, to gradual social transformations, for example. It is therefore difficult to examine discontinuity other than through examples. These analytical complications make it difficult to judge whether a scenario is discontinuity-rich or not. Like epistemological ambiguity, the analytical problems associated with the idea of discontinuity apply to all types of scenario development.

Contextual hurdles

The context - institutional, cultural, and political, for example – can exert pressure on a scenario study that compromises its exploratory character. The VISIONS reconstruction highlighted the benefits of a research environment relatively free of contextual constraints. The study's sponsor did not impose demands regarding the conduct of the study. A study's output often becomes more conservative when subjected to contextual influences such as peer or political pressure, and unconventional ideas, including those about discontinuity, are frequently filtered out. We addressed a number of such studies in Chapter 4. Another type of contextual challenge is the social dynamics between those involved in a scenario process. Again, the VISIONS reconstruction proved insightful by offering examples of obstructive behaviour that hindered discontinuity-rich thought.

Procedural hurdles

The procedural complications were a focus of our research, which produced insights about the interplay of inspiring, impairing, and double-edged factors. These include factors such as group composition, structure, discontinuity guardianship, and underdeveloped methods. The procedural difficulties involved in discontinuity-oriented scenario development are tied to the other three types of complications. From an epistemological and analytical point of view, the difficulty involves the manner in which an ambiguous and counter-paradigmatic idea can be made concrete enough to use in a scenario process. With regards to the contextual hurdles, no procedure for discontinuity-oriented scenario development is successful if it is not supported by the institutional and political context in which it is carried out. The complications are exacerbated by the absence of established discontinuity-oriented procedures.

How might hurdles be overcome?

What does the set of hurdles involved in the exploration of discontinuity mean for scenario methodology? In this thesis we argued that discontinuity-oriented scenario development is not solely a matter of methods and techniques. The reconstruction of VISIONS and the DISCO 1.0. experiment demonstrated that a broad methodological scope is necessary for discontinuity-oriented scenario development. However, in hindsight we observe that DISCO 1.0. focussed mainly on broadening procedural methodology for exploring the idea of discontinuity. We paid attention to some contextual factors in our selection of the case study in our effort to make the experiment relatively true to life. This is exemplified in our efforts to involve stakeholders rather than substitutes, and to ensure that there be little interference from the experiment's sponsor. We did not overcome all epistemological and analytical complications of the idea of discontinuity.

To conclude, we contend that our relatively broad methodological approach was still not broad enough, and epistemological, analytical and contextual aspects proved more important than we had anticipated. Further experimentation with discontinuity-oriented scenario development would benefit from a more explicit, systematic exploration of these aspects.

3 Rising to the challenge: fostering cultures of curiosity

We argue that an appreciation of the idea of discontinuity and its complications on epistemological and analytical levels is necessary if it is to be adequately addressed on a procedural and contextual level. Procedural improvements are unlikely to stimulate the exploration of discontinuity if the frame of mind of those involved in the scenario study is indifferent or hostile to the idea of discontinuity. Therefore, the common focus in scenario practice on procedural aspects as expressed in rhetoric about 'tools', 'toolboxes', methods, and techniques is simple and naïve. We propose that methodological improvement should focus more broadly on the development and fostering of cultures of curiosity in scenario studies, in which an interest in future discontinuity is created, facilitated, and fostered on epistemological, analytical, procedural, and contextual levels.

Cultures of curiosity

We propose the idea of 'cultures of curiosity' as a way to facilitate discontinuity-oriented scenario development. Cultures of curiosity in discontinuity-oriented scenario processes are environments driven by inquisitiveness and imaginative thinking about future discontinuity. Such a culture involves an interaction between a set of epistemological, analytical, procedural, and contextual factors in a self-reinforcing manner.

On an epistemological level, cultures of curiosity work from a desire to explore the concept of discontinuity in future contexts. The basic assumption is that the future might well be structurally different from the present; few certainties about societal development are presumed, thereby challenging the evolutionary paradigm. In curiosity-driven processes, the interest in discontinuity is also reflected in the vocabulary used. Terms, metaphors and examples denoting change are common; those conveying continuity are rare. On an analytical level, the ambiguous nature of discontinuity is a source of interest, rather than of discomfort. Cultures of curiosity rely on a process with an open structure to facilitate inquisitiveness and imaginative thinking. Such a process is designed to foster the interplay of influential factors whereby inspiring ones are mobilised and impairing ones are quashed. These factors include those that we addressed in Chapters 5 and 6, such as group variety, team work and spirit, and discontinuity guardianship. They also include the positive aspects of the double-edged factors: knowledge and expertise, methods and concepts, and the scenario writing process. On a contextual level, for a culture of curiosity to flourish the institutional and political constraints should be minimal.

The DISCO 1.0. prototype was a first step in creating a culture of curiosity for discontinuity-oriented scenario development. However, the experiment with DISCO 1.0 was ad hoc and not embedded in an organisation or full-fledged scenario process. A culture of curiosity needs to be grounded in an organisational and/or strategic context, if it is not to be short-lived.

Fostering cultures of curiosity

Creating, facilitating, and fostering cultures of curiosity makes certain demands on a scenario process design. On an epistemological level, interest in the idea of discontinuity would need to be stimulated. Eye-catching events and developments in recent years might have already contributed to such an increased interest. The current thesis might make a contribution as well. In any event, on an epistemological level, interest in discontinuity would require a realisation that thinking in terms of discontinuity is counter-paradigmatic. Such a realisation might also involve questioning such basic tenants of scenario practice as the notions of plausibility and consistency, since these might involve ignoring the possibility of discontinuity.

Given the counter-paradigmatic nature of reasoning from discontinuity, the notion needs to be nurtured if it is become embedded in a scenario process.

From an analytical point of view a scenario process might benefit from a rudimentary concept of discontinuity used as a dummy or straw man at the start of the study to stimulate thinking about the notion. DISCO 1.0 did not include a concept of discontinuity in part to avoid the danger that workshop participants feel constrained. However, time might be allocated at the start of a scenario process so that those people involved in the study can explore and agree on a concept of discontinuity. The concept should not be rigid, but adaptable as the scenario study progresses. Those involved in a scenario process should keep an open mind throughout and avoid a dogmatic adherence to concepts or ideas, since such behaviour might constrain the exploratory process. A shared concept can help to make the idea of discontinuity concrete, to create a vocabulary for discontinuity-oriented discussions, and to provide a basis for exchanging ideas and examples during a scenario study. A shared concept of discontinuity might help raise an awareness of discontinuity and ensure its guardianship during the course of the study.

On a contextual level, it is important to nurture those environments that foster independent curiosity-driven research. These appear to be diminishing at present [1]. Curiosity-driven research has traditionally been the task of universities. However, today's universities are being pressured to work in a more market-oriented and customer-driven manner, and there are fewer opportunities for research that deviates from established paradigms. Nor are cultures of curiosity usually found in contexts of client-based research, because the type of output is often constrained by the desires of the client. These cultures are also generally absent in regulatory institutions, interested in the optimal functioning of the existent system. The idea of discontinuity is often unwelcome to those who have an interest in maintaining the status quo. Little deviation from the path is possible in client-based and regulatory contexts because the desired output is usually in tune with conventional paradigms. As a result, thoughts that do not conform to the paradigm are dismissed. Possibilities for creating environments of curiosity-driven research might include buttressing independent research at universities as well as setting up platforms for multi-stakeholder dialogue about societal issues and their future. Such platforms are currently being experimented with in the context of transition management in various parts of the Dutch civil service[2].

On a procedural level, the experience of DISCO 1.0 provides a valuable basis from which to experiment with new methodological options for creating cultures of curiosity and producing insights about discontinuity. A scenario team might introduce an explicit discontinuity-oriented component in a design phase of a scenario process. This

---

[1] The comments about curiosity-driven research are inspired by a discussion with Poul Harremoës and David Gee.

might include an awareness-raising session preceding the scenario development process. Such a session would aim to familiarise those involved in the scenario process with the idea of discontinuity and the epistemological, analytical, and contextual challenges raised. The session might further help the exploration of future discontinuity during the scenario study. Besides establishing a shared concept of discontinuity, the scenario team might agree on some rules of conduct, including giving yellow and red cards – like in football – to those who dismiss the possibility of discontinuous developments occurring. Such rules might help team members assume a joint responsibility for discontinuity guardianship. Further research might experiment with such an awareness-raising session or other alternatives to ensure that a positive attitude towards the idea of discontinuity is embedded in a scenario process.

Other methodological options include those that we identified earlier but did not incorporate in the design of DISCO 1.0 For instance, potentially valuable insights might be gained from such novel modelling techniques as Chance Discovery[3] and asking experts what future developments would surprise them. Besides raising awareness about the concept of discontinuity, these techniques might help establish insights about possible future discontinuities.

Also Braudel's three-layered conceptual model of time might be used as an aid for overcoming analytical hurdles in exploring discontinuity. Through our discussion of the September 11th attacks and the rise of environmental concern in chapter 3, we showed how discontinuous developments often involve the interaction of a variety of events and societal processes on different time scales. Braudel's model appears to be a useful heuristic for analysing how discontinuities might arise and for identifying possible future discontinuities. Although a similar model to Braudel's is referred to in some scenario literature[4;5], we have not found evidence of its use or Braudel's in the studies that we examined.

4 Issues for further interdisciplinary research

There are other, more general issues than those related to cultures of curiosity that are worthy of further investigations. In the DISCO 1.0 experiment, we omitted factors such as obstructive behaviour, teamwork, and institutional barriers. The analysis of other scenario studies than in the current thesis might bring to light more inspiring, impairing, or double-edged factors, or elaborate those that we identified. Therefore, we recommend the investigation of studies that produced discontinuity-rich scenarios with a view to establishing better insight into the inspiring or impairing factors that contribute to particular outputs.

It might be useful to investigate the personal qualities and group dynamics that influence thinking about discontinuity in the context of a scenario process. Establishing a better understanding of the effect of these factors with a view to developing cultures of curiosity requires cognitive and social psychological research. Although some psychological research of scenario development has taken place[6;7;8;9], as far as we know, there has not been any such investigation of discontinuity-oriented processes. Psychological and sociological research might also shed more light on the epistemological complications of thinking in terms of discontinuity.

The DISCO 1.0 experiment did not lead to full-fledged scenarios. Instead, discontinuity-rich input that can be used to draft scenarios was produced. The VISIONS reconstruction demonstrated that the writing and revising of scenarios and the negotiations this involves are important parts of discontinuity-oriented scenario development and sometimes serve to diminish ideas about discontinuity. We propose the writing phase as an issue for further research. To research it adequately would involve analysing the socio-cultural influences that motivate behaviour in a scenario process. The ethnographic research that this requires was beyond the scope of our research². Ethnographic research might also provide insights into specific influences of institutional contexts in which discontinuity-oriented scenario development is carried out. For example, attitudes and decisions made by sponsors of a scenario study can have a strong influence on curiosity-driven research, one that cannot be fully understood from the research data that we collected. A further investigation of these factors would also benefit from ethnographic research of scenario processes. A rare example of such research is Dobbinga's[10] organisational anthropological study of a scenario process at a Dutch ministry³.

Lastly, our research focussed on discontinuity-oriented scenario development, rather than the use of scenarios. It is possible that the influencing factors that we identified, as well as others, also play a role in the use of discontinuity-rich scenarios in decision-making contexts. The use of scenarios in decision-making has not been the subject of much research[11;12]. Such research might provide valuable insights into the epistemological and contextual obstacles for discontinuity-oriented scenario development in policy-making environments. Investigating these questions would require the involvement of policy scientists and business administrators, among others, in the interdisciplinary research of foresight and integrated assessment. Current research by policy scientists Hoppe et al.[13] involves the study from a policy scientific perspective of Dutch policy advisory institutes that also conduct scenario studies. Although the research does not focus specifically on the use of scenarios, it might provide interesting policy scientific insights for the use of discontinuity-rich scenarios in policy-making.

---

² In contrast to our research, Van der Duin's upcoming thesis of scenario processes in the private sector will include some ethnographic components. The publication of his thesis is expected in 2005.
³ Moreover, ethnographic research is currently being carried out by Van Asselt and Van't Klooster in the public sector as part of the research programme on foresight methodology, of which the current thesis is a product.

In summary, besides the type of research described in the current thesis, further experimentation with discontinuity-oriented scenario methodology would require other types of disciplines, research strategies and tests; a few of which we propose in this section.

5 Towards deciphering the writing on the wall

To conclude, we contend that efforts to improve discontinuity-oriented scenario development should concentrate on the creation and fostering of cultures of curiosity rather than the design of the ultimate 'discontinuity tool'. To achieve this, we emphasise the need for an open, creative methodology for stimulating discontinuity-oriented thinking. We underscore this with a liberal use of Alfred Whitney Griswold's words[14]:

> *Could Hamlet have been written by a committee, or the Mona Lisa painted by a club? Could the New Testament have been composed as a conference report?*

In the introductory chapter we discussed the writing on the wall at King Belshazzar's feast, warning of an imminent discontinuity. Deciphering the writing proved to be difficult, and of all the king's magicians only Daniel was successful. Similarly challenging is the exploration of discontinuity in the context of scenario development. However, we hope that this thesis will contribute to an increased capacity to consider the writing on the wall in times of discontinuity.

References for chapter 1

[1] The White House - Office of the Press Secretary (September 20th, 2001). Address to a Joint Session of Congress and the American People. Washington, D.C.
[2] Schwartz, P.: *Inevitable Surprises*. The Free Press, London, 2003.
[3] Soros, G.: The Bubble of American Supremacy, *The Atlantic Monthly*, 292(5) (2003).
[4] Boorstin, D. J.: *The Americans: The Democratic Experience*. Random House, New York, 1973.
[5] Huntingdon, S. P.: *The clash of civilizations and the remaking of world order*. Simon & Schuster, New York, 1996.
[6] Barber, B. R. and Schulz, A.: *Jihad vs. McWorld: How Globalism and Tribalism Are Reshaping the World*. Ballantine Books, New York, 1996.
[7] Nowotny, H., Scott, P. and Gibbons, M.: *Re-Thinking Science: Knowledge and the public in an age of uncertainty*. Polity Press in assoc. with Blackwell, Cambridge (UK), 2001.
[8] Rotmans, J.: Integrated thinking and acting: a necessary good (in Dutch), *ICIS*, Maastricht, the Netherlands (1998).
[9] Drucker, P. F.: *The Age of Discontinuity*. Harper and Row, New York, 1968.
[10] Mazlish, B.: *The Fourth Discontinuity: The Co-Evolution of Humans and Machines*. Yale University Press, New Haven and London, 1993.
[11] Fukuyama, F.: *The great disruption: human nature and the reconstitution of social order*. The Free Press, New York, 1999.
[12] Dammers, E.: *Leren van de toekomst. Over de rol van scenario's bij strategische beleidsvorming (Learning from the future: the role of scenarios in strategic policy making)*. Eburon, Delft., 2000.
[13] Wiedemann, P. M., Karger, C. R. and Clauberg, M.: Early Risk Detection in Environmental Health: Feasibility Study. Report of the Action Programme "Environment and Health", Report number 200 61 218/09, (2002).
[14] De Wilde, R.: *De Voorspellers: een kritiek op de toekomstindustrie (The Predictors: a critique of the futures industry*. de balie, Amsterdam, 2000.
[15] Toffler, A.: *Future Shock*. Bantam Books, New York, 1970.
[16] Wells, H. G.: The discovery of the future, *Nature*, 15(1684) (1902).
[17] Kahn, H.: *On Thermonuclear War*. Princeton University Press, Princeton, 1961.
[18] Kahn, H.: *Thinking about the Unthinkable*. Weidenfeld and Nicolson, London, 1962.
[19] Kahn, H., The alternative world futures approach, in *Search for Alternatives: Public Policy and the Study of the Future*. F. Tugwell, Witrop, Cambridge 1973.
[20] Kahn, H. and Wiener, A. J.: *The Year 2000*. MacMillan, New York, 1967.
[21] Aligicia, P. D.: The challenge of the future and the institutionalization of interdisciplinarity: notes on Herman Kahn's legacy, *Futures*, 36(1), 67-83 (2004).
[22] Fuller, T., Future Studies and Foresight, in *Rescuing all our Futures*. Z. Sardar, Praeger, Westport, 134-145, 1999.
[23] Horton, A.: A simple guide to successful foresight, *Foresight*, 1(1) (1999).
[24] Bell, W.: *Foundations of Futures Studies: Human Science for a New Era. History, Purposes, and Knowledge*. Second printing 1997, Transaction Publishers, New Brunswick, 1997.
[25] Marien, M.: Futures studies in the 21st Century: a reality-based view, *Futures*, 34(3/4), 261-281 (2002).
[26] Bell, W.: Advancing future studies: a reply to Michael Marien, *Futures*, 34(5), 435-447 (2002).
[27] Bell, W.: A community of futurists and the state of the futures field, *Futures*, 34(3/4), 235-247 (2002).
[28] Slaughter, R. A.: Futures Studies as a civilization catalyst, *Futures*, 34(3/4), 349-363 (2002).
[29] Meadows, D. H., Meadows, D. L., Randers, J. and Behrens, W. W.: *The Limits to Growth*. Universe Books, New York, USA, 1972.
[30] Van der Heijden, K.: Can internally generated scenarios accelerate organisational learning?, *Futures*, 36(2), 145-159 (2004).
[31] Berkhout, F. and Hertin, J.: Foresight Futures Scenarios, *Greener Management International*, (37), 37-52 (2002).
[32] Berkhout, F., Hertin, J. and Jordan, A.: Socio-economic futures in climate change impact assessment: using scenarios as 'learning machines', Science and Technology Policy Research, University of Sussex, Brighton (1998).
[33] Department of Trade and Industry: Foresight Futures 2020: Revised scenarios and guidance, *Department of Trade and Industry*, London (2002).

[34] UNEP: *Global Environment Outlook 3: Past, present and future perspectives.* Earthscan, London, 2002.
[35] Van Asselt, M. B. A.: *Perspectives on Uncertainty and Risk: The PRIMA approach to decision support.* Kluwer, Dordrecht, The Netherlands, 2000.
[36] Rotmans, J.: *Transitiemanagement: sleutel voor een duurzame samenleving (Transition management: key to a sustainable society).* Van Gorcum, Assen, 2003.
[37] Vennix, J.: *Group Model Building: Facilitating Team Learning Using System Dynamics.* Wiley, Chichester, 1996.
[38] Rittel, H. W. J. and Webber, M. M.: Dilemmas in a general theory of planning, *Policy Sciences*, 4, 155-169 (1973).
[39] Bovens, M. and 't Hart, P.: *Understanding policy fiascoes.* Transaction Publishers, New Brunswick, 1996.
[40] Mason, R. and Mitroff, I., Complexity: The Nature of Real World Problems, in *Strategy Synthesis: Resolving strategy paradoxes to create competitive advantage.* B. De Wit and R. Meyer, International Thomson Business Press, London 1999.
[41] Hisschemöller, M. and Hoppe, R.: Coping with Intractable Controversies: the case for problem structuring in policy design and analysis, *Knowledge and Policy*, 8(4), 40-60 (1996).
[42] Rotmans, J.: Geintegreerd denken en handelen: een noodzakelijk goed (Integrated thinking and acting: a necessary good), ICIS, Maastricht, the Netherlands (1998).
[43] Rotmans, J.: Methods for IA: The challenges and opportunities ahead, *Environmental Modelling and Assessment*, 3(3), 155-179 (1998).
[44] Van Asselt, M. B. A., Rotmans, J. and Greeuw, S. C. H., Eds. *Puzzle solving for policy. A provisional handbook for Integrated Assessment.* ICIS, Maastricht, The Netherlands, 2001.
[45] Van Eijndhoven, J. C. M.: *The unbearable lightness of the debate: The contribution of Technology Assessment to the debate on science and technology (in Dutch).* Rathenau Institute, The Hague, the Netherlands, 1995.
[46] Risk Analysis., Blackwell Publishers.
[47] Geurts, J. L. A.: Omkijken naar de Toekomst: Lange-termijn verkenningen in beleidsexercities, *Katholieke Universiteit Brabant*, Tilburg, the Netherlands (1993).
[48] van Asselt, M. B. A. and Rijkens-Klomp, N.: A Look in the Mirror: Reflection on participation in Integrated Assessment from a methodological perspective, *Global Environmental Change*, 107-180 (2002).
[49] Blass, E.: Researching the future: method or madness?, *Futures*, 35, 1041-1054 (2003).
[50] Schneider, S. H., Turner II, B. L. and Morehouse Garriga, H.: Imaginable Surprise in Global Change Science, *Journal of Risk Research*, 1(2), 165-185 (1998).
[51] Kates, R. W. and Clark, W.: Environmental Surprise: Expecting the Unexpected, *Environment*, 38(2), 6-11 (1996).
[52] Myers, N.: Environmental Unknowns, *Science*, 269(21 July), 358-360 (1995).
[53] Holroyd, P.: Change and Discontinuity, *Futures*, 10(1), 31-43 (1978).
[54] Schmidt-Gernig, A., The Cybernetic Society, in *What the Future Holds: Insights from Social Sciences.* R. N. Cooper and R. Layard, The MIT Press, Cambridge 2002.
[55] Ester, P., Geurts, J. L. A. and Vermeulen, M.: *De makers van de toekomst: Over nut en noodzaak van toekomstverkenningen voor beleidsonderzoek (The makers of the future: The value and need for futures research for policy research).* Tilburg University Press, Tilburg, 1997.
[56] Van der Staal, P. M. and Van Vught, F. A.: Vijftien jaar toekomstonderzoek door de WRR: de uitgestelde methodologische reflectie, Deel 1 (Fifteen years of futures research at the WRR: the postponed methodological reflection, Part 1), *Beleidsanalyse*, 87(4), 16-25 (1987).
[57] Van Asselt, M. B. A. and Rotmans, J.: Uncertainty in integrated assessment modelling, from positivism to pluralism, *Climatic Change*, 54, 75-105 (2002).
[58] Stevenson, T.: The futures of futures studies, *Futures*, 33, 665-669 (2001).
[59] Davis, G.: Creating Scenarios for Your Company's Future, in: *The 1998 Conference on Corporate Environmental, Health, and Safety Excellence: Bringing Sustainable Development Down to Earth*, (1998) New York City
[60] Van Notten, P. W. F., Rotmans, J., Van Asselt, M. B. A. and Rothman, D. S.: An updated scenario typology, *Futures*, 35(5), 423-443 (2003).
[61] Kleiner, A.: *The Age of Heretics.* Doubleday, New York, 1996.
[62] Ringland, G.: *Scenario Planning.* John Wiley & Sons, Chichester, 1998.

[63] Popper, K.: *Conjectures and Refutations.* Roueledge, London, UK, 1963.
[64] Davis, G.: Scenarios as a tool for the 21st Century, in: *Probing the Future: Developing Organizational Foresight in the Knowledge Economy,* (2002) The University of Strathclyde Graduate School of Business, Glasgow
[65] Schwartz, P.: *The Art of the Long View: Planning for the Future in an Uncertain World.* Currency Doubleday, New York, 1991.
[66] Wack, P.: Scenarios: Shooting the Rapids, *Harvard Business Review,* 63(6), 139-150 (1985).
[67] Wack, P.: Scenarios: Uncharted Waters Ahead, *Harvard Business Review,* 63(5), 72-79 (1985).
[68] Greeuw, S. C. H., van Asselt, M. B. A., Grosskurth, J., Storms, C. A. M. H., Rijkens-Klomp, N., Rothman, D. S. and Rotmans, J.: Cloudy crystal balls : An assessment of recent European and global scenario studies and models, Copenhagen, Denmark : European Environmental Agency (EEA) Experts' corner report no. 4 : Prospects and scenarios (2000).
[69] Heinzen, B.: Political Experiments of the 1990s: The Use of Scenarios in the Public Domain, *The Deeper News,* (September 1994).
[70] Heinzen, B.: Pioneers of Persuasion: A Review of the Use of Scenarios in the Public Sector, *Scottish Enterprise,* Glasgow and London (1994).
[71] Stuurgroep Toekomstonderzoek en Strategisch Omgevingsbeleid: *Terugblik op toekomstverkenningen (A retrospective look at foresight studies).* Netherlands Scientific Council for Government Policy (WRR), The Hague, 2000.
[72] Futures of Future Studies: *Futures,* 34(3/4) (2002).
[73] Van Asselt, M. B. A., Storms, C. A. H. M., Rijkens-Klomp, N. and Rotmans, J.: Towards Visions for a Sustainable Europe: An overview and assessment of the last decade of European scenario studies, *ICIS,* Maastricht (1998).
[74] Babbie, E. R.: *The practice of social research.* Belmont, Wandsworth, 1975.
[75] Van Asselt, M. B. A., Bijker, W., Van 't Klooster, S. A., Van Notten, P. W. F. and Sleegers, A. M.: Discussienota: Vernieuwingsimpuls - Methodologie voor Toekomstverkenning (Discussion document: Innovational Research Incentive Scheme - Futures research methodology), *Faculty of Arts and Sciences, Maastricht University,* Maastricht (2003).

References for chapter 2

[1] Ringland, G.: *Scenario Planning*. John Wiley & Sons, Chichester, 1998.
[2] Kleiner, A.: *The Age of Heretics*. Doubleday, New York, 1996.
[3] De Geus, A.: *The Living Company: Growth, Learning and Longevity*. Nicholas Brealey, London, 1997.
[4] Van der Heijden, K., Bradfield, R., Burt, G., Cairns, G. and Wright, G.: *The Sixth Sense: Accelerating Organisational Learning with Scenarios*. Wiley & Sons, Chichester, 2002.
[5] Kahn, H., The alternative world futures approach, in *Search for Alternatives: Public Policy and the Study of the Future*. F. Tugwell, Witrop, Cambridge 1973.
[6] Wack, P.: Scenarios: Uncharted Waters Ahead, *Harvard Business Review*, 63(5), 72-79 (1985).
[7] Wack, P.: Scenarios: Shooting the Rapids, *Harvard Business Review*, 63(6), 139-150 (1985).
[8] Van Steenbergen, B.: *De Nieuwe Mens in de Toekomstige Wereldmaatschappij: Uitdagingen voor de Toekomstonderzoeker (The New Human in the Future World Society: Challenges for the Futures researcher)*. Nyenrode University, Breukelen, 2003.
[9] European Environment Agency and ICIS: Cloudy Crystal Balls: An assessment of recent European and global scenario studies and models,, (2000).
[10] Marien, M.: Futures studies in the 21st Century: a reality-based view, *Futures*, 34(3/4), 261-281 (2002).
[11] Masini, E. B. and Vasquez, J. M.: Scenarios as Seen from a Human and Social Perspective, *Technological Forecasting & Social Change*, (65), 49-66 (2000).
[12] Sparrow, O.: Making use of scenarios - From the vague to the concrete, *Scenario & Strategy Planning*, 2(5), 18 - 21 (2000).
[13] Godet, M. and Roubelat, F.: Creating the future: The use and misuse of scenarios, *Long Range Planning*, 29(2), 164-171 (1996).
[14] Van der Heijden, K. and Schutte, P.: Look before you leap: key questions for designing scenario applications, *Scenario & Strategy Planning*, 1(6) (2000).
[15] Jungermann, H.: Psychological Aspects of Scenarios, *NATO ASI series*, Vol G4(Environmental Risk Assessment, Technology Assessment and Risk Analysis) (1985).
[16] Jungermann, H.: Inferential Processes in the Construction of Scenarios, *Journal of Forecasting*, 4, 321-327 (1985).
[17] Jungermann, H. and Thuring, M., The Use of Mental Models for Generating Scenarios, in *Judgmental Forecasting*. G. Wright, John Wiley & Sons Ltd, Chichester, 245-266, 1987.
[18] Kahn, H. and Wiener, A. J.: *The Year 2000*. MacMillan, New York, 1967.
[19a] Schoemaker, P. J. H.: Multiple scenario development: Its conceptual and behavioural foundation, *Strategic Management Journal*, 14, 193 - 213 (1993).
[19b] Becker, H.A.: Handleiding voor het ontwerpen van scenario's (Guidebook for the development of scenarios), Vakgroep Planning en Beleid (Dept. of Planning and Policy, Utrecht University), Utrecht 1982
[20] Godet, M. and Roubelat, F.: Scenario Planning: An Open Future, *Technological Forecasting and Social Change*, 65(1), 1-2 (2000).
[21] Van der Heijden, K.: *Scenarios: the Art of Strategic Conversation*. Wiley, Chichester, 1996.
[22] Postma, T. J. B. M., et al: Toekomstverkenning met scenario's (Exploring the future using scenarios), *Bedrijfskunde*, 67(2), 2 - 19 (1995).
[23] Fahey, L. and Randall, M., What is scenario Learning?, in *Learning from the future*. L. Fahey and M. Randall, Wiley, USA, 3-21, 1998.
[24] Global Business Network: www.gbn.org, accessed on October 15th, 2003
[25] Rotmans, J.: Methods for IA: The challenges and opportunities ahead, *Environmental Modelling and Assessment*, 3(3), 155-179 (1998).
[26] Ringland, G.: *Scenarios in Business*. John Wiley & Sons, Chichester, 2002.
[27] Ringland, G.: *Scenarios in Public Policy*. John Wiley & Sons, Chichester, 2002.
[28] Berkhout, F. and Hertin, J.: Foresight Futures Scenarios, *Greener Management International*, (37), 37-52 (2002).
[29] Shell International: Scenarios: An Explorer's Guide, London (2003).
[30] Mendonça, S., Cunha, M. P., Kaivo-oja, J. and Ruff, F.: Wild cards, weak signals and organisational improvisation, *Futures*, 36(2), 201–218 (2004).
[31] Fuller, T., Argyle, P. and Morgan, P., Entrepreneurial Foresight; a case study in reflexivity, experiments, sensitivity and reorganisation, in *Developing Strategic Foresight in the Knowedge Economy: Probing the Future*. H. Tsoukas and J. Shepherd, Blackwell, Oxford 2003.

REFERENCES

[32] Schwartz, P.: *The Art of the Long View: Planning for the Future in an Uncertain World*. Currency Doubleday, New York, 1991.

[33] Dasgupta, S., Wang, H. and Wheeler, D.: Surviving Success: Policy Reform and the Future of Industrial Pollution in China, *The World Bank*, (1997).

[34] UNEP: *Global Environment Outlook 3: Past, present and future perspectives*. Earthscan, London, 2002.

[35] Ruokanen, T. and Nurmio, A.: *Finland - New Realities, Alternative Futures*. Sitra, Helsinki, 1996.

[36] De Bruin, J.: personal communication, January 21st, 2002

[37] Le Roux, P., et al.: The Mont Fleur Scenarios, *Weekly Mail and The Guardian Weekly*, (1992).

[38] Kahane, A., Imagining South Africa's Future: How Scenarios Helped Discover Common Ground, in *Learning from the Future: Competitive Foresight Scenarios*. L. Fahey and R. Randall, John Wiley & Sons, New York, 1998.

[39] Global Business Network: Destino Colombia, *Deeper News* 9(1) (1998).

[40] Institute of Economic Affairs and Society for International Development: *Kenya at the Crossroads*. Nairobi, 2000.

[41] Gallopin, G., Hammond, A., Raskin, P. and Swart, R.: Branch Points: Global Scenarios and Human Choice - A Resource Paper of the Global Scenario Group, *Stockholm Environment Institute, Sweden*, (1997).

[42] Intergovernmental Panel on Climate Change: *Emissions Scenarios*. Cambridge University Press, Cambridge, 2000.

[43] Bell, W.: Advancing future studies: a reply to Michael Marien, *Futures*, 34(5), 435-447 (2002).

[44] Bell, W.: A community of futurists and the state of the futures field, *Futures*, 34(3/4), 235-247 (2002).

[45] Marien, M.: My differences with Wendell Bell, *Futures*, 34(5), 449-456 (2002).

[46] Fahey, L. and Randall, R.: *Learning from the Future: competitive foresight scenarios*. John Wiley & Sons, USA, 1998.

[47] Heinzen, B.: *Pioneers of Persuasion: A Review of the Use of Scenarios in the Public Sector, Scottish Enterprise*, Glasgow and London (1994).

[48] Heinzen, B.: Political Experiments of the 1990s: The Use of Scenarios in the Public Domain, *The Deeper News* (September 1994).

[49] Stuurgroep Toekomstonderzoek en Strategisch Omgevingsbeleid: *Terugblik op toekomstverkenningen (A retrospective look at foresight studies)*. Netherlands Scientific Council for Government Policy (WRR), The Hague, 2000.

[50] Futures of Future Studies: *Futures*, 34(3/4) (2002).

[51] Ducot, C. and Lubben, H. J.: A typology for scenarios, *Futures*, 12(1), 15-57 (1980).

[52] Duncan, N. E. and Wack, P.: Scenarios Designed to Improve Decision Making, *Planning Review*, 22(4), 18-25, 46 (1994).

[53] Heugens, P. M. A. R. and van Oosterhout, J.: To boldly where no man has gone before: integrating cognitive and physical features in scenario studies, *Futures*, 33(10), 861-872 (2001).

[54] Dobbinga, E.: *Weerbarstigheid van organisatiecultuur: een organisatie-antropologische studie naar betekenisgeving aan moderne managementinstrumenten (Stubbornness of organisational culture)*. Eburon, Delft, 2001.

[55] Schoemaker, P. J. H., Twenty Common Pitfalls in Scenario Planning, in *Learning from the Future: competitive foresight scenarios*. L. Fahey and R. M. Randall, John Wiley & Sons, New York, 422-431, 1998.

[56] Rotmans, J., van Asselt, M. B. A., Anastasi, C., Greeuw, S., Mellors, J., Peters, S., Rothman, D. and Rijkens, N.: Visions for a sustainable Europe, *Futures*, 32(9-10), 809-831 (2000).

[57] Van Notten, P. and Rotmans, J.: The future of scenarios, *Scenario and Strategy Planning*, 1(3), 4-8 (2001).

[58] Hammond, A.: *Which World? Scenarios for the 21st century. Global destinies, regional choices*. Earthscan Publications Ltd, London, 1998.

[59] McKiernan, P., et al.: The low road: Scenarios for Scotland part II, *Scenario & Strategy Planning* 2(6) (2001).

[60] McKiernan, P., et al.: Scenarios for Scotland, *Scenario and Strategy Planning* 2(5) (2001).

[61] McKiernan, P., et al.: The high road, *Scenario and Strategy Planning* 3(1) (2001).

[62] Gertner, R. and Knez, M.: Speltheorie in de realiteit (Game theory in reality), *Het Financieele Dagblad: Supplement on strategy*, 12 - 13 (2000).

[63] Brussaard, T.: personal communication, 23 April 2002

[64] Van Notten, P. W. F.: Create the future: 21- 22 June workshop report, *ICIS*, Maastricht (2000).

[65] Rotmans, J. and Dowlatabadi, H., Integrated Assessment of Climate Change: Evaluation of Methods and Strategies, in *Human Choice and Climate Change: An International Social Science Assessment*. S. Rayner and E. Malone, Battelle Press, Washington, USA 1998.

[66] Ruff, F. and Mendonça, S., Futures Research at the Driver's Seat: Scenario Planning at DaimlerChrysler, in *Puzzle solving for policy. A provisional handbook for Integrated Assessment*. M. B. A. Van Asselt and J. Rotmans, ICIS, Maastricht 2001.

[67] Fink, A. and Schalke, O.: Scenario Management - An Approach for Strategic Foresight, *Competitive Intelligence Review*, 11(1), 37-45 (2000).

[68] Gausemeier, J., Fink, A. and Schalke, O.: Scenario Management: An Approach to Develop Future Potentials, *Technological Forecasting & Social Change*, 59, 111-130 (1998).

[69] Anastasi, C., van Asselt, M. B. A., Peters, S. S. M., Mellors, J., Ravetz, J. and Rotmans, J.: From Wild Storyline Material to Integrated Visions: The first steps have been taken, *ICIS*, Maastricht, the Netherlands (1999).

[70] Bood, R. P. and Postma, T. J. B. M.: Leren met scenario's? (Learning using scenarios?), *Bedrijfskunde*, (2), 45-53 (1995).

[71] De Jong, R.: De geschiedenis van de toekomst: De ontwikkeling van vier scenarios voor intemediairs op de arbeidsmarkt van 2010 (The history of the future: the development of four scenarios for intermediaries on the job market in 2010), Faculteit Bedrijfskunde (Faculty of Business Administration), University of Groningen, Groningen (1998).

[72] De Jong, R.: personal communication, 13 February 2001

[73] Van Asselt, M. B. A., Rotmans, J. and Rothman, D. S.: *Scenario innovation: Experiences from a European experimental garden*. Taylor & Francis, London, 2005.

[74] Godet, M.: *Scenarios and strategic management*. Butterworth, 1987.

[75] Rotmans, J. and de Vries, H. J. M.: *Perspectives on Global Change: The TARGETS approach*. Cambridge University Press, Cambridge, 1997.

[76] Janssen, M. A.: *Meeting Targets: Tools to support Integrated Assessment Modeling of global change*. Maastrict University, Maastricht, The Netherlands, 1996.

[77] CPB Netherlands Bureau for Economic Policy Analysis: WorldScan. The Core Version, *CPB Netherlands Bureau for Economic Policy Analysis*, The Hague (1999).

[78] Bobbitt, P.: *The Shield of Achilles: War, Peace and the Course of History*. Penguin, London, 2002.

[79] McRae, H.: *The world in 2020: power, culture and prosperity. A vision of the future*. Harper Collins, London, 1995.

[80] Breunesse, E., et al.: Koersen op de toekomst: vier toekomstscenarios voor modern leiderschap (Navigating our way to the future: four scenarios for modern leadership), *NIVE*, (2000).

[81] Godet, M.: Manuel de prospective stratégique, Tome 2 : L'art et la méthode, http://www.cnam.fr/depts/te/dso/lecture/godet.htm, accessed on 13th July 2001

[82] European Environment Agency: Environment in the European Union at the turn of the Century, *European Environment Agency*, Copenhagen (1999).

[83] Mercer, D.: Simpler scenarios, *Management Decision*, 33(4), 32-40 (1995).

[84] Coates, J. F.: Scenario Planning, *Technological Forecasting and Social Change*, 65(1), 115-123 (2000).

[85] Vleugel, J.: *Design of Transport and Land-use Scenarios: Principles and Applications*. Eburon, Delft, 2000.

[86] Schoemaker, P. J. H.: Scenario Planning: A Tool for Strategic Thinking, *Sloan Management Review*, (Winter), 25-39 (1995).

[87] Anastasi, C., Van Notten, P. W. F. and Higginson, S., Think the Unthinkable: A Practical Introduction to Scenario Thinking, in *Puzzle solving for policy. A provisional handbook for Integrated Assessment*. M. B. A. Van Asselt and J. Rotmans, ICIS, Maastricht 2001.

[88] Van der Heijden, K.: Scenarios and Forecasting: Two Perspectives, *Technological Forecasting & Social Change*, (65), 31-36 (2000).

[89] Hiltunen, E.: Weak Signals, in: *Seminar on Scenario Building*, (2001) Turku, Finland

[90] Van Steenbergen, B.: Looking into the seeds of time, *Futures*, 28(6-7), 679-683 (1996).

[91] Harremoës, P., Gee, D., MacGarvin, M., Stirling, A., Keys, J., Wynne, B. and Guedes Vaz, S.: Late lessons from early warnings: the precautionary principle 1896 - 2000, *European Environment Agency*, Copenhagen (2002).

[92] Molitor, G. T. T.: How to Spot, Track, and Forecast Change, in: *Strategies for the New Millennium: A World Future Society Conference*, Chicago (1998)

REFERENCES

[93] Wilson, I.: From Scenario Thinking to Strategic Action, *Technological Forecasting & Social Change*, (65), 23-29 (2000).
[94] European Environment Agency and Alcamo, J.: Scenarios as tools for international environmental assessments, *European Environment Agency*, Copenhagen (2001).
[95] Robinson, J.: personal communication, 25 July 2002
[96] Shell International: People and Connections: Global Scenarios to 2020 - Public summary, London (2002).
[97] CPB Netherlands Bureau for Economic Policy Analysis: *The Netherlands in Triplicate: a scenario study of the Dutch economy (In Dutch)*. Sdu Uitgeverij, The Hague, The Netherlands, 1992.
[98] Höjer, M. and Mattsson, L.-G.: Determinism and backcasting in future studies, *Futures*, 32(7), 613-634 (2000).
[99] Dreborg, K.: Essence of backcasting, *Futures*, 28(9), 813-828 (1996).
[100] Robinson, J.: Futures under glass: A recipe for people who hate to predict, *Futures*, 22(8), 820-842 (1990).
[101] Banister, D., Stead, D., Steen, P., Akerman, J., Dreborg, K., Nijkamp, P. and Schleicher-Tappeser, R.: *European Transport Policy and Sustainable Mobility*. Spon, London and New York, 2000.
[102] Pardoe, G. K. C., et al: *Technology and the future of Europe: the impact of emerging technologies and the activity and economy of the member states beyond 1992*. Luxembourg, Luxembourg, 1992.
[103] World Business Council for Sustainable Development: *Exploring Sustainable Development. Global scenarios 2000-2050*. WBCSD, London, 1998.
[104] Digital Thinking Network: The future of television, www.dtn.net, accessed on October 20th, 2001
[105] Digital Thinking Network: The future of crime, www.dtn.net, accessed on August 28th, 2000
[106] McCorduck, P. and Ramsey, N.: *The Futures of Women: scenarios for the 21st century*. Warner Books, New York, 1996.
[107] Nakamae International Economic Research: The future of Japan, www.nier.co.jp/reports/pro-e.html, accessed on October 20th, 2000
[108] Nakamae, T.: Three Futures for Japan: Views from 2020, *The Economist* (1998).
[109] VROM: The Netherlands in 2030 - Exploration of spatial perspectives (in Dutch), *Ministry of Housing, Spatial Planning and the Environment (VROM)*, The Hague, the Netherlands (1997).
[110] Godet, M.: Scenarios and Strategies: A Toolbox for Scenario Planning, Conservatoire National des Arts et Métiers (CNAM) www.cnam.fr/lips/toolbox,accessed
[111] Achebe, C., Hyden, G., Magadza, C., Okeyo, A. P. and (eds): *Beyond Hunger in Africa: Conventional Wisdom and an Alternative Vision*. Heinemann, Portsmouth, N.H., 1990.
[112] Svedin, U. and Aniansson, B.: *Surprising Futures: Notes from an International Workshop on Long-Term World Development*. Swedish Council for Planning and Coordination of Research, Stockholm, 1987.
[113] Rotmans, J., Van Asselt, M. B. A., de Bruin, A. J., den Elzen, M. G. J., de Greef, J., Hilderink, H., Hoekstra, A. Y., Janssen, M. A., Koster, H. W., Martens, W. J. M., Niessen, L. W. and de Vries, H. J. M.: Global Change and Sustainable Development: A Modelling Perspective for the Next Decade, *National Institute of Public Health and the Environment (RIVM)*, Bilthoven, The Netherlands (1994).
[114] Schneider, S.: Integrated Assessment Modeling of Climate Change. Transparent rational tool for policy making or opaque screen hiding value-laden assumptions?, *Environmental Modelling and Assessment*, 2(4), 229-250 (1997).
[115] Dammers, E.: *Leren van de toekomst. Over de rol van scenario's bij strategische beleidsvorming (Learning from the future: the role of scenarios in strategic policy making)*. Eburon, Delft., 2000.
[116] CPB Netherlands Bureau for Economic Policy Analysis: *Scanning the Future: A long term scenario study of the world economy 1990-2015*. Sdu Uitgeverij, The Hague, The Netherlands, 1992.
[117] Moss, S.: Canonical Tasks, Environments and Models for Social Simulation., *Computational & mathematical Organization Theory*, 6(3), 249-275 (2000).
[118] Gilbert, N. and Troitzsch, K. G.: *Simulation for the Social Scientist*. Open University Press, Buckingham, UK, 1999.
[119] Conte, R. and Castelfranchi, C.: *Cognitive and social action*. UCL Press ltd, London, 1995.
[120] Van Asselt, M.B.A., Mellors, J., Rijkens-Klomp, N., Greeuw, S.C.H., Molendijk, K.G.P., Beers, P.J. and Van Notten, P. W. F.: Building Blocks for Participation in Integrated Assessment, *ICIS*, Maastricht (2001).
[121] van Asselt, M.B.A. and Rijkens-Klomp, N.: A Look in the Mirror: Reflection on participation in Integrated Assessment from a methodological perspective, *Global Environmental Change*, 107-180 (2002).

REFERENCES

[122] European Environment Agency and Toth, F.: Participatory integrated assessment methods: An assessment of their usefulness to the European Environment Agency, *European Environment Agency*, Copenhagen (2001).

[123] De Niet, R., De Nijs, T., De Hollander, G., Greeuw, S., van Asselt, M. and Rotmans, J.: The Green Heart Region towards 2050 : Three scenarios for the Green Heart Region, *RIVM & ICIS*, Maastricht, the Netherlands (2000).

[124] De Niet, R., de Nijs, A.C.M., De Hollander, A.E.M.: Visions for the Green Heart, Methodology Report, *RIVM*, Bilthoven (2001).

[125] Rotmans, J., van Asselt, M. B. A., Rothman, D., Greeuw, S. C. H. and van Bers, C.: Integrated Visions for a Sustainable Europe: Change Mental Maps. VISIONS Final Report, *ICIS*, Maastricht (2001).

[126] OECD: *Citizens as Partners: OECD Handbook on information, consultation and public participation in policy-making.* OECD, Paris, 2001.

[127] Street, P.: Scenario workshops: A participatory approach to sustainable urban living?, *Futures*, 29(2), 139-158 (1997).

[128] Vennix, J.: *Group Model Building: Facilitating Team Learning Using System Dynamics.* Wiley, Chichester, 1996.

[129] The Millennium Institute: www.threshold21.com, accessed on September 10th, 2004

[130] Schwartz, P., Leyden, P. and Hyatt, J.: *The Long Boom: A Vision for the Coming Age of Prosperity.* Perseus, Boulder, 1999.

[131] Ashby, W. R.: *An Introduction to Cybernetics.* Wiley, New York, 1963.

[132] Barbanente, A., Khakee, A. and Puglisi, M.: Scenario building for Metropolitan Tunis, *Futures*, 34, 583-596 (2002).

[133] Vervuurt, G.: personal communication, 26 July 2002

[134] Bertrand, G. and Michalski, A., Governance in a larger and more diverse European Union: lessons from scenarios Europe 2010, in *Governance in the European Union*. O. De Schutter, et al., Forward Studies Unit/ European Commission 2001.

[135] Bertrand, G., et al.: Scenarios Europe 2010, *European Commission Forward Studies Unit*, Brussels (1999).

[136] Munasinghe, M.: Environmental Economics and Sustainable Development, *The World Bank*, Washington, USA (1993).

[137] OECD: Environmental Indicators: Basic Concepts and Terminology, in: *Indicators for use in environmental performance reviews*, (1993) Paris, France

[138] Netherlands Scientific Council for Government Policy (WRR): *Sustained Risks: A Lasting Phenomenon.* SDU Uitgeverij, The Hague, The Netherlands, 1994.

[139] World Business Council for Sustainable Development: *Biotechnology Scenarios.* Conches-Geneva, 2000.

[140] Rotmans, J., van Asselt, M., Anastasi, C., Rothman, D., Greeuw, S. and van Bers, C.: Integrated Visions for a Sustainable Europe: Change Mental Maps: VISIONS Final Report, *ICIS*, VISIONS, Maastricht (2001).

[141] Rotmans, J., van Asselt, M. B. A. and van Notten, P., VISIONS scenarios on the future of Europe, in *Scenario Planning in Public Policy*. G. Ringland, John Wiley, Chichester, UK 2002.

[142] Øverland, E. F., Neumann, I. B., Dokk Holm, E. and Høviskeland, T.: Norway 2030, *Royal Ministry of Labour and Government Administration*, Oslo (2000).

[143] Ministry of Transport and Public Works: Verplaatsen in de Toekomst (Mobility in the Future): Project Questa, The Hague (1998).

[144] Dobbinga, E.: personal communication, March 2001

[145] Bruun, H., Hukkinen, J. and Ekland, E.: Scenarios for coping with contingency: The case of aquaculture in the Finnish Archipelago Sea, *Technological Forecasting & Social Change*, (69), 107-127 (2002).

References for chapter 3

[1] Feyerabend, P.: *Against Method.* Verso, London, 1975.
[2] Clark, W. C.: Visions of the 21st Century: Conventional Wisdom and Other Surprises in the Global Interactions of Population, Technology, and Environment, in: *Perspective 2000: Proceedings of a Conference Sponsored by the Economic Council of Canada,* K. Newton, T. Schweitzer and J. P. Voyer (eds) (1988), Economic Council of Canada.
[3] Clark, W. C., Sustainable development of the biosphere: themes for a research program, in *Sustainable Development of the Biosphere.* W. C. Clark and R. E. Munn, Cambridge University Press, Cambridge, UK, 1986.
[4] Davis, G.: Creating Scenarios for Your Company's Future, in: *The 1998 Conference on Corporate Environmental, Health, and Safety Excellence: Bringing Sustainable Development Down to Earth,* New York City (1998)
[5] Berkhout, F. and Hertin, J.: Foresight Futures Scenarios, *Greener Management International,* (37), 37-52 (2002).
[6] Global Business Network: www.gbn.org, accessed on October 15th, 2003
[7] Berkhout, F., Hertin, J. and Jordan, A.: Socio-economic futures in climate change impact assessment: using scenarios as 'learning machines', *Science and Technology Policy Research, University of Sussex,* Brighton (1998).
[8] Bell, W.: *Foundations of Futures Studies: Human Science for a New Era: History, Purposes, and Knowledge.* Second printing 1997,Transaction Publishers, New Brunswick, 1997.
[9] Dammers, E.: *Leren van de toekomst. Over de rol van scenario's bij strategische beleidsvorming (Learning from the future: the role of scenarios in strategic policy making).* Eburon, Delft, 2000.
[10] Wiedemann, P. M., Karger, C. R. and Clauberg, M.: Early Risk Detection in Environmental Health: Feasibility Study. Report of the Action Programme "Environment and Health", Report number 200 61 218/09, (2002).
[11] Brooks, H., The Typology of Surprises in Technology, Institutions, and Development, in *Sustainable Development of the Biosphere.* W. C. Clark and R. E. Munn, Cambridge University Press, Cambridge, UK, 325-350, 1986.
[12] European Environment Agency and ICIS: Cloudy Crystal Balls: An assessment of recent European and global scenario studies and models, (2000).
[13] Marien, M.: Futures studies in the 21st Century: a reality-based view, *Futures,* 34(3/4), 261-281 (2002).
[14] Bruun, H., Hukkinen, J. and Ekland, E.: Scenarios for coping with contingency: The case of aquaculture in the Finnish Archipelago Sea, *Technological Forecasting & Social Change,* (69), 107-127 (2002).
[15] Zeisler, S. and Dyer, H.: Order from chaos: part two, *Scenario & Strategy Planning,* 2(2), 14-17 (2000).
[16] Ayres, R. U.: On Forecasting Discontinuities, *Technological Forecasting & Social Change,* (65), 81-97 (2000).
[17] Schwartz, P.: *The Art of the Long View: Planning for the Future in an Uncertain World.* Currency Doubleday, New York, 1991.
[18] Drucker, P. F.: *The Age of Discontinuity.* Harper and Row, New York, 1968.
[19] The Collins English Dictionary: HarperCollins, New York, 2000.
[20] Merriam-Webster's Collegiate Dictionary: http://www.m-w.com/cgi-bin/dictionary
[21] Oxford English Dictionary: 2nd,Oxford University Press, New York, 1989.
[22] Gallopin, G., Hammond, A., Raskin, P. and Swart, R.: Branch Points: Global Scenarios and Human Choice - A Resource Paper of the Global Scenario Group, *Stockholm Environment Institute, Sweden,* (1997).
[23] Davis, G.: Scenarios as a tool for the 21st Century, in: *Probing the Future: Developing Organizational Foresight in the Knowledge Economy,* (2002) The University of Strathclyde Graduate School of Business, Glasgow
[24] Rotmans, J., van Asselt, M. B. A., Rothman, D., Greeuw, S. C. H. and van Bers, C.: Integrated Visions for a Sustainable Europe: Change Mental Maps. VISIONS Final Report, *ICIS,* Maastricht (2001).
[25] Mendonça, S., Cunha, M. P., Kaivo-oja, J. and Ruff, F.: Wild cards, weak signals and organisational improvisation, *Futures,* 36(2), 201–218 (2004).
[26] Dansereau, P., The Edge of Dreams, in *Perspective 2000: Proceedings of a Conference Sponsored by the Economic Council of Canada.* K. Newton, T. Schweitzer and J. P. Voyer, Canadian Government Publishing Centre, Ottawa, 32-37, 1988.

REFERENCES

[27] Polak, F.: *The image of the future.* Elsevier, Amsterdam, 1971.

[28] Banister, D., Stead, D., Steen, P., Akerman, J., Dreborg, K., Nijkamp, P. and Schleicher-Tappeser, R.: *European Transport Policy and Sustainable Mobility.* Spon, London and New York, 2000.

[29] Ringland, G., Edwards, M., Hammond, L., Heinzen, B., Rendell, A., Sparrow, O. and White, E.: Shocks and Paradigm Busters (Why Do We Get Surprised?), *Longe Range Planning,* 32(4), 403-413 (1999).

[30] Moyer, K.: Scenario Planning at British Airways - A Case Study, *Long Range Planning* 29(2) 172-181 (1996).

[31] Ringland, G.: *Scenario Planning.* John Wiley & Sons, Chichester, 1998.

[32] Achebe, C., Hyden, G., Magadza, C., Okeyo, A. P. and (eds): *Beyond Hunger in Africa: Conventional Wisdom and an Alternative Vision.* Heinemann, Portsmouth, N.H., 1990.

[33] Svedin, U. and Aniansson, B.: *Surprising Futures: Notes from an International Workshop on Long-Term World Development.* Swedish Council for Planning and Coordination of Research, Stockholm, 1987.

[34] UNEP: *Global Environment Outlook 3: Past, present and future perspectives.* Earthscan, London, 2002.

[35] Rotmans, J., van Asselt, M. B. A., Anastasi, C., Greeuw, S., Mellors, J., Peters, S., Rothman, D. and Rijkens, N.: Visions for a sustainable Europe, *Futures,* 32(9-10), 809-831 (2000).

[36] Streets, D. G. and Glantz, M. H.: Exploring the concept of climate surprise, *Global Environmental Change,* (10), 97-107 (2000).

[37] Kieken, H.: Integrating structural changes in future research and modeling on the Seine River Basin in Integrated Assessment and Decision Support., in: *Proceedings of the 1st biennal meeting of the International Environmental Modelling and Software Society* 2 37-42, A. E. Rizzoli and A. J. Jakeman (eds) (2002)

[38] Holling, C. S., The resilience of terrestrial ecosystems: local surprise and global change, in *Sustainable Development in the Biosphere.* W. C. Clark and R. E. Munn, International Institute for Applied Systems Analysis, Laxenburg, 1986.

[39] Schneider, S. H., Turner II, B. L. and Morehouse Garriga, H.: Imaginable Surprise in Global Change Science, *Journal of Risk Research,* 1(2), 165-185 (1998).

[40] Glantz, M. H., Streets, D. G., Stewart, T. R., Bhatti, N., Moore, C. M. and Rosa, C. H.: Exploring the Concept of Climate Surprises: A Review of the Literature on the Concept of Surprise and How It Is Related to Climate Change, *Environmental and Societal Impacts Group, National Center for Atmospheric Research,* Boulder, CO, USA (1998).

[41] Kates, R. W. and Clark, W.: Environmental Surprise: Expecting the Unexpected, *Environment,* 38(2), 6-11 (1996).

[42] Myers, N.: Environmental Unknowns, *Science,* 269(21 July), 358-360 (1995).

[43] Hassol, S. J. and Katzenberger, J.: Elements of Change 1994, Part 2: Anticipating Global Change Surprises, *Aspen Global Change Institute,* Aspen, Colorado (1995).

[44] Rotmans, J.: Methods for IA: The challenges and opportunities ahead, *Environmental Modelling and Assessment,* 3(3), 155-179 (1998).

[45] Faber, M., Manstetten, R. and Props, J. L. R.: Humankind and the Environment: An Anatomy of Surprise and Ignorance, *Environmental Values,* 1(3), 217-241 (1992).

[46] Schneider, S.: Integrated Assessment Modeling of Climate Change: Transparent rational tool for policy making or opaque screen hiding value-laden assumptions?, *Environmental Modelling and Assessment,* 2(4), 229-250 (1997).

[47] Timmerman, P., Mythology and surprise in the sustainable development of the biosphere, in *Sustainable Development of the Biosphere.* W. C. Clark and Munn R. E., Cambridge University Press, Cambridge, UK, 1986.

[48] Thompson, M., Ellis, R. and Wildavsky, A.: *Cultural Theory.* Westview Press, Boulder, USA, 1990.

[49] Easterling, W. E. and Kok, K., Emergent Properties of Scale in Global Environmental Modeling - Are There Any?, in *Scaling in Integrated Assessment.* J. Rotmans and D. S. Rothman, Swets & Zeitlinger Publishers, Lisse, 263-292, 2003.

[50] Von Clausewitz, C.: *On War.* Princeton University Press, Princeton, 1991.

[51] Sun Tzu: *The Art of War.* Oxford University Press, London, 1971.

[52] O'Leary, J.: Surprise and Intelligence: Towards a clearer understanding, *Aerospace Power Journal,* (Spring issue) (1994).

[53] McCorduck, P. and Ramsey, N.: *The Futures of Women: scenarios for the 21st century.* Warner Books, New York, 1996.

[54] Petersen, J. L.: *Out of the blue. How to anticipate big future surprises.* Madison Books, Lanham, 1999.

[55] Global Business Network: Wild Cards (1996) San Francisco, Global Business Network.

[56] Scott, A.: 11 September, 2001, *Scenario and Strategy Planning* 3(5) 4-8 (2002).
[57] Western Australian Planning Commission: Future Perth. Scenarios of our Future: Challenges for Western Australian Society, *John Curtin International Institute*, Perth (2000).
[58] Slaughter, R. A.: Beyond the mundane: reconciling breadth and depth in futures enquiry, *Futures*, 34(6), 493-507 (2002).
[59] Braudel, F.: *On History*. Wiedenfeld and Nicolson, London, 1980.
[60] Vries, P., De zegetocht van de *Annales*, in *Geschiedschrijving in the twintigste eeuw: Discussie zonder eind*. H. Beliën and G. J. Van Setten, Agon, Amsterdam, 181-222, 1991.
[61] Braudel, F.: *The Mediterranean and the Mediterranean World in the Age of Philip II*. Harper and Row, New York, 1972.
[62] Cannon, J., Davis, R. H. C., Doyle, W. and Greene, J. P.: *The Blackwell Dictionary of Historians*. Basil Blackwell Inc, New York, 1988.
[63] Boyd, K.: *Encyclopedia of Historians and Historical Writing*. Fitzroy Dearborn Publishers, London, 1999.
[64] Macfarlane, A.: Fernand Braudel and Global History, in: *Seminar on Global History*, (1996) Institute of Historical Research
[65] Van der Heijden, K.: *Scenarios: the Art of Strategic Conversation*. Wiley, Chichester, 1996.
[66] Van der Heijden, K., Bradfield, R., Burt, G., Cairns, G. and Wright, G.: *The Sixth Sense: Accelerating Organisational Learning with Scenarios*. Wiley & Sons, Chichester, 2002.
[67] Slaughter, R. A.: Futures Studies as a civilization catalyst, *Futures*, 34(3/4), 349-363 (2002).
[68] Braudel, F.: *Afterthoughts on Material Civilization and Capitalism*. The Johns Hopkins University Press, Baltimore, 1977.
[69] Mazlish, B.: *The Fourth Discontinuity: The Co-Evolution of Humans and Machines*. Yale University Press, New Haven and London, 1993.
[70] Kuhn, T. S.: *The Structure of Scientific Revolutions*. University of Chicago Press, Chicago, USA, 1970.
[71] Jacques, E., Gibson, R. O. and Isaac, D. J.: *Levels of Abstraction in Logic and Human Action: A theory of discontinuity in the structure of mathematical logic, psychological behaviour, and social organization*. Heinemann, London, 1978.
[72] Nicolas, G. and Prigogine, I.: *Exploring complexity: An introduction*. Freeman, New York, 1989.
[73] Gleick, J.: *Chaos : making a new science*. Viking, New York, 1987.
[74] Kaminsky, G. L.: Currency and Banking Crises: The Early Warnings of Distress,, (1998).
[75] MacGarvin, M., Fisheries: taking stock, in *Late lessons from early warnings: the precautionary principle 1896 - 2000*. P. Harremoës, D. Gee, M. MacGarvin et al., European Environment Agency, Copenhagen, 17-30, 2001.
[76] Mandelbrot, B. B.: *Fractals and Scaling in Finance: Discontinuity, Concentration, Risk*. Springer, New York, 1997.
[77] Palmer, R. R. and Colton, J.: *A history of the modern world*. Knopf, New York, 1978.
[78] Rotmans, J., Kemp, R. and Van Asselt, M. B. A.: More evolution than revolution: transition management in public policy, *Foresight*, 3(1), 15-32 (2001).
[79] Rotmans, J., Kemp, R., Van Asselt, M. B. A., Geels, F., Verbong, G., Molendijk, K. G. P. and Van Notten, P. W. F.. Transitions & Transition Management. The case for a low emission energy supply, ICIS, Maastricht (2001).
[80] Fukuyama, F.: *The great disruption: human nature and the reconstitution of social order*. The Free Press, New York, 1999.
[81] The Economist: Seeing the world anew, (25th October 2001).
[82] Perlez, J. and Sanger, D.: Powell says U.S. had signs, but not clear ones, of a plot, *The New York Times*, (3rd October 2001).
[83] The National Commission on Terrorist Attacks Upon the United States, Rice's Testimony before the Sept. 11 Commission, http://wid.ap.org/transcripts/rice.html, Washington, 2004
[84] Schwartz, P.: *Inevitable Surprises*. The Free Press, London, 2003.
[85] Watkins, M. D. and Bazerman, M. H.: Predictable Surprises: The Disasters You Should Have Seen Coming, *Harvard Business Review*, 81(3), 72-80 (2003).
[86] National Commission on Terrorist Attacks: *The 9/11 Commission Report: The Final Report of the National Commission on Terrorist Attacks upon the United States*. Norton, W. W. & Company, Inc., Washington, 2004.

REFERENCES

[87] Crockatt, R.: *America Embattled: September 11, anti-Americanism, and the global order.* Routledge, London, 2003.
[88] Boorstin, D. J.: *The Americans: The Democratic Experience.* Random House, New York, 1973.
[89] Huntingdon, S. P.: *The clash of civilizations and the remaking of world order.* Simon & Schuster, New York, 1996.
[90] Barber, B. R. and Schulz, A.: *Jihad vs. McWorld: How Globalism and Tribalism Are Reshaping the World.* Ballantine Books, New York, 1996.
[91] Buruma, I. and Margalit, A.: *Occidentalism: The West in the Eyes of its Enemies.* Penguin Press, New York, 2004.
[92] The Economist: A drug on the market, (1st March 2002).
[93] The Economist: Silver linings, (29th September 2001).
[94] The Economist: Re-edit, (22nd September 2002).
[95] The Economist: Night fell on a different world, (5th September 2002).
[96] Clarke, L., Introduction: 9.11 as Disaster: On Worst Cases, Terrorism, and Catastrophe, in *Terrorism and Disaster: New Threats, New Ideas.* L. Clarke, Elsevier, Amsterdam, 1-6, 2003.
[97] Michaels, A.: Terrorism threat boosts investment in insurers, *Financial Times*, (6th November 2001).
[98] Elsner, A., An Anxious Nation, in *After September 11: New York and the World.* Reuters, Prentice Hall, Upper Sadle River, 2003.
[99] Cohen, A.: A flight to corporate jets, *Financial Times*, (6th November 2001).
[100] Luce, E.: Hot money flooding into Pakistan, *The Financial Times*, 3 (2001).
[101] Soros, G.: The Bubble of American Supremacy, *The Atlantic Monthly*, 292(5) (2003).
[102] The Economist: Six months on, (7th May 2002).
[103] Larabee, A., Empire of Fear: Imagined Community and the September 11 Attacks, in *Terrorism and Disaster: New Threats, New Ideas.* L. Clarke, Elsevier, Amsterdam, 19-31, 2003.
[104] Harremoës, P., Gee, D., MacGarvin, M., Stirling, A., Keys, J., Wynne, B. and Guedes Vaz, S.: Late lessons from early warnings: the precautionary principle 1896 - 2000, *European Environment Agency*, Copenhagen (2002).
[105] Van Notten, Ph.W.F, *To Learn from Early Warnings*, in: Nieuwe Risico's in Zicht (New Risks in Sight), Raad voor Ruimtelijk Milieu- en Natuuronderzoek (Advisory Council for Research on Spatial Planning, Nature, and the Enviroment) (ed.), Lemma, Utrecht (2005)
[106] Farman, J., Halocarbons, the ozone layer and the precautionary principle, in *Late lessons from early warnings: the precautionary principle 1896 - 2000.* P. Harremoës, D. Gee, M. MacGarvin et al., European Environment Agency, Copenhagen, 76-83, 2001.
[107] Molina, M. J. and Rowland, F. S.: Stratospheric sink for chlorofluoromethanes: chlorine atome catalyzed destruction of ozone, *Nature*, (249), 810-812 (1974).
[108] Rotmans, J., van Asselt, M., Anastasi, C., Rothman, D., Greeuw, S. and van Bers, C.: Integrated Visions for a Sustainable Europe : Change Mental Maps : VISIONS Final Report, *ICIS, VISIONS*, Maastricht (2001).
[109] Van Zwanenberg, P. and Millstone, E., 'Mad cow disease' 1980s–2000: how reassurances undermined precaution, in *Late lessons from early warnings: the precautionary principle 1896 - 2000.* P. Harremoës, D. Gee, M. MacGarvin et al., European Environment Agency, Copenhagen, 157-167, 2001.
[110] Broekhans, B.: *How Dutch environmental science became history: Demarcation of a socially relevant science 1970-2000.* Nijmegen University Press, Ede, 2003.
[111] Gee, D. and Greenberg, M., Asbestos: from 'magic' to malevolent mineral, in *Late lessons from early warnings: the precautionary principle 1896 - 2000.* P. Harremoës, D. Gee, M. MacGarvin et al., European Environment Agency, Copenhagen, 52-63, 2001.
[112] Meadows, D. H., Meadows, D. L., Randers, J. and Behrens, W. W.: *The Limits to Growth.* Universe Books, New York, USA, 1972.
[113] Pieterman, R. and Hanekamp, J.: The Cautious Society: An essay on the Rise of the Precautionary Culture, *Heidelberg Appeal Nederland*, (2001).
[114] Beck, U.: *Risk Society: Towards a New Modernity.* Sage, London, UK, 1986.

References for chapter 4

[1]   Berkhout, F., Hertin, J. and Jordan, A.: Socio-economic futures in climate change impact assessment: using scenarios as 'learning machines', *Science and Technology Policy Research, University of Sussex*, Brighton (1998).
[2]   Global Business Network: www.gbn.org, accessed on October 15th, 2003
[3]   Davis, G.: Creating Scenarios for Your Company's Future, in: *The 1998 Conference on Corporate Environmental, Health, and Safety Excellence: Bringing Sustainable Development Down to Earth*, (1998) New York City
[4]   Bruun, H., Hukkinen, J. and Ekland, E.: Scenarios for coping with contingency: The case of aquaculture in the Finnish Archipelago Sea, *Technological Forecasting & Social Change*, (69), 107-127 (2002).
[5]   Postma, T. J. B. M., Vijverberg, A. M. M., Bood, R. P. and Terpstra, S.: Toekomstverkenning met scenario's: Een hulpmiddel bij de bepaling van de strategische koers van een organisatie (Foresight using scenarios: an aid in determining the strategy of an organisation), *Bedrijfskunde*, 2, 13-19 (1995).
[6]   Van der Heijden, K.: *Scenarios: the Art of Strategic Conversation*. Wiley, Chichester, 1996.
[7]   Ducot, C. and Lubben, H. J.: A typology for scenarios, *Futures*, 12(1), 15-57 (1980).
[8]   Bood, R. P. and Postma, T. J. B. M.: Leren met scenario's? (Learning using scenarios?), *Bedrijfskunde*, (2), 45-53 (1995).
[9]   Jungermann, H. and Thuring, M., The Use of Mental Models for Generating Scenarios, in *Judgmental Forecasting*. G. Wright, John Wiley & Sons Ltd, Chichester, 245-266, 1987.
[10] Schwartz, P.: *The Art of the Long View: Planning for the Future in an Uncertain World*. Currency Doubleday, New York, 1991.
[11] European Environment Agency and ICIS: Cloudy Crystal Balls: An assessment of recent European and global scenario studies and models, (2000).
[12] Marien, M.: Futures studies in the 21st Century: a reality-based view, *Futures*, 34(3/4), 261-281 (2002).
[13] Mendonça, S., Cunha, M. P., Kaivo-oja, J. and Ruff, F.: Wild cards, weak signals and organisational improvisation, *Futures*, 36(2), 201-218 (2004).
[14] Petersen, J. L.: *Out of the blue. How to anticipate big future surprises*. Madison Books, Lanham, 1999.
[15] Van Steenbergen, B.: Looking into the seeds of time, *Futures*, 28(6-7), 679-683 (1996).
[16] Ansoff, I. H. (1982). Strategic Response in Turbulent Environments. Working Paper, European Institute for Advanced Studies in Management.
[17] Harremoës, P., Gee, D., MacGarvin, M., Stirling, A., Keys, J., Wynne, B. and Guedes Vaz, S.: Late lessons from early warnings: the precautionary principle 1896 - 2000, *European Environment Agency*, Copenhagen (2002).
[18] Semb, A., Sulphur dioxide: from protection of human lungs to remote lake restoration, in *Late lessons from early warnings: the precautionary principle 1896 - 2000*. P. Harremoës, D. Gee, M. MacGarvin et al., European Environment Agency, Copenhagen, 101-109, 2002.
[19] Salus, P. H.: *Casting the Net: From ARPANET to INTERNET and Beyond*. Addison-Wesley, Boston, 1995.
[20] Molitor, G. T. T.: How to Spot, Track, and Forecast Change, in: *Strategies for the New Millennium: A World Future Society Conference*, (1998) Chicago
[21] Gee, D. and Greenberg, M., Asbestos: from 'magic' to malevolent mineral, in *Late lessons from early warnings: the precautionary principle 1896 - 2000*. P. Harremoës, D. Gee, M. MacGarvin et al., European Environment Agency, Copenhagen, 52-63, 2001.
[22] Ibarreta, D. and Swan, S. H., The DES story: long-term consequences of prenatal exposure, in *Late lessons from early warnings: the precautionary principle 1896 - 2000*. P. Harremoës, D. Gee, M. MacGarvin et al., European Environment Agency, Copenhagen, 2002.
[23] Harremoës, P. and Gee, D.: personal communication, June 13th, 2003
[24] De Wilde, R.: personal communication, January 26th, 2003
[25] Braudel, F.: *On History*. Wiedenfeld and Nicolson, London, 1980.
[26] Braudel, F.: *The Mediterranean and the Mediterranean World in the Age of Philip II*. Harper and Row, New York, 1972.
[27] Braudel, F.: *Afterthoughts on Material Civilization and Capitalism*. The Johns Hopkins University Press, Baltimore, 1977.
[28] Schwartz, P.: *Inevitable Surprises*. The Free Press, London, 2003.

REFERENCES

[29] Brooks, H., The Typology of Surprises in Technology, Institutions, and Development, in *Sustainable Development of the Biosphere*. W. C. Clark and R. E. Munn, Cambridge University Press, Cambridge, UK, 325-350, 1986.

[30] Kates, R. W. and Clark, W.: Environmental Surprise: Expecting the Unexpected, *Environment*, 38(2), 6-11 (1996).

[31] Clark, W. C., Sustainable development of the biosphere: themes for a research program, in *Sustainable Development of the Biosphere*. W. C. Clark and R. E. Munn, Cambridge University Press, Cambridge, UK, 1986.

[32] Van Steenbergen, B.: *De Nieuwe Mens in de Toekomstige Wereldmaatschappij: Uitdagingen voor de Toekomstonderzoeker (The New Human in the Future World Society: Challenges for the Futures researcher)*. Nyenrode University, Breukelen, 2003.

[33] Kieken, H.: Integrating structural changes in future research and modeling on the Seine River Basin in Integrated Assessment and Decision Support., in: *Proceedings of the 1st biennal meeting of the International Environmental Modelling and Software Society* 2 37-42, A. E. Rizzoli and A. J. Jakeman (eds) (2002),

[34] McBurney, P. and Parsons, S.: Chance discovery and scenario analysis, *New Generation Computing, special issue on Chance Discovery*, Vol. 21, 13-22 (2003).

[35] McBurney, P.: personal communication, 13 July 2002

[36] Easterling, W. E. and Kok, K., Emergent Properties of Scale in Global Environmental Modeling - Are There Any?, in *Scaling in Integrated Assessment*. J. Rotmans and D. S. Rothman, Swets & Zeitlinger Publishers, Lisse, 263-292, 2003.

[37] Maso, I.: *De zin van het toeval (The meaning of chance)*. Ambo, Baarn, 1997.

[38] Abaza, H. and Baranzini, A.: *Implementing Sustainable Development: Integrated Assessment and Participatory Decision-making Processes*. Edward Elgar, Cheltenham, 2002.

[39] Van Asselt, M. B. A., Mellors, J., Rijkens-Klomp, N., Greeuw, S. C. H., Molendijk, K. G. P., Beers, P. J. and Van Notten, P. W. F.: Building Blocks for Participation in Integrated Assessment, *ICIS*, Maastricht (2001).

[40] Kasemir, B., Jäger, J. and Jaeger, C., Eds. *Public Participation in Sustainability Science* Cambridge University Press, 2002.

[41] Hyde-Price, A. G. V.: *European security beyond the Cold War: four scenarios for the year 2010*. Sage, London, 1991.

[42] Buchan, A.: *Europe's Futures, Europe's Choices: Models for Western Europe in the 1970s*. Chatto and Windus for the Institute of Strategic Studies, London, 1969.

[43] Moyer, K.: Scenario Planning at British Airways - A Case Study, *Long Range Planning* 29(2) 172-181 (1996).

[44] Global Business Network: Port of Rotterdam scenario workshop report, (1996).

[45] Jongman, P. J.: personal communication, June 10th, 2002

[46] Ringland, G.: *Scenario Planning*. John Wiley & Sons, Chichester, 1998.

[47] Berkhout, F. and Hertin, J.: Foresight Futures Scenarios, *Greener Management International*, (37), 37-52 (2002).

[48] Department of Trade and Industry: Foresight Futures 2020: Revised scenarios and guidance, *Department of Trade and Industry*, London (2002).

[49] Dobbinga, E.: *Weerbarstigheid van organisatiecultuur: een organisatie-antropologische studie naar betekenisgeving aan moderne managementinstrumenten (Stubbornness of organisational culture)*. Eburon, Delft, 2001.

[50] Dobbinga, E.: personal communication, March 2001

[51] Ministry of Transport and Public Works: Verplaatsen in de Toekomst (Mobility in the Future): Project Questa, The Hague (1998).

[52] Stuurgroep Toekomstonderzoek en Strategisch Omgevingsbeleid: *Terugblik op toekomstverkenningen (A retrospective look at foresight studies)*. Netherlands Scientific Council for Government Policy (WRR), The Hague, 2000.

[53] Vleugel, J.: *Design of Transport and Land-use Scenarios: Principles and Applications*. Eburon, Delft, 2000.

[54] European Environment Agency: Environment in the European Union at the turn of the Century, *European Environment Agency*, Copenhagen (1999).

[55] European Environment Agency and DHV: Documentation and Evaluation of the EU98 scenarios process, *DHV Environment and Infrastructure*, Amersfoort (2000).

REFERENCES

[56] Bertrand, G., et al.: Scenarios Europe 2010, *European Commission Forward Studies Unit*, Brussels (1999).

[57] Bertrand, G. and Michalski, A., Governance in a larger and more diverse European Union: lessons from scenarios Europe 2010, in *Governance in the European Union*. O. De Schutter, et al., Forward Studies Unit/ European Commission, 2001.

[58] European Environment Agency and Alcamo, J.: Scenarios as tools for international environmental assessments, *European Environment Agency*, Copenhagen (2001).

[59] Intergovernmental Panel on Climate Change: *Emissions Scenarios*. Cambridge University Press, Cambridge, 2000.

[60] Breunesse, E., et al.: Koersen op de toekomst: vier toekomstscenarios voor modern leiderschap (Navigating our way to the future: four scenarios for modern leadership), *NIVE,,* (2000).

[61] Banister, D., Stead, D., Steen, P., Akerman, J., Dreborg, K., Nijkamp, P. and Schleicher-Tappeser, R.: *European Transport Policy and Sustainable Mobility*. Spon, London and New York, 2000.

[62] OECD: Schooling for Tomorrow: What Schools for the Future?, *OECD*, Paris (2001).

[63] Miller, R.: The Future of the Tertiary Education Sector: Scenarios for a Learning Society, *OECD-CERI*, Paris (2003).

[64] De Ruijter, P.: personal communication, April 19th, 2002

[65] Vervuurt, G.: personal communication, 26 July 2002

[66] Barbanente, A., Khakee, A. and Puglisi, M.: Scenario building for Metropolitan Tunis, *Futures*, 34, 583-596 (2002).

[67] De Mooij, R. and Tang, P.: Four futures of Europe, *CPB Netherlands Bureau for Economic Policy Analysis,,* Den Haag (2003).

[68] De Mooij, R.: personal communication, February 6th, 2004

[69] Myers, N.: Environmental Unknowns, *Science*, 269(21 July), 358-360 (1995).

[70] Morgan, D.: Images of the future: a historical perspective, *Futures*, 34(9/10), 883-893 (2002).

[71] Kahn, H. and Wiener, A. J.: *The Year 2000*. MacMillan, New York, 1967.

[72] Schoonenboom, J.: Toekomstscenario's en beleid (Scenarios and policy), *Beleid, politiek en maatschappij (Policy, politics, and society)*, 30(4), 212-218 (2003).

[73] Svedin, U. and Aniansson, B.: *Surprising Futures: Notes from an International Workshop on Long-Term World Development*. Swedish Council for Planning and Coordination of Research, Stockholm, 1987.

[74] Achebe, C., Hyden, G., Magadza, C., Okeyo, A. P. (eds): *Beyond Hunger in Africa: Conventional Wisdom and an Alternative Vision*. Heinemann, Portsmouth, N.H., 1990.

[75] McCorduck, P. and Ramsey, N.: *The Futures of Women: scenarios for the 21st century*. Warner Books, New York, 1996.

[76] De Jong, R.: De geschiedenis van de toekomst: De ontwikkeling van vier scenarios voor intemediairs op de arbeidsmarkt van 2010 (The history of the future: the development of four scenarios for intermediaries on the job market in 2010), Faculteit Bedrijfskunde (Faculty of Business Administration), University of Groningen, Groningen (1998).

[77] De Jong, R.: personal communication, 13 February 2001

[78] World Business Council for Sustainable Development. *Biotechnology Scenarios*. Conches Geneva, 2000.

[79] Øverland, E. F., Neumann, I. B., Dokk Holm, E. and Høvlskeland, T.: Norway 2030, *Royal Ministry of Labour and Government Administration*, Oslo (2000).

[80] Schwartz, P. and Ogilvy, J., Plotting your scenarios, in *Learning from the future*. L. Fahey and M. Randall, Wiley, USA, 57-80, 1998.

[81] Shell International: People and Connections: Global Scenarios to 2020 - Public summary, London (2002).

[82] Rotmans, J., Anastasi, C., van Asselt, M., Rothman, D. S., Mellors, J., Greeuw, S. C. H. and van Bers, C.: The European Scenarios, *ICIS, VISIONS*, Maastricht, the Netherlands (2001).

[83] Rotmans, J., Anastasi, C., van Asselt, M. B. A., Rothman, D. S., Mellors, J., Greeuw, S. and van Bers, C.: VISIONS: The European Scenarios, *ICIS*, Maastricht (2001).

[84] Rotmans, J., van Asselt, M. B. A., Anastasi, C., Greeuw, S., Mellors, J., Peters, S., Rothman, D. and Rijkens, N.: Visions for a sustainable Europe, *Futures*, 32(9-10), 809-831 (2000).

[85] Van Notten, P. W. F., Rotmans, J., Van Asselt, M. B. A. and Rothman, D. S.: An updated scenario typology, *Futures*, 35(5), 423-443 (2003).

[86] Van Asselt, M. B. A., Rotmans, J. and Rothman, D. S.: *Scenario innovation: Experiences from a European experimental garden*. Taylor & Francis, London, 2005.

[87] Bobbitt, P.: *The Shield of Achilles: War, Peace and the Course of History*. Penguin, London, 2002.
[88] Le Roux, P., et al.: The Mont Fleur Scenarios, *Weekly Mail and The Guardian Weekly*, (1992).
[89] Kahane, A., Imagining South Africa's Future: How Scenarios Helped Discover Common Ground, in *Learning from the Future: Competitive Foresight Scenarios*. L. Fahey and R. Randall, John Wiley & Sons, New York, 1998.
[90] Global Business Network: Destino Colombia, *Deeper News* 9(1) (1998).
[91] Hammond, A.: *Which World? Scenarios for the 21st century. Global destinies, regional choices*. Earthscan Publications Ltd, London, 1998.
[92] Van Notten, P. W. F.: Create the future: 21- 22 June workshop report, *ICIS*, Maastricht (2000).
[93] Brussaard, T.: personal communication, 23 April 2002
[94] UNEP: *Global Environment Outlook 3: Past, present and future perspectives*. Earthscan, London, 2002.
[95] Rothman, D. S.: personal communication, March 18th, 2004
[96] Fontela, E.: Bridging the gap between scenarios and models, *Foresight*, 2(10), 10-14 (2000).
[97] Rotmans, J.: Methods for IA: The challenges and opportunities ahead, *Environmental Modelling and Assessment*, 3(3), 155-179 (1998).
[98] Shell International: Scenarios: An Explorer's Guide, London (2003).
[99] Davis-Floyd, R. E.: Storying Corporate Futures: The Shell Scenarios, *International Journal of Futures Studies*, 1, 1995-1997 (1996).
[100] Neustadt, R. E. and E. R. May, *Thinking in Time: The Uses of History for Decision Makers*. New York, The Free Press, 1988.

References for chapter 5

[1] Ayres, R. U.: On Forecasting Discontinuities, *Technological Forecasting & Social Change*(65), 81-97 (2000).

[2] Van Asselt, M. B. A., Rotmans, J. and Rothman, D. S.: *Scenario innovation: Experiences from a European experimental garden.* Taylor & Francis, London, 2005.

[3] Ratcliffe, J.: Scenario planning: strategic interviews and conversations, *Foresight*, 4(1), 19-30 (2002).

[4a] Babbie, E.R.: *The practice of Social Research*, Belmont, Wandsworth, 1975.

[4b] Van Asselt, M. B. A., Van 't Klooster, S. A. and Van Notten, P. W. F.: Verkennen in onzekerheid (Exploring contexts of uncertainty), *Beleid, politiek en maatschappij (Policy, politics, and society)*, 30(4), 230-241 (2003).

[5] Rotmans, J.: Integrated Visions for a Sustainable Europe: An Integrated Assessment proposal, *European Union, DG XII, Work Programme Environment and Climate (second phase)*, Brussels, Belgium,(1997).

[6] Kasemir, B., Behringer, J., de Marchi, B., Deuker, C., Durrenberger, D., Funtowicz, S., Gerger, A., Giaoutzi, M., Haffner, Y., Nillson, M., Querol, C., Schule, R., Tabara, D., van Asselt, M., Vassilarou, D., Willi, N. and Jaeger, C.: Focus Groups in Integrated Assessment: The ULYSSES pilot experience, *Darmstadt University of Technology*, Darmstadt, Germany, (1997).

[7] Rotmans, J. and Dowlatabadi, H., Integrated Assessment of Climate Change: Evaluation of Methods and Strategies, in *Human Choice and Climate Change: An International Social Science Assessment.* S. Rayner and E. Malone, Battelle Press, Washington, USA, 1998.

[8] Janssen, M. A.: *Meeting Targets: Tools to support Integrated Assessment Modeling of global change.* Maastrict University, Maastricht, The Netherlands, 1996.

[9] Schneider, S. H., Turner II, B. L. and Morehouse Garriga, H.: Imaginable Surprise in Global Change Science, *Journal of Risk Research*, 1(2), 165-185 (1998).

[10] Van Asselt, M. B. A., Storms, C. A. H. M., Rijkens-Klomp, N. and Rotmans, J.: Towards Visions for a Sustainable Europe: An overview and assessment of the last decade of European scenario studies, *ICIS*, Maastricht,(1998).

[11] Nijstad, B. A.: *How the group affects the mind.* Interuniversity Center for Social Science Theory and Methodology, Utrecht, 2000.

[12] Van Asselt, M., Peters, S., Mellors, J. and Rotmans, J.: From Wild storyline material to Integrated VISIONS: VISIONS Euro-workshop report, *ICIS*, Maastricht,(1999).

[13] Anastasi, C., Rotmans, J., van Asselt, M. B. A., Greeuw, S., Mellors, J., Peters, S. and Rothman, D.: Global Format: position paper, *ICIS*, Maastricht,(1999).

[14] CPB Netherlands Bureau for Economic Policy Analysis: WorldScan. The Core Version, *CPB Netherlands Bureau for Economic Policy Analysis*, The Hague,(1999).

[15] Rotmans, J., Anastasi, C., van Asselt, M. B. A., Rothman, D. S., Mellors, J., Greeuw, S. and van Bers, C.: VISIONS: The European Scenarios, *ICIS*, Maastricht,(2001).

[16] Gallopin, G., Hammond, A., Raskin, P. and Swart, R.: Branch Points: Global Scenarios and Human Choice - A Resource Paper of the Global Scenario Group, *Stockholm Environment Institute, Sweden*, (1997).

[17] Rotmans, J. and Van Asselt, M. B. A.: Bifurcations, *ICIS*, Maastricht,(2000).

[18] Nicolas, G. and Prigogine, I.: *Exploring complexity: An introduction.* Freeman, New York, 1989.

[19] Rotmans, J., van Asselt, M., Anastasi, C., Rothman, D., Greeuw, S. and van Bers, C.: Integrated Visions for a Sustainable Europe : Change Mental Maps : VISIONS Final Report, *ICIS, VISIONS*, Maastricht,(2001).

[20] Kasemir, B., Mellors, J. and Ravetz, J.: Surprises in Scenarios: A report for the Visions project, *ICIS*, Maastricht,(2000).

[21] Clark, W. C., Sustainable development of the biosphere: themes for a research program, in *Sustainable Development of the Biosphere.* W. C. Clark and R. E. Munn, Cambridge University Press, Cambridge, UK 1986.

[22] Kates, R. W. and Clark, W.: Environmental Surprise: Expecting the Unexpected, *Environment*, 38(2), 6-11 (1996).

[23] Van Steenbergen, B.: *De Nieuwe Mens in de Toekomstige Wereldmaatschappij: Uitdagingen voor de Toekomstonderzoeker.* Nyenrode University, Breukelen, 2003.

[24] Sleegers, A. M.: The Future Shocks: On the role of discontinuity in scenario analysis, International Centre for Integrative Studies & Faculty of Economics and Business Administration, Maastricht University,

Maastricht (2003).

[25] Van der Heijden, K.: Scenarios and Forecasting: Two Perspectives, *Technological Forecasting & Social Change*(65), 31-36 (2000).
[26] Van der Heijden, K.: *Scenarios: the Art of Strategic Conversation*. Wiley, Chichester, 1996.
[27] Maso, I.: *De zin van het toeval (The meaning of chance)*. Ambo, Baarn, 1997.
[28] Schwartz, P.: *The Art of the Long View: Planning for the Future in an Uncertain World*. Currency Doubleday, New York, 1991.
[29] Brooks, H., The Typology of Surprises in Technology, Institutions, and Development, in *Sustainable Development of the Biosphere*. W. C. Clark and R. E. Munn, Cambridge University Press, Cambridge, UK, 325-350, 1986.
[30] Dammers, E. (2000). *Leren van de toekomst. Over de rol van scenario's bij strategische beleidsvorming* (Learning from the future: the role of scenarios in strategic policy making). Delft., Eburon.
[31] Van Steenbergen, B., Looking into the seeds of time, *Futures*, 28(6-7): 679-683 (1996).

References for chapter 6

[1] Vellema, S. and Van Notten, P.: Transparent Transitions: Designing the future of aquacultural production systems and farmed fish supply chains, *KLICT*, (2003).

[2] Macalister Elliott and partners: Forward study of community aquaculture Summary report, *European Commission Fisheries Directorate General*, Brussels (1999).

[3] Stel, J. H. (2002). Mare Nostrum - Mare Liberum - Mare sit Aeternum: Duurzaam gebruik van de oceanische ruimte (Mare Nostrum - Mare Liberum - Mare sit Aeternum: Sustainable use of ocean space). *Inaugural address*. Maastricht.

[4] Food and Agriculture Organisation (FAO): The state of world fisheries and aquaculture 2000, *FAO*, Rome (2000).

[5] Luiten, E.: Controverses rond kweek van vis in Nederland? (Controversy regarding fish farming in the Netherlands), *Stichting Toekomstbeeld der Techniek*, The Hague (2002).

[6] Lindeboom, H. J., Fonds, M., Wolff, W. J. and van Zon, J. C. J.: Zeeën van mogelijkheden? Drie essays over benutting van aquatische biomassa (Three essays about the exploitation of aquatic biomass), *NRLO*, (1998).

[7] Girling, R.: Is this fish or is it foul?, *The Sunday Times Magazine*, (September 30th, 2001).

[8] CEFAS: Vegetarian fish, *downloaded from www.ceas.co.uk/news/news041102.htm*, (November 4th, 2002).

[9] Black, K. D., Sustainability of aquaculture, in *Environmental impacts of aquaculture*. K. D. Black, Sheffield Academic Press, Sheffield, 199-212, 2001.

[10] Naylor, R., Goldburg, R., Primavera, J., Kautsky, N., Beveridge, M., Clay, J., Folke, C., Lubchenco, J., Mooney, H. A. and Troell, M.: Effect of aquaculture on world fish supplies, *Nature*, 405, 1017-1024 (2000).

[11] Berry, C. and Davison, A.: Bitter harvest: a call for reform in Scottish aquaculture, *World Wildlife Fund*, Geneva (2001).

[12] British Broadcasting Corporation (2001). Warning from the Wild: The Price of Salmon.

[13] EU Scientific Committee On Animal Nutrition: Dioxin contamination of feeding stuffs and their contribution to the contamination of food of animal origin, *European Commission*, Brussels (2001).

[14] Stroebe, W. and Diehl, M., Why groups are less effective than their members: On productivity losses in idea-generating groups, in *European Review of Social Psychology, volume 5*. W. Stroebe and M. Hewstone, John Wiley, London, 271-303, 1994.

[15] Nijstad, B. A.: *How the group affects the mind*. Interuniversity Center for Social Science Theory and Methodology, Utrecht, 2000.

[16ª] Vennix, J. (1996). *Group Model Building: Facilitating Team Learning Using System Dynamics*. Chichester, Wiley.

[16ᵇ] Osborn, A. F.: *Applied Imagination*, 2nd edition. Scribner, New York, 1957.

[17] Osborn, A. F.: *Applied Imagination*. Scribner, New York, 1953.

[18] Lamm, H. and Trommsdorff, G.: Group versus individual performance on a task requiring ideational proficiency (brainstorming): A review, *European Journal of Social Psychology*, 25, 1579-1596 (1973).

[19] Schwartz, P.: *The Art of the Long View: Planning for the Future In an Uncertain World*. Currency Doubleday, New York, 1991.

[20] Neustadt, R. E. and May, E. R.: *Thinking in Time: The Uses of History for Decision Makers*. The Free Press, New York, 1988.

[21] Gilbertson, M., The precautionary principle and early warnings of chemical contamination of the Great Lakes, in *Late lessons from early warnings: the precautionary principle 1896 - 2000*. P. Harremoës, D. Gee, M. MacGarvin et al., European Environment Agency, Copenhagen, 126-133, 2002.

[22] Santillo, D., Johnston, P. and Langston, W. J., Tributyltin (TBT) antifoulants: a tale of ships, snails and imposex, in *Late lessons from early warnings: the precautionary principle 1896 - 2000*. P. Harremoës, D. Gee et al., European Environment Agency, Copenhagen, 135-144, 2002.

[23] Kates, R. W. and Clark, W.: Environmental Surprise: Expecting the Unexpected, *Environment*, 38(2), 6-11 (1996).

[24] Clark, W. C., Sustainable development of the biosphere: themes for a research program, in *Sustainable Development of the Biosphere*. W. C. Clark and R. E. Munn, Cambridge University Press, Cambridge, UK, 1986.

[25] Van Steenbergen, B.: *De Nieuwe Mens in de Toekomstige Wereldmaatschappij: Uitdagingen voor de Toekomstonderzoeker (The New Human in the Future World Society: Challenges for the Futures researcher)*. Nyenrode University, Breukelen, 2003.

[26] Achebe, C., Hyden, G., Magadza, C., Okeyo, A. P. (eds): *Beyond Hunger in Africa: Conventional Wisdom and an Alternative Vision*. Heinemann, Portsmouth, N.H., 1990.

[27] Svedin, U. and Aniansson, B.: *Surprising Futures: Notes from an International Workshop on Long-Term World Development*. Swedish Council for Planning and Coordination of Research, Stockholm, 1987.

[28] Hales, S. D. and Welshon, R.: *Nietzsche's Perspectivism*. University of Illinois Press, Champaign, 2000.

[29] Solomon, R. C., Nietzsche *ad hominem*: Perspectivism, personality and *ressentiment*, in *The Cambridge Companion to Nietzsche*. B. Magnus and K. M. Higgens, Cambridge University Press, Cambridge, 180-222, 1996.

[30] Kuhn, T. S.: *The Structure of Scientific Revolutions*. University of Chicago Press, Chicago, USA, 1970.

[31] Johnson-Laird, P. N.: *Mental models: Towards a cognitive science of language, inference, and consciousness*. Cambridge University Press, 1983.

[32] Cohen, I. B., Newton's concepts of force and mass, with notes on the Laws of motion, in *The Cambridge Companion to Newton*. I. B. Cohen and G. E. Smith, Cambridge University Press, Cambridge, 57-84, 2002.

[33] Senge, P.: *The Fifth Discipline*. Century Business, London, 1993.

[34] van Asselt, M. B. A. and Rotmans, J.: Uncertainty in Perspective, *Global Environmental Change*, 6(2), 121-157 (1996).

[35] Rotmans, J. and de Vries, H. J. M.: *Perspectives on Global Change: The TARGETS approach*. Cambridge University Press, Cambridge, 1997.

[36] Van Asselt, M. B. A.: *Perspectives on Uncertainty and Risk: The PRIMA approach to decision support*. Kluwer, Dordrecht, The Netherlands, 2000.

[37] Van Asselt, M. B. A. and Rotmans, J.: Uncertainty in integrated assessment modelling, from positivism to pluralism, *Climatic Change*, 54, 75-105 (2002).

[38] Schwarz, M. and Thompson, M.: *Divided We Stand: Redefining Politics, Technology and Social Choice*. Harvester Wheatsheaf, New York, USA, 1990.

[39] Douglas, M. and Wildavsky, A.: *Risk and Culture: Essays on the Selection of Technical and Environmental Dangers*. University of California Press, Berkley, USA, 1982.

[40] Thompson, M., Ellis, R. and Wildavsky, A.: *Cultural Theory*. Westview Press, Boulder, USA, 1990.

[41] Janssen, M. A.: *Meeting Targets: Tools to support Integrated Assessment Modeling of global change*. Maastrict University, Maastricht, The Netherlands, 1996.

[42] Hoekstra, A. Y.: *Perspectives on Water: An integrated model-based exploration of the future*. International Books, Utrecht, 1998.

[43] van Asselt, M. B. A., Middelkoop, H., van 't Klooster, S. A., van Deursen, W. P. A., Haasnoot, M., Kwadijk, J. C. J., Buiteveld, H., Können, G. P., Rotmans, J., van Gemert, N. and Valkering, P.: Integrated water management strategies for the Rhine and Meuse basins in a changing environment : Final report of the NRP project 0/958273/01, *ICIS*, Maastricht/Utrecht (2001).

[44] Bobbitt, P.: *The Shield of Achilles: War, Peace and the Course of History*. Penguin, London, 2002.

[45] Øverland, E. F., Neumann, I. B., Dokk Holm, E. and Høviskeland, T.: Norway 2030, *Royal Ministry of Labour and Government Administration*, Oslo (2000).

References for chapter 7

[1] Kahn, H. and Wiener, A. J.: *The Year 2000.* MacMillan, New York, 1967.
[2] Rotmans, J., Kemp, R. and Van Asselt, M. B. A.: More evolution than revolution: transition management in public policy, *Foresight*, 3(1), 15-32 (2001).
[3] Kates, R. W. and Clark, W.: Environmental Surprise: Expecting the Unexpected, *Environment*, 38(2), 6-11 (1996).
[4] Van der Heijden, K.: *Scenarios: the Art of Strategic Conversation.* Wiley, Chichester, 1996.
[5] Van der Heijden, K., Bradfield, R., Burt, G., Cairns, G. and Wright, G.: *The Sixth Sense: Accelerating Organisational Learning with Scenarios.* Wiley & Sons, Chichester, 2002.
[6] Jungermann, H. and Thuring, M., The Use of Mental Models for Generating Scenarios, in *Judgmental Forecasting.* G. Wright, John Wiley & Sons Ltd, Chichester, 245-266, 1987.
[7] Jungermann, H.: Psychological Aspects of Scenarios, *NATO ASI series*, Vol G4(Environmental Risk Assessment, Technology Assessment and Risk Analysis) (1985).
[8] Jungermann, H.: Inferential Processes in the Construction of Scenarios, *Journal of Forecasting*, 4, 321-327 (1985).
[9] Eden, C. and Ackermann, F.: *Making Strategy: the Journey of Strategic Management.* Sage Publications, London, 1998.
[10] Dobbinga, E.: *Weerbarstigheid van organisatiecultuur: een organisatie-antropologische studie naar betekenisgeving aan moderne managementinstrumenten (Stubbornness of organisational culture).* Eburon, Delft, 2001.
[11] Schoonenboom, J.: Toekomstscenario's en beleid (Scenarios and policy), *Beleid, politiek en maatschappij (Policy, politics, and society)*, 30(4), 212-218 (2003).
[12] Van Asselt, M. B. A., Van 't Klooster, S. A. and Van Notten, P. W. F.: Verkennen in onzekerheid (Exploring contexts of uncertainty), *Beleid, politiek en maatschappij (Policy, politics, and society)*, 30(4), 230-241 (2003).
[13] Bakker, W.: Scenario's tussen rationaliteit, systeemdwang en politieke rede (Scenarios in contexts of rationality, system pressure, and political reason), *Beleid en Maatschappij*, 30(4), 219-229 (2003).
[14] Nijstad, B. A.: *How the group affects the mind.* Interuniversity Center for Social Science Theory and Methodology, Utrecht, 2000.

APPENDIX I
SOURCES OF CONSULTED SCENARIO STUDIES

The 30 studies used in the comparative review

1   SURPRISING FUTURES
    Svedin, U. and Aniansson, B., *Surprising Futures: Notes from an International Workshop on Long-Term World Development.* Swedish Council for Planning and Coordination of Research, Stockholm, 1987.

2   BEYOND HUNGER IN AFRICA
    Achebe, C., et al. (eds), *Beyond Hunger in Africa: Conventional Wisdom and an Alternative Vision.* Heinemann, Portsmouth, N.H., 1990.

3   EUROPEAN SECURITY BEYOND THE COLD WAR
    Hyde-Price, A. G. V., *European security beyond the Cold War: four scenarios for the year 2010.* Sage, London, 1991.

4   MONT FLEUR
    - Le Roux, P., et al., The Mont Fleur Scenarios, *Weekly Mail and The Guardian Weekly,* (July 1992).
    - Kahane, A., Imagining South Africa's Future: How Scenarios Helped Discover Common Ground, in: *Learning from the Future: Competitive Foresight Scenarios.* L. Fahey and R. Randall, John Wiley & Sons, New York 1998.
    - Ringland, G., *Scenario Planning.* John Wiley & Sons, Chichester, 1998.

5   BRITISH AIRWAYS
    Moyer, K., Scenario Planning at British Airways - A Case Study, *Long Range Planning* 29(2): 172-181 (1996).

6   ICL
    Ringland, G., *Scenario Planning.* John Wiley & Sons, Chichester, 1998.

7   PORT OF ROTTERDAM
    Global Business Network, Port of Rotterdam scenario workshop report, (1996).
    Jongman, P. J., personal communication, 10 June 2002

8   THE FUTURES OF WOMEN
    McCorduck, P. and Ramsey, N., *The Futures of Women: scenarios for the 21st century.* Warner Books, New York, 1996.

9 DESTINO COLOMBIA

Global Business Network, Destino Colombia, *Deeper News* 9(1) (1998).

10 KPMG EBBINGE

- De Jong, R., De geschiedenis van de toekomst: De ontwikkeling van vier scenarios voor intemediairs op de arbeidsmarkt van 2010 (The history of the future: the development of four scenarios for intermediaries on the job market in 2010), Faculteit Bedrijfskunde (Faculty of Business Administration), University of Groningen, Groningen (1998).
- De Jong, R., personal communication, 13 February 2001

11 QUESTA

- Ministry of Transport and Public Works, Verplaatsen in de Toekomst (Mobility in the Future): Project Questa, The Hague (1998).
- Stuurgroep Toekomstonderzoek en Strategisch Omgevingsbeleid, *Terugblik op toekomstverkenningen (A retrospective look at foresight studies)*. Netherlands Scientific Council for Government Policy (WRR), The Hague, 2000.
- Vleugel, J., *Design of Transport and Land-use Scenarios: Principles and Applications*. Eburon, Delft, 2000.
- Dobbinga, E., *Weerbarstigheid van organisatiecultuur: een organisatie-antropologische studie naar betekenisgeving aan moderne managementinstrumenten (Stubbornness of organisational culture)*. Eburon, Delft, 2001.
- Dobbinga, E., personal communication, March 2001

12 SCENARIOS EUROPE 2010

- Bertrand, G., et al., Scenarios Europe 2010, *European Commission Forward Studies Unit*, Brussels (1999).
- Bertrand, G. and Michalski, A., Governance in a larger and more diverse European Union: lessons from scenarios Europe 2010, *in Governance in the European Union*. O. De Schutter, et al., Forward Studies Unit/ European Commission 2001.
- Scenarios as tools for international environmental assessments, *European Environment Agency*, Copenhagen (2001).

13 THE EUROPEAN ENVIRONMENT AT THE TURN OF THE CENTURY

- Environment in the European Union at the turn of the Century, *European Environment Agency*, Copenhagen (1999).
- Documentation and Evaluation of the EU98 scenarios process, *DHV Environment and Infrastructure*, Amersfoort (2000).

14 WHICH WORLD?

Hammond, A., *Which World? Scenarios for the 21st century. Global destinies, regional choices.* Earthscan Publications Ltd, London, 1998.

15 BIOTECHNOLOGY SCENARIOS

World Business Council for Sustainable Development, *Biotechnology Scenarios*, Conches-Geneva, 2000.

16 IPCC/SRES

- Intergovernmental Panel on Climate Change, *Emissions Scenarios.* Cambridge University Press, Cambridge, 2000.
- Scenarios as tools for international environmental assessments, *European Environment Agency*, Copenhagen (2001).

17 NIVE NAVIGATING THE FUTURE

Breunesse, E., et al.: Koersen op de toekomst: vier toekomstscenarios voor modern leiderschap (Navigating our way to the future: four scenarios for modern leadership), *NIVE*, (2000).

18 NORWAY 2030

Øverland, E. F., Neumann, I. B., Dokk Holm, E. and Høviskeland, T., Norway 2030, *Royal Ministry of Labour and Government Administration*, Oslo (2000).

19 NUTRITION

- Van Notten, Ph. W. F., Create the future: 21- 22 June workshop report, *ICIS*, Maastricht (2000).
- Brussaard, T., personal communication, 23 April 2002

20 POSSUM

- Banister, D., Stead, D., Steen, P., Akerman, J., Dreborg, K., Nijkamp, P. and Schleicher-Tappeser, R., *European Transport Policy and Sustainable Mobility.* Spon, London and New York, 2000.
- Cloudy Crystal Balls: An assessment of recent European and global scenario studies and models, *European Environment Agency*, (2000).

21 TELECOM

- Vervuurt, G., personal communication, 26 July 2002
- Author's participation in scenario process

APPENDIX I SOURCES OF CONSULTED SCENARIO STUDIES

22 SCHOOLING FOR TOMORROW
- OECD, Schooling for Tomorrow: What Schools for the Future?, *OECD*, Paris (2001).
- Miller, R., The Future of the Tertiary Education Sector: Scenarios for a Learning Society, *OECD-CERI*, Paris (2003).

23 SHELL GLOBAL SCENARIOS
Shell International, People and Connections: Global Scenarios to 2020 - Public summary, London (2002).

24 FINNISH AQUACULTURE
Bruun, H., Hukkinen, J. and Ekland, E., Scenarios for coping with contingency: The case of aquaculture in the Finnish Archipelago Sea, *Technological Forecasting & Social Change* (69), 107-127 (2002).

25 FORESIGHT FUTURES
- Berkhout, F., Hertin, J. and Jordan, A., Socio-economic futures in climate change impact assessment: using scenarios as 'learning machines', *Science and Technology Policy Research, University of Sussex*, Brighton (1998).
- Berkhout, F. and Hertin, J., Foresight Futures Scenarios, *Greener Management International* (37), 37-52 (2002).
- Department of Trade and Industry, Foresight Futures 2020: Revised scenarios and guidance, *Department of Trade and Industry*, London (2002).

26 GEO-3
- UNEP, *Global Environment Outlook 3: Past, present and future perspectives*. Earthscan, London, 2002.
- Rothman, D. S., personal communication, March 18th, 2004

27 THE SHIELD OF ACHILLES
Bobbitt, P., *The Shield of Achilles: War, Peace and the Course of History*. Penguin, London, 2002.

28 TUNIS
Barbanente, A., Khakee, A. and Puglisi, M., Scenario building for Metropolitan Tunis, *Futures* 34, 583-596 (2002).

29 CPB NETHERLANDS BUREAU FOR ECONOMIC POLICY ANALYSIS

- De Mooij, R. and Tang, P., Four futures of Europe, *CPB Netherlands Bureau for Economic Policy Analysis,* The Hague (2003).
- De Mooij, R., personal communication, February 6th, 2004

30 VISIONS

- Rotmans, J., Anastasi, C., Van Asselt, M. B. A., Rothman, D. S., Mellors, J., Greeuw, S. and Van Bers, C., VISIONS: The European Scenarios, *ICIS,* Maastricht (2001).
- Rotmans, J., Van Asselt, M. B. A., Anastasi, C., Greeuw, S., Mellors, J., Peters, S., Rothman, D. and Rijkens, N., Visions for a sustainable Europe, *Futures* 32(9-10), 809-831 (2000).
- Van Notten, Ph. W. F., Rotmans, J., Van Asselt, M. B. A. and Rothman, D. S.: An updated scenario typology, *Futures* 35(5), 423-443 (2003).
- Van Asselt, M. B. A., Rotmans, J. and Rothman, D. S.: *Scenario innovation: Experiences from a European experimental garden.* Taylor & Francis, London, 2004.

Other consulted sources

ALTERNATIVE FUTURES FINLAND
Ruokanen, T. and A. Nurmio . *Finland - New Realities, Alternative Futures.* Helsinki, Sitra, 1996.

AMD SCENARIOS
Gertner, R. and M. Knez, Speltheorie in de realiteit (Game theory in reality). *Het Financieele Dagblad: Supplement on strategy,* 12-13, (2000).

AUSTRALIA 2050
Cocks, D., *Future Makers, Future Takers: Life in Australia 2050.* Sydney, University of New South Wales, 1999.

BRANCH POINTS
Gallopin, G., A. Hammond, et al. (1997). Branch Points: Global Scenarios and Human Choice - A Resource Paper of the Global Scenario Group, Stockholm Environment Institute, Sweden.

CHINA'S FUTURES
Ogilvy, J., P. Schwartz, et al., *China's Futures: Scenarios for the World's Fastest Growing Economy, Ecology, and Society,* San Francisco, Jossey-Bass, 2000.

APPENDIX I SOURCES OF CONSULTED SCENARIO STUDIES

EUROFUTURES
Smith, D., *Eurofutures: Five scenarios for the next millennium*, Oxford, Capstone Publishing Limited, 1997.

EXPLORING SUSTAINABLE DEVELOPMENT
World Business Council for Sustainable Development, *Exploring Sustainable Development. Global scenarios 2000-2050*, London, 1998.

FUTURE PERTH
- Barker, J. Scenarios for the sustainability of Perth, Western Australia, *Scenario and Strategy Planning* 3(2), (2000).
- Western Australian Planning Commission (2000). *Future Perth. Scenarios of our Future: Challenges for Western Australian Society*. Perth, John Curtin International Institute

KENYA AT THE CROSSROADS
Institute of Economic Affairs and Society for International Development, *Kenya at the Crossroads*. Nairobi, (2000).

KPN SCENARIOS ON THE FUTURE OF THE CONSUMER
Abeln, M. E. M., Telekomklant in perspectief (Telecom customer in perspective), *Informatie en informatiebeleid* 16(2): 48-52 (1998).

SCENARIOS FOR THE TESTING EN DEVELOPMENT OF DYNAMIC POLICY
Janssen, N. et al., *Scenario's voor toetsing en ontwikkeling van dynamisch beleid (Scenarios for the testing en development of dynamic policy)*. Ministery of Justice, The Hague, (2002).

NETHERLANDS IN TRIPLICATE
CPB Netherlands Bureau for Economic Policy Analysis, *Nederland in Drievoud (The Netherlands in Triplicate)*. Sdu Uitgeverij, The Hague, (1992).

PERSPECTIVE-BASED SCENARIOS FOR THE RHINE AND MEUSE
- Buiteveld, H., et al.. *Perspective-based scenarios for the Rhine and Meuse - model results*. Arnhem, RIZA, 2001.
- Kwadijk, J. C. J., H. Buiteveld, et al.. *Perspective-based scenarios. Analysis of a-priori sensitivity of water demand and the hydrological system to global change*. WL/Delft Hydraulics, Delft, (2000).

PRESTON

Street, P., Scenario workshops: A participatory approach to sustainable urban living?, *Futures* 29(2), 139-158 (1997).

RUSSIA 2010

Yergin, D. and T. Gustafson, *Russia 2010 and What It Means for the World*. New York, Vintage, 1995.

SCANNING THE FUTURE

CPB Netherlands Bureau for Economic Policy Analysis, *Scanning the Future: A long term scenario study of the world economy 1990-2015*. Sdu Uitgeverij, The Hague, 1992.

SCENARIOS FOR THE FRENCH AGRI-FOODSTUFF SECTOR

Lafourcade, B., and P. Chapuy, Scenarios and Actors´ Strategies: The Case of the Agri-Foodstuff Sector, *Technological Forecasting and Social Change*, 65(1), 67-80 (2000).

SCENARIOS FOR SCOTLAND

- McKiernan, P., et al., Scenarios for Scotland, *Scenario and Strategy Planning*, January 26th, 2001.
- McKiernan, P., et al., The high road, *Scenario and Strategy Planning*, April 26th, 2001.
- McKiernan, P., et al., The low road: Scenarios for Scotland part II., *Scenario & Strategy Planning*, March, 27th, 2001.
- University of St Andrews and University of Strathclyde, Scenarios for Scotland - a journey to 2015. Edinburgh, 1999.

SMITH AND HAWKEN

Schwartz, P., *The Art of the Long View: Planning for the Future in an Uncertain World*. New York, Currency Doubleday, 1991.

STATOIL

Stokke, P. R., et al., Visioning (and Preparing for) the Future: The Introduction of Scenarios-Based Planning into Statoil, *Technological Forecasting & Social Change* 40: 73-86, (1991).

STRING-SCENARIOS

Holst Jørgensen, B., Foresight in Cross-Border Cooperation, *The IPTS Report* (59): 22-30, (2001).

APPENDIX 1 SOURCES OF CONSULTED SCENARIO STUDIES

THE FUTURE OF JAPAN
- Nakamae International Economic Research, www.nier.co.jp/reports/pro-e.html, The future of Japan, accessed on October 20th, 2000.
- Nakamae, T., Three Futures for Japan: Views from 2020, *The Economist*, March 21st, 1998.

THE FUTURE OF CRIME
Digital Thinking Network, www.dtn.net, The future of crime, accessed on August 28th, 2000.

THE FUTURE OF TELEVISION
Digital Thinking Network, www.dtn.net, The future of television, accessed on October 20th, 2001.

THE LONG BOOM
Schwartz, P., Leyden, P. and Hyatt, J.: *The Long Boom: A Vision for the Coming Age of Prosperity*. Perseus, Boulder, 1999.

THE WORLD IN 2020 (OECD)
OECD, *The world in 2020. Towards a new global age*. Paris, OECD Publications, 1997.

THE WORLD IN 2020 (MCRAE)
McRae, H., *The world in 2020: power, culture and prosperity. A vision of the future*. London, Harper Collins, 1995.

TRANSPORT IN A GLOBALISED WORLD
CPB Netherlands Bureau for Economic Policy Analysis, *Globalization, International Transport and the Global Environment: four quantitative scenarios*. The Hague, 1999.

VISIONS GREEN HEART
- De Niet, R., T. de Nijs, et al. (2000). The Green Heart Region towards 2050 : Three scenarios for the Green Heart Region. Maastricht, the Netherlands, RIVM & ICIS.
- Van Asselt, M. B. A., et al., *(Op weg naar scenario's voor het Groene Hart. Stof voor verhalen) On the Way to Scenarios for the Green Heart: Food for stories*. ICIS/RIVM, Bilthoven, 1999.

VISIONS NORTH WEST UK
Gough, C., et al., *VISONS for the NW UK: Interim report*. UMIST and Manchester University, Manchester, September 1999.

A collection of approximately 30 other studies that were consulted is described in:
- European Environment Agency, *Cloudy Crystal Balls: An assessment of recent European and global scenario studies and models,* Copenhagen, 2000.
- Heinzen, B., *Poineers of Persuasion: A Review of the Use of Scenarios in the Public Sector.* Glasgow and London, Scottish Enterprise, 1994.
- Heinzen, B., *Political Experiments of the 1990s: The Use of Scenarios in the Public Domain. The Deeper News,* (September 1994).
- Ringland, G., *Scenario Planning.* Chichester, John Wiley & Sons, 1998.
- Stuurgroep Toekomstonderzoek en Strategisch Omgevingsbeleid, *Terugblik op toekomstverkenningen (A retrospective look at foresight studies).*Netherlands Scientific Council for Government Policy (WRR), The Hague, 2000.

APPENDIX 2
INTERVIEW FORMAT FOR VISIONS PROCESS RECONSTRUCTION

OPENING QUESTION:
1   What was your role in VISIONS?

QUESTIONS ON THE GOAL OF THE STUDY:
2   Why was there an emphasis on discontinuity in the VISIONS?
3   What is your opinion about the emphasis placed on surprise/bifurcations?
4   Was there too much/ too little emphasis?
5   Why?
6   At what stage in the process did discontinuity become an issue of interest?
7   Who placed it on the agenda?
8   How was it placed on the agenda?

QUESTIONS ON DEFINITION OF DISCONTINUITY:
9   What is your definition of discontinuity?
10 How was discontinuity defined in VISIONS?
11 How was the definition subsequently used in the project?
12 Did the definition evolve during the project or did it stay the same?
13 How were the definitions interpreted in the context of the project, namely the future for a sustainable Europe?
14 Please give examples of the discontinuities that were considered.

QUESTIONS ON THE PROCESS:
15 What approach was used to integrate discontinuity in the scenario development process?
16 Was the approach preconceived or did it evolve during the project?
17 How was the choice for the approach made?
18 What were the steps taken and how successful were they?
19 How was the choice made for the discontinuities that were ultimately used?
20 Was the choice arbitrary of was it systematic?

QUESTIONS ON INFLUENCING FACTORS:
21 What factors influenced the way discontinuity was addressed in the project? Please explain.
22 To what degree did the following factors influence how discontinuity was addressed? Please explain.
    Group composition, group dynamics, individual qualities, bias (eg through group

APPENDIX 2 INTERVIEW FORMAT FOR VISIONS PROCESS RECONSTRUCTION

think), knowledge and expertise, process design and method, facilitation.
23 What other factors influenced the way discontinuity was addressed in the project?

QUESTIONS ON PRECONDITIONS FOR DISCONTINUITY-ORIENTED SCENARIO DEVELOPMENT:
24 To what degree are the following preconditions necessary to ensure that discontinuity are addressed systematically in scenario development processes? Please explain. Group variety, expertise and knowledge, resources (e.g. time and money), method and approach?
25 What other preconditions are necessary?
26 Under ideal circumstances, how is discontinuity best addressed in scenario development processes in your opinion?
27 Which of the above preconditions were present that facilitated the integration of discontinuity in VISIONS?
28 Were there other preconditions present that facilitated the integration of discontinuity in VISIONS?
29 Which of the above preconditions were missing?
30 Other than the above, were there preconditions missing in VISIONSthat would have helped facilitated the integration of surprise?

CLOSING QUESTIONS:
31 In hindsight, how do you evaluate your role in the with regards to discontinuity in VISIONS?
32 What would you do differently with regards to discontinuity if you were to repeat the project? Why?
33 What would you do the same? Why?

CURRICULUM VITAE

Philip was educated in the United Kingdom. He received his Bachelor of Arts degree in History from The College of William and Mary, Virginia, USA, in 1993. In 1996, he received his Master's Degree in History at Leiden University, The Netherlands. His specialisation was twentieth century American politics with a focus on foreign policy.

From 1996 to 2000 he worked in consulting and corporate training. Philip was introduced to scenario development in 1997 while working for a KPMG daughter company. He started his doctoral research at the International Centre for Integrative Studies (ICIS), Maastricht University in April 2000. Philip was a visiting scientist with the European Environment Agency in Copenhagen in 2001. Other activities during his doctoral research included the establishment of the COST European Network for Foresight Methodology, and projects for the OECD and UNEP.

PEER REVIEWED PUBLICATIONS

- Van Notten, Ph.W.F., et al., *The Future Shocks: On Discontinuity and Scenario Development,* Technological Forecasting and Social Change 72(2), 175-194
- Van Notten, Ph. W.F., et al., *An updated scenario typology,* Futures 35 (2003), 423-443
- Van Asselt, M.B.A., Van 't Klooster, S., Van Notten, Ph.W.F., *Verkennen in onzekerheid (Exploring under conditions of uncertainty),* Beleid, Politiek en Maatschappij, 30 (4), 230-241

OTHER PUBLICATIONS INCLUDE

- Van Notten, Ph.W.F., *To Learn from Early Warnings,* in: Nieuwe Risico's in Zicht (New Risks in Sight), Raad voor Ruimtelijk, Milieu en Natuuronderzoek (Advisory Council for Research on Spatial Planning, Nature, and the Environment)(ed.), Lemma, Utrecht (2005)
- Van Notten, Ph.W.F. and J. Rotmans (2001). "The future of scenarios." Scenario and Strategy Planning 1(3): 4-8.
- Dobbinga, E. and Ph.W.F. van Notten (2002). "A crunch of gears: scenarios and organisational cultures." Scenario & Strategy Planning 3(6): 24-26.
- Rotmans, J., M. B. A. van Asselt, van Notten, Ph.W.F., (2002). *VISIONS scenarios on the future of Europe.* Scenario Planning in Public Policy. G. Ringland, John Wiley, Chichester, UK.

INDEX

'9/11'	3, 4, 58-62, 161
Aquaculture	129-135
Finnish aquaculture	38, 39, 87, 01, 163
Analogies	75, 144-145, 148, 154
Bellamy, Edward	4
Belshazzar	8, 172
Beyond Hunger in Africa	38, 39, 83, 91, 163
Biotechnology	38, 39, 83, 91
Brainstorming/-writing	142-144, 148, 149-151, 153-154
Braudel, Fernand	51-53
Brent Spar	152, 139, 156
British Airways	38, 39, 78-87, 91, 163
BSE	64-65, 144
Chance Discovery	75
CFCs	64, 72-73
Club of Rome	5, 66
CPB	see *Netherlands Bureau of Economic Policy Analysis*
Cultural Theory	146
Cultures of curiosity	167-170
Curiosity- driven research	169
Destino Colombia	38, 39, 89, 163
Discontinuity	3-4, chapter 3
Abrupt discontinuity	55-56
Discontinuity guardianship	125, 140-141, 148
Gradual discontinuity	56, 57
Early Warnings	see *Weak signals*
Environmental concern	65-66
European Environment Agency (EEA)	38, 39, 63, 79, 82, 91, 163
European Commission	38, 39, 91
Evolutionary paradigm	82, 121, 124, 140, 165
Fish stocks	63
Free spirits	122, 138-139, 156-157
Foresight	4-7
Foresight Futures	38, 39, 78, 163
Futures research	see *Foresight*
Futures studies	see *Foresight*
Global Environmental Outlook	38, 39, 90, 91, 163

Historical analogy	see *Analogies*
Huxley, Aldous	4
ICL	38, 39, 78
Institutional constraints	82-83, 125, 169
Integrated Assessment	4-7
Intergovernmental Panel on Climate Change (IPCC)	38, 39, 79, 81, 82, 163
Intransigence	116, 125
Kahn, Herman	5, 17, 19, 165
Knowledge & expertise	125
KPMG	38, 84, 91
Group variety	138-139, 156-157
Mont Fleur	38, 88-89, 91
More, Thomas	4
Multi-scale analysis	75
Netherlands Bureau of Economic Policy Analysis (CPB)	38, 39, 52, 80, 91, 63
NIVE	38, 39, 79, 91, 163
Norway 2030	38, 39, 91, 85, 163
Nutrition	38, 39, 90, 91, 163
Open structure	125, 135, 141-142, 148,
Orwell, George	4
Ozone layer	see *CFCs*
Perspective-based imaging	145-147, 148, 152-153, 155
Possum	38, 39, 79, 91
Programming	see *Discontinuity guardianship*
Questa	38, 39, 78, 81, 91
Requisite variety	35
Rotterdam, Port of	38, 39, 78, 81, 91, 163
Salmon	see *Aquaculture*
Salmon aquaculture	see *Aquaculture*
Salmon farming	see *Aquaculture*
Scenarios Europe 2010	38, 39, 79, 91, 163
Schooling for tomorrow	38, 39, 80, 91, 163
Security, European	38, 39, 77, , 81, 91, 163
September 11th, 2001	see '9/11'
Signals	see *Weak signals*
Special Report on Emissions Scenarios (SRES)	see *Intergovernmental Panel on Climate Change*
Surprise	47-49
Surprising Futures	38, 39, 83, 91, 163
Shell International	5, 17, 38, 39, 85, 91, 92

INDEX

'Spirit of the times'	125
Shield of Achilles, The	38, 39, 87, 163
Synergy	115, 125
TARGETS	105
Telecom	38, 39, 80, 81, 91
Transitions	see *Gradual discontinuity*
Tunis	38, 39, 80
VISIONS	38, 39, 86, 91
Weak signals	71-74
Wells, H.G.	4
Which World?	38, 39, 89
Wild cards	49-50
Women, The Futures of	38, 39, 84, 163
World Business Council for Sustainable Development	see *Biotechnology*